Understanding UK Annual Reports and Accounts

OWL

HALL

Understanding UK Annual Reports and Accounts

A Case Study Approach

John Laidler
and
Peter Donaghy

INTERNATIONAL THOMSON BUSINESS PRESS

I(T)P® An International Thomson Publishing Company

London ● Bonn ● Boston ● Johannesburg ● Madrid ● Melbourne ● Mexico City ● New York ● Paris
Singapore ● Tokyo ● Toronto ● Albany, NY ● Belmont, CA ● Cincinnati, OH ● Detroit, MI

Understanding UK Annual Reports and Accounts ·

Copyright © 1998 John Laidler and Peter Donaghy

First published by International Thomson Business Press

I(T)P® A division of International Thomson Publishing Inc.
The ITP logo is a trademark under licence

British Library Cataloguing-in-Publication Data
A catalogue record for this book is available from the British Library

First edition 1998

Typeset by LaserScript Limited, Mitcham, Surrey
Printed in the UK by The Alden Press, Oxford

ISBN 1–86152–109–X

International Thomson Business Press
Berkshire House
168–173 High Holborn
London WC1V 7AA
UK

http://www.itbp.com

Contents

Preface

This book is intended for those who need to familiarize themselves with the basic concepts and terminology of financial reporting.

We hope it will help to serve the increasing number of UK undergraduate and postgraduate students who require an appreciation of accounts as part of their degree programmes. At the same time it should be of use to foreign students who wish to extend their knowledge of the UK system of financial reporting as well as their command of the appropriate English terminology.

With the wider distribution of share ownership in the UK in recent years, we have also had in mind the needs of the increasing number of people who feel they want to gain a greater understanding of the structure and contents of annual reports and accounts.

The emphasis of this book, therefore, is on providing clear explanations of the main business and accounting concepts and terms which are found in annual reports and accounts, in a way that makes their meaning clear to both the non-accountant and the non-native speaker of English.

We have chosen to adopt a case study approach in order to give readers confidence in dealing with real situations, and in doing so we have used the 1997 annual report of Scottish & Newcastle plc in order to illustrate the typical format and contents found in the annual reports of major UK companies. At the same time, we have selected examples from other leading companies when we have felt the need to draw attention to important differences and varieties in presentation.

We have included exercises which are designed to reinforce the material provided in the main text and to give readers an opportunity to develop confidence in handling financial statements. The exercises are based on the extracts from the Scottish & Newcastle (S&N) 1997 annual report and accounts in Appendix 3. Solutions to all the exercises are provided, thus facilitating the use of the material for independent study purposes.

For those who are new to the subject matter, we have included a glossary of terms which contains some expressions found within the text which may be used with a specific meaning in the context of financial reports.

We would like to thank Scottish & Newcastle plc for permission to reproduce their 1997 annual report and accounts and for providing technical assistance in this regard. Last but not least, we are very grateful to our families for their support and encouragement.

John Laidler and Peter Donaghy

List of abbreviations

ACT	Advance corporation tax
AGM	Annual general meeting
ASB	Accounting Standards Board
ASC	Accounting Standards Committee
CBI	Confederation of British Industry
EMU	European Monetary Union
EPS	Earnings per share
ESOP	Employee share ownership plan
EU	European Union
FASB	Financial Accounting Standards Board
FRED	Financial Reporting Exposure Draft
FRS	Financial Reporting Standard
GAAP	Generally accepted accounting principles
IASC	International Accounting Standards Committee
IOSCO	International Organization of Securities Commissions
Plc	Public limited company
P/E	Price/earnings
ROCE	Return on capital employed
S	Section
Sch	Schedule
S&N	Scottish & Newcastle
SI	Statutory instrument
SSAP	Statement of Standard Accounting Practice
UITF	Urgent Issues Task Force
VAT	Value added tax

Financial reporting in the UK

Introduction

We can define financial reporting as the communication of information about the financial position and performance of an entity to interested parties.

For a business entity the traditional means of communication has been by the issue of a balance sheet and profit and loss account, but it is now the practice to issue these together with additional statements. The balance sheet, profit and loss account and other statements may be referred to as the *financial statements*. However, they are often called the *annual accounts* or, more simply, the *accounts*. They are made publicly available in the form of the document which is the subject of this book, the *annual report and accounts*, often referred to as the *annual report*.

Interested parties, otherwise called the users of accounts, may include personnel from within a company, for example directors and managers, and people from outside the business. In practice, the term *financial reporting* is usually employed in a more restricted sense to mean reporting to users from outside the business.

Users of accounts

There are various groups of people from outside the company who are recognized as being interested in the facts and figures contained in the accounts produced by UK companies. In a recent publication (*Statement of Principles for Financial Reporting*, Accounting Standards Board, 1995) the following were identified as being user groups who may use company accounts to satisfy some of their different needs for information:

- investors
- employees
- lenders
- suppliers and other creditors
- customers
- governments and their agencies
- the public

We shall now deal with each of these in turn.

Investors

Investors are those individuals or institutions who buy shares in a company and, as shareholders, are members of that company. Those investors who buy ordinary shares take a risk in the hope of making a return. The risk is that the value of their shares will fall. The return, if there is one, will be in the form of a dividend or an increase in the market value of the shares or a combination of both. Investors and potential investors need information to assess the performance of the company's managers and to assess the likelihood of receiving dividends and whether they should buy or sell the shares.

In the UK, investors are perceived as being the main users of the information in the accounts and much of the UK law on company accounts is concerned with the informational needs of the company's shareholders. Having said that, it is generally accepted that much of the information which is presumed to be needed by other user groups will be met from the existing financial statements, even though they have been prepared primarily for investors.

Employees

Employees and trade unions are interested in the ability of firms to continue to provide employment at appropriate levels of remuneration. This involves a knowledge of the financial stability and profitability of the employing company. The recent introduction of European works councils by the European Union has led to a greater interest in the comparative performance of the subsidiaries of multinational companies from this group of users.

Lenders

Institutions, such as banks, and individuals can lend money to a company, for example by buying bonds or loan stock when it is issued by the company. The most relevant information for lenders is that which helps them to answer questions such as whether the company will be able to pay interest on the loans and in due course repay the loans.

Suppliers and other creditors

Anyone supplying goods and services to a company will need to have reasonable assurance that they will be paid by the company when the amounts are due. Hence, they are interested in the financial stability of the company.

Customers

Customers, for example other businesses which intend to buy goods and services from a company, will be interested in the ability of the company to continue to be able to supply the goods and services as and when they are required. Hence, like suppliers, customers will be interested in the continued financial stability of the company.

Governments and their agencies

The informational needs of governments include statistical data and information for the regulation of activities and the assessment of taxes. Company accounts are of particular significance for the assessment of corporation tax and certain indirect taxes.

The public

The activities of companies can affect members of the public in a number of ways. For example, inward investment into an area might bring extra employment and an increase in the opportunities available to local suppliers. Sometimes these benefits might be associated with economic costs such as a possible increase in pollution. The local population and their representatives will be very interested in the financial position and prospects of the company which is bringing the inward investment into the area.

Any of the above users, but perhaps particularly investors, might draw on the services of specialist analysts and advisers, who may themselves be designated as a separate user group.

User groups will not restrict themselves to looking only at the accounts but will seek other sources of information. However, the annual accounts are seen as one of the most important sources of publicly available information about UK companies. The responsibility for their preparation lies with the directors of the company.

Preparers of accounts

In the UK the directors of every company have a legal duty to prepare accounts for each financial year of the company. In addition, if, at the end of the financial year, the company is a parent company, the directors must also prepare group accounts. However, provided certain conditions in the Companies Act are complied with, the documents that must be published may be restricted to the balance sheet of the parent company, the group balance sheet and the group profit and loss account (i.e. the parent company profit and loss account need not be published).

There are legal rules which set out whether or not a company is a parent company. Some of these rules can be quite difficult to interpret in practice. One of the most basic rules is that a company will be a parent if it 'holds a majority of the voting rights' in another company. This is illustrated in Example 1.1.

Example 1.1 Parent companies	Company A owns 70% of the shares of company B. Each share in company B gives the shareholder one vote at company meetings. In this situation, company A 'holds a majority of the voting rights' in company B and is, therefore, the *parent company* of company B. Company B is called the *subsidiary* of company A. At the end of its financial year, the directors of company A must prepare: • accounts for the *individual company*, i.e. company A, and • accounts for the *group*, which aggregate the figures of company A and company B.

The directors also have a duty to keep proper accounting records on a day-to-day basis. These records must be such that they enable the directors to prepare the required annual accounts.

The basic legal requirement to prepare annual accounts applies to all companies, whether private or public. One of the distinguishing features of a public company is that it may offer its shares to the public. Those public companies which seek a quotation on the Stock Exchange are often referred to as *quoted companies* or *listed companies*.

In this book we are principally concerned with the accounts of listed companies. When the directors of companies prepare accounts they have to make sure that these comply with various rules which are set out in company law, accounting standards and Stock Exchange regulations, as well as with codes of best practice concerning corporate governance. We can refer to these as the *authoritative sources* with regard to disclosure requirements for annual accounts.

Authoritative sources of disclosure requirements for annual accounts

The authoritative sources for information which is to be disclosed in the accounts of UK listed companies are discussed below under the following headings:

- legal requirements
- accounting standards
- Stock Exchange rules
- corporate governance: codes of best practice

There is no regulatory term to embrace the rules set out in the authoritative sources. However, the term *generally accepted accounting principles* (GAAP) is beginning to be used in practice in the UK. This is not defined in the Companies Act although reference to 'principles generally accepted' is used in the Act in the context of realized profits. In the US the term has a specific meaning and US GAAP is a defined part of the regulatory framework of accounting in the US.

The acronym UK GAAP is used increasingly. There is some debate about what this term covers but it is probably usually understood to mean the body of rules and regulations laid down by the authoritative sources discussed below.

Legal requirements

In the UK the primary law relating to the disclosure of information in company accounts is the Companies Act 1985 as amended by the Companies Act 1989 (referred to hereafter as the Companies Act). In addition to the original Act subordinate legislation may be enacted by means of a statutory instrument (SI). For example, a statutory instrument might be used to issue detailed rules in order to put into effect a requirement in the Act.

The basic legal requirements for the preparation of UK company accounts are listed below. References are to the Companies Act 1985 as amended by the Companies Act 1989. The Companies Act contains detailed provisions regarding the application of these basic accounting requirements. These provisions will be discussed under their appropriate headings throughout this book. (Note that S stands for Section and Sch for Schedule.)

1. *Preparation of accounts of individual companies.* The directors of every UK company must prepare a balance sheet and a profit and loss account which give a true and fair view (S227, S228).

2. *Preparation of accounts of groups.* If a company is a parent company at the end of its financial year, group accounts must also be prepared. These are to be a consolidated balance sheet and a consolidated profit and loss account which give a true and fair view (S229, S230).

3. *Notes to the accounts.* Any information required shall (if not given in the company's accounts) be given by way of notes to the accounts (Sch 4).

4. *Accounts to be in standard formats.* Individual company accounts and group accounts are to be in a standard format. A choice of formats is given in the Act; two balance sheet formats and four profit and loss account formats are permitted (S228, S230) (These formats are reproduced in Appendix 1.)

5. *Accounting rules which may be used.* Two sets of accounting rules are provided: historical cost accounting rules and alternative accounting rules (Sch 4).

6. *Accounting principles to be applied.* The following accounting principles are to be applied when accounts are prepared:

   - going concern
   - consistency
   - prudence
   - accruals
   - separate determination

   (Sch 4).

7. *Accounting policies are to be shown.* The accounting policies which the company has adopted in determining the amounts included for all material items in the balance sheet and in determining the profit or loss must be stated in a note to the accounts (Sch 4).

8. *Compliance with applicable accounting standards.* The accounts must contain a statement that they have been prepared in accordance with applicable accounting standards. Particulars must be given of any material departure from those standards (Sch 4, 36A).

9. *Definition of accounting standards.* 'Accounting standards' means statements of standard accounting practice issued by such body or bodies as may be prescribed by regulations (S256,1).

10. *Prescription of standard setting body.* The Accounting Standards Board is prescribed as a standard setting body (SI 1990, no. 1667).

Some of the terms used in the list above need further explanation and are discussed below.

True and fair view

This means that the accounts reflect what has actually happened and that the information presented is not misleading. To demonstrate that the accounts do give a true and fair view, it is expected that they have been prepared on the basis of fundamental accounting principles and comply with accounting standards.

Notes to the accounts

In addition to the items specified in Sch 4, Part III, there are several other references in the Companies Act to items which have to be shown by way of note. In practice, companies use the notes to the accounts to amplify and extend the figures in the accounts beyond the legal minimum disclosure requirements.

Accounting rules

The Companies Act refers to two sets of rules: historical cost rules and alternative accounting rules. Most of the detailed rules are set out in Schedule 1 of the 1989 Act. It is not legally necessary to state which set of rules has been applied. However, virtually all companies refer in their accounts to which rules they have used, usually describing these as the convention which has been followed. For example, Scottish & Newcastle's (S&N's) 1997 accounts state:

> The accounts are prepared under the historical cost convention except that certain properties are included at valuation.

Accounting principles

In the context of the Companies Act, accounting principles are the broad basic assumptions on which the annual accounts are prepared. They are discussed in detail in Chapter 7.

- The *going concern* principle assumes that the company will continue to operate for the foreseeable future.
- The application of the *consistency* principle means that users of a company's accounts can make comparisons on a like-for-like basis.
- Using the *prudence* principle means that profits may not be anticipated but that anticipated liabilities (expenses and losses) must be brought into account.
- The *accruals* principle is applied by the inclusion of sales and costs in the profit and loss account of the year to which they relate rather than simply including all monies received and paid.

An example of the principle of *separate determination* is the calculation of the figure for 'stock' in the balance sheet. Each individual stock item must be valued separately and the individual values added together to arrive at the total value for stocks. The application of the principle does not permit a global valuation of this or any other asset.

Accounting policies

As we have seen, a company's accounts are prepared on certain broad basic assumptions, i.e. accounting principles. Within the framework of these principles each company must decide what its policy will be with regard to the various transactions it enters into. This is necessary because, in many cases, there will be a number of bases to chose from. For example, there are different methods by which stocks can be valued and there are different ways of calculating the depreciation of assets. If we look at Note 1(c)(iv) of the S&N accounts we can see that the company's accounting policy for the depreciation of its leisure plant is to write it off over the plant's anticipated useful life of between 10 and 15 years.

For any company, its accounting policies are the particular accounting bases it has adopted as being most appropriate to its circumstances.

Accounting standards

Accounting standards are sets of rules and regulations for the measurement and/or disclosure of particular types of transactions. They are set by standard setting bodies with the objective of achieving some level of standardization and, hence, comparability between annual accounts from different companies.

As previously noted, in the context of the UK Companies Act the specified accounting standards are those set by the Accounting Standards Board (ASB). The standards for which the ASB has responsibility are now discussed as the second of the authoritative sources of the information which is to be disclosed in the annual accounts of UK companies.

The standard setting regime in the UK was revised in 1990. The present system is shown in Figure 1.1.

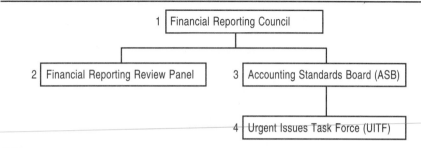

KEY:
1 The Financial Reporting Council guides the Accounting Standards Board (ASB).
2 The Financial Reporting Review Panel enquires into annual accounts where it appears that the requirements of the Companies Act, including the requirement that annual accounts shall show a true and fair view, might have been breached.
3 The ASB develops, issues and withdraws accounting standards.
4 The Urgent Issues Task Force (UITF) assists the ASB in areas where an accounting standard or Companies Act provision exists, but where unsatisfactory or conflicting interpretations have developed or seem likely to develop.
Source: Adapted from Accounting Standards 1998, Coopers & Lybrand (1997)

Figure 1.1 The standard setting regime in the UK

The ASB is the only standard setting body recognized for the purpose of the Companies Act. The recognized accounting standards are those for which the ASB has responsibility, which means the standards of the ASB and the still existing standards of its predecessor body, the Accounting Standards Committee (ASC). The relevant standards are:

- Statements of Standard Accounting Practice (SSAPs) – issued by the ASC.
- Financial Reporting Standards (FRSs) – issued by the ASB.

The process of the development of accounting standards includes the issuing of a Financial Reporting Exposure Draft (FRED) to enable interested parties to comment on the proposed standard.

In addition, the promulgations issued by the UITF by means of published abstracts are considered by the ASB 'to be part of the corpus of practices forming the basis of what constitutes a true and fair view'. The standards and abstracts in issue are shown in Figure 1.2.

Statements of Standard Accounting Practice (SSAPs)
SSAP 1: Accounting for associated companies
SSAP 2: Disclosure of accounting policies
SSAP 3: Earnings per share
SSAP 4: Accounting for government grants
SSAP 5: Accounting for value added tax
SSAP 8: The treatment of taxation under the imputation system in the accounts of companies
SSAP 9: Stocks and long-term contracts
SSAP 12: Accounting for depreciation
SSAP 13: Accounting for research and development
SSAP 15: Accounting for deferred tax
SSAP 17: Accounting for post-balance sheet events
SSAP 18: Accounting for contingencies
SSAP 19: Accounting for investment properties
SSAP 20: Foreign currency translation
SSAP 21: Accounting for leases and hire purchase contracts
SSAP 22: Accounting for goodwill
SSAP 24: Accounting for pension costs
SSAP 25: Segmental reporting

Financial Reporting Standards (FRSs)
FRS 1: Cash flow statements (revised 1996)
FRS 2: Accounting for subsidiary undertakings
FRS 3: Reporting financial performance
FRS 4: Capital instruments
FRS 5: Reporting the substance of transactions
FRS 6: Acquisitions and mergers
FRS 7: Fair values in acquisition accounting

UITF Abstracts
UITF Abstract 3: Treatment of goodwill on disposal of a business
UITF Abstract 4: Presentation of long-term debtors in current assets
UITF Abstract 5: Transfers from current assets to fixed assets
UITF Abstract 6: Accounting for post-retirement benefits other than pensions
UITF Abstract 7: True and fair view override disclosures
UITF Abstract 9: Accounting for operations in hyper-inflationary economies
UITF Abstract 10: Disclosure of directors' share options
UITF Abstract 11: Capital instruments: issuer call options
UITF Abstract 12: Lessee accounting for reverse premiums and similar incentives
UITF Abstract 13: Accounting for ESOP trusts
UITF Abstract 14: Disclosure of changes in accounting policy
UITF Abstract 15: Disclosure of substantial acquisitions
UITF Abstract 16: Income and expenses subject to non-standard rates of tax

---

Figure 1.2 UK accounting standards and abstracts

Two accounting standards, FRS 1 and FRS 3, include requirements for the production of specific financial statements in addition to the balance sheet and profit and loss account required by the Companies Act. A list of the individual statements needed is shown in the summary at the end of this chapter.

AUTHORITATIVE SOURCES OF DISCLOSURE REQUIREMENTS FOR ANNUAL ACCOUNTS

Stock Exchange rules

When a company's shares are listed on a stock exchange the company will need to comply with the regulations of the stock exchange on which it is listed.

UK companies listed on the London Stock Exchange have to comply within their annual accounts with the informational requirements set out in *Admissions of Securities to Listing* (known as the 'Yellow Book'). In addition, listed companies must produce a half-yearly or interim report.

Compliance with the Companies Act and ASB requirements will meet the Stock Exchange's main listing rules. However, in a fairly limited number of areas different disclosures are needed to comply with the Stock Exchange rules, for example with regard to a difference between actual results and published forecast.

The Stock Exchange requires all listed UK companies to state in their annual report whether they are complying with the code of best practice on corporate governance and to give reasons for any areas of non-compliance. The code was established following the Cadbury Report, which is discussed below under *Corporate governance.*

Corporate governance: codes of best practice

As a result of public and investor dissatisfaction, a series of Companies Acts between 1948 and 1989 resulted in gradually more information being required to be disclosed in company annual reports. This increased disclosure was not sufficient to meet the broader criticisms about the way companies were run, i.e. about systems of corporate governance, especially with regard to the communication of information between directors and shareholders. This general lack of confidence, coupled with a number of well-publicized company failures, led to the setting up of the Cadbury Committee to examine these matters.

The *Report of the Cadbury Committee on the Financial Aspects of Corporate Governance* (December 1992) included a code of best practice. The code aims 'to achieve the necessary high standards of corporate behaviour' and, *inter alia*, requires boards to report on the responsibilities of directors with regard to the preparation of accounts and the effectiveness of the company's internal control procedures, and to present a balanced and understandable assessment of the company's position.

Despite the fairly wide sweep of the code of best practice, public dissatisfaction continued to be expressed about a number of issues, not least the question of directors' pay. In 1995, the Confederation of British Industry (CBI) set up a committee under the chairmanship of Sir Richard Greenbury, to draw up best practice guidelines for UK company directors' pay. The committee reported in July 1995 and its report included a code of best practice for determining and reporting on directors' remuneration. Subsequently, the Stock Exchange listing rules were amended to implement the Greenbury recommendations and the accounts of listed companies should now contain the required disclosures.

The broad thrust of revisions to systems of corporate governance in the UK has been to place more reliance on non-executive directors and institutional shareholders as overseers of company boards, as well as to establish disclosure and other requirements. The extent to which these moves have overcome public and investor dissatisfaction remains to be seen.

Summary

In the context of this book, financial reporting in the UK is concerned with the communication of information about the financial position and performance of UK companies to interested parties. Interested parties include investors, employees, lenders, suppliers and other creditors, customers and governments and their agencies. The principal means of communication is by the issue of the annual report and accounts, which is aimed primarily at the company's shareholders but which also serves to meet some of the informational needs of other users.

The directors are responsible for preparing accounts which must show a true and fair view of the state of the company's financial position and results. Rules and regulations regarding the format, content and the methods of measurement used to arrive at the figures to be included in the accounts are set out in the Companies Act, accounting standards, Stock Exchange rules and codes of best practice on corporate governance.

Within the annual report and accounts document, the accounts, sometimes called *financial statements*, consist of:

- group profit and loss account
- group balance sheet
- company balance sheet
- group cash flow statement
- statement of total recognized gains and losses
- note on historical cost profit and losses
- reconciliation of movements in shareholders' funds
- notes to the accounts

The amount of information in the accounts is dependent upon the disclosure requirements in the authoritative sources and the voluntary disclosures made by management. Many of the most interesting details are found in the notes to the accounts.

It is important for interested parties to obtain as much information about a company as they can, and not restrict themselves to information found in the annual report and accounts. However, an understanding of the annual accounts is an essential prerequisite to further investigation.

The annual reports and accounts

Introduction

Scottish & Newcastle plc- hereafter referred to as S&N- has been selected to provide authentic examples of the contents of an annual report and accounts and extracts from the 1997 annual report and accounts have been reproduced in Appendix 3.

S&N became the UK's largest brewer, with a market share of over 30%, as a result of its takeover of Courage in August 1995. This position was consolidated by the Government's decision in June 1997 to block the takeover of Carlsberg-Tetley by Bass, which, in turn, seemed to herald a tough new line on competition policy. It was established as a group company under its present name as recently as 1960, but the origins of some of its constituent parts date back almost 150 years. It has grown to become a leading UK company, combining interests at home and abroad in brewing, retailing of food and drink and leisure facilities, with an annual turnover in 1997 of £3349 million and a workforce of over 45 000.

Contents of the annual report and accounts

The annual reports and accounts of most UK companies contain similar items and, in order to obtain an overview of the type of headings which we can expect to find, the contents page of the S&N Group 1997 annual report and accounts is shown in Table 2.1.

Although these are not specifically referred to in the table of contents, S&N also includes the two other financial statements which it is required to disclose, namely, the note on historical cost profits and losses and the reconciliation of movements in shareholders' funds.

The contents of the annual report can be classified under two broad types of information:

- information required based on authoritative sources (discussed in Chapter 1)
- information supplied on a voluntary basis

Table 2.1 Contents page of S&N Group 1997 annual report

* These sections are reproduced in Appendix 3.

Information required based on authoritative sources

The authoritative sources shaping the nature of financial reporting which are described in Chapter 1, namely the Companies Act, accounting standards, Stock Exchange rules and corporate governance codes of best practice, determine the minimum information that publicly quoted companies must disclose in their accounts. From these sources we can see that the annual report of a company has to contain certain specific sections. These sections are listed in Table 2.2 together with a reminder of their sources and reference to the chapters in which they are dealt with in this book.

Information supplied on a voluntary basis

In addition to those sections of annual reports of companies specifically required by the authoritative sources, most companies include a substantial amount of further information under a variety of headings. These items contain some basic factual information which may help the reader to build up a clearer picture of the organization and structure of the company, as well as to obtain a general and less technical idea of its performance, than that contained in the detailed financial reports and statements.

The S&N annual report contains a number of such headings, as shown in Table 2.3:

Table 2.2 Information required based on authoritative sources

Section	Source	Chapter in this book
Financial review	Code of best practice	Chapter 3
Report of the remuneration committee	Code of best practice	Chapter 3
Corporate governance	Code of best practice	Chapter 3
Statement of directors' responsibilities	Code of best practice	Chapter 3
Directors' report*	Companies Act	Chapter 3
Auditors' report	Companies Act	Chapter 3
Balance sheet	Companies Act	Chapters 4, 5, 6
Profit and loss account	Companies Act	Chapter 7
Cash flow statement	Accounting standards	Chapter 8
Statement of total recognized gains and losses	Accounting standards	Chapter 9
Note on historical cost profits and losses	Accounting standards	Chapter 9
Reconciliation of movements in shareholders' funds	Accounting standards	Chapter 9
Notes to the accounts	Companies Act	Chapter 10

*Note:** The directors' report has to include a review of the business of the company during the year in question together with an indication of likely future developments. S&N, in line with other major companies, fulfils this requirement by means of a chairman's statement and a chief executive's review, reference to both of which is found in Chapter 3.

Table 2.3 Information supplied on a voluntary basis

Group financial highlights
Brand building and divisional highlights
Retail division
Beer division
Leisure division
Community and environment
Board of Directors
Five-year record
Shareholder information
Notice of meeting
Financial calendar

These sections of the S&N annual report, which are now discussed below, are typical of those which seek to meet the needs of the normal shareholder. The page numbers referred to are those of Appendix 3.

Group financial highlights

This, as the title suggests, is a summary of the major financial achievements of the company in terms of profit, earnings per share, dividends and capital expenditure illustrated by means of graphs to reflect the growth in these areas over the last five years.

Brand building and divisional highlights

Brand building is displayed on the front cover as the theme of the 1997 annual report and this section contains a cash flow chart emphasizing the importance of investment in brand development in the three divisions of the company. This is accompanied by a summary of the results in terms of operating profit and turnover for each division with an indication of the change from the previous year.

Retail, beer and leisure divisions

These pages enable the reader to form a very clear picture of the group and we can see that they are organized under three divisions corresponding to the three activities (retail – pubs and restaurants – brewing and leisure), which in turn embrace a significant number of individual brand names. The divisions, activities and brands of S&N are summarized in Table 2.4.

It is in these pages that the reader will be able to learn about the performance during the previous year and the future plans and prospects of the distinctive areas of business. In this way it is possible to build up a profile of the company with reference to product development, brand names, outlets, market segments, exports, restructuring, and acquisitions and disposals, as well as the capacity and occupancy of the holiday villages.

Thus, in the case of the retail division we can appreciate that 'managed houses' forms by far the most significant sector, with increasing sales and profits, while the number of 'tenancies' and their corresponding turnover and profits are falling. There are now some 400 establishments owned by the company, which carry brand names such as the 25 Chef and Brewer and the 33 John Barras pubs. The company is clearly attempting to cater for different segments of the restaurant market with its 69 Country Carveries for the older persons 'empty nester' market and 36 family eating sites through its Homespreads chain.

Table 2.4 Summary of S&N divisions, activities and brands

Division	Activity	Examples of brands
Scottish & Newcastle Retail	Retail (pubs & restaurants)	Chef & Brewer Rat & Parrot Finnegan's Wake Old Orleans Country Carvery
Scottish Courage Ltd	Beer (brewing)	McEwan's Foster's Kronenbourg John Smith's Beamish
Center Parcs	Leisure	Center Parcs-Holland Center Parcs-Germany Center Parcs-France Holiday Club Pontins

In the community (pages 154–5)

Major companies are becoming more aware both of their responsibilities in regard to the environment and of the public relations value of green issues. S&N is no exception and, while these issues were generally addressed in the chief executive's review in earlier years, in 1997 S&N took the opportunity to dedicate a separate section of the

INFORMATION SUPPLIED ON A VOLUNTARY BASIS

report for the first time to include some details of its environmental policy and its involvement in community projects.

There are references to direct donations to charities and examples of the company's support for education and young people, the disabled and disadvantaged. Energy saving initiatives are highlighted, as is direct financial assistance to a number of environmental projects.

Board of directors

Here the company takes the opportunity to remind shareholders who the directors are. There are photographs and brief biographical details of the chairman, deputy chairman and chief executive, five executive directors who have specific senior posts within the organization (i.e. chairmen of the three respective divisions, the group finance director, and the group personnel and services director), two non-executive directors who contribute their expertise from a range of businesses in an advisory capacity and the company secretary, who is the person responsible for the company's administrative and legal affairs. The user of the annual report can thus begin to form an opinion about the age, experience and connections of the leading figures in the company.

Five-year record (page 183)

This is in the form of a table with a checklist of key statistics for each of the past five years. Here, at a glance, is a summary of indicators which the potential investor can study in order to assess the progress of the company over a reasonable period of time. This gives a broader context in which one can consider the performance of the current year both in terms of the company itself and in relation to other companies with which the reader is familiar. S&N include comparative figures under the following headings:

- assets employed
- financed by share capital/share premium and reserves
- turnover
- operating profit
- profit on ordinary activities before interest
- profit before taxation
- profit after taxation
- profit attributable to ordinary shareholders
- profit/(loss) retained
- basic earnings per share
- dividends per share
- dividend cover

Shareholder information (page 184)

This section may be of interest to anyone wanting to know about the distribution of shareholdings in the company. It provides an analysis which, among other things, tells us that 84.6% of shareholders hold no more than 2500 shares each and that 110 shareholdings control between them 57.75% of the company.

There are also details of the share price at various times of the year, capital gains tax values, personal equity plans and S&N's share dealing service.

Notice of meeting (page 185)

This is specifically directed at current shareholders but it may provide some information of interest to general observers of the company as well.

In addition to details of the time and place of the annual general meeting, there is a list of the resolutions to be considered at the meeting, including the election or re-election of directors and any proposed changes to the company's articles of association.

Financial calendar

Again, while this is directed at shareholders, it does alert other users to key dates when they can expect to discover something about the progress of the company.

Thus we find here a list of dates for the payment of interim and final dividends as well as an indication of when the annual results will be announced.

Comparison with other companies

Broadly speaking, S&N is in line with most other companies in regard to the form and content of its annual report. However, certain information may be subsumed under one heading rather than another. Thus, for example, in the case of HSBC details of directors' remuneration is within the directors' report rather than under a separate section. Companies may choose to provide some information, such as notice of their annual meeting or details of subsidiaries, in other company publications. The amount of information contained under the various headings may also vary as companies choose to give more space to certain aspects of their activities rather than to others. Again it has to be borne in mind that this may vary from year to year depending on the significance of the information which companies wish to highlight at any one time. All of these issues need to be taken into consideration when making a comparison of the contents of annual reports.

Table 2.5 shows the distribution of contents according to the percentage of pages in the annual reports of a selection of leading companies. As can be seen in Table 2.5, there are clearly two predominant sections, namely, reports on operations and notes to the accounts. The reports on operations generally take the form of a review of the performance and prospects of the various product divisions of the company along the lines of that discussed in the case of S&N above (see 'Retail, beer and leisure divisions' above). The notes to the accounts section, which is considered in Chapter 10, occupies by far the largest proportion of the contents of all the reports and this is generally the case for major companies. If we compare the percentage of the contents dedicated to particular items in the case of the ten companies which feature in Table 2.5, it is interesting to note that five companies (S&N, Zeneca, M&S, Hanson and T&N) have chosen to draw attention to health and safety and/or the environment. A further three companies (M&S, HSBC and T&N) have provided separate sections on staff training and works councils. The latter is an area of increasing interest, particularly in the light of European Union legislation on increased consultation with employees.

Table 2.5 Comparison of contents of recent annual reports (percentage to nearest whole number of pages per section)

	S&N	Zeneca	Bass	M&S	HSBC	Hanson	B Gas	T&N	TT	BT
Financial highlights	2	4	2	3	1	3	2	1	3	4
Chairman's statement	3	3	–	3	4	3	5	1	3	3
Chief executive's review	3	3	–	–	10	2	2	1	10	~3
Reports on operations	23	18	13	27	3	16	15	35	10	10
Financial review	7	6	6	3	15	3	5	3	3	11
Board of directors	3	1	–	3	2	3	3	1	3	3
Report of directors	3	8	7	3	12	6	3	4	7	1
Remuneration committee	8	–	10	8	–	–	–	8	8	10
Corporate governance	2	–	–	1	–	–	2	1	–	4
Auditors' report	2	1	2	1	1	2	2	1	2	1
Financial statements	7	4	7	5	5	8	8	7	8	6
Notes to the accounts	26	34	37	23	38	32	42	23	30	29
Health & safety, environment	2	4	–	6	–	3	–	1	–	–
Additional information for US	–	4	6	–	–	10	–	–	–	3
Staff, community	3	1	–	6	3	–	–	1	–	–
Principal subsidiaries	–	1	2	–	2	–	–	1	3	3
Shareholder information	2	1	–	1	1	3	2	3	–	3
Notice of meeting	2	–	–	1	–	3	–	1	3	–
Five-year review	2	1	6	–	1	–	3	1	3	–
Other	–	6	2	6	2	3	6	6	4	6

Of particular interest is the reference in the reports of four companies (Zeneca, Bass, Hanson and T&N) to additional information for US investors. This is because companies whose shares are quoted on the New York Stock Exchange are subject to the regulations of the Securities and Exchange Commission (SEC). The accounting principles generally accepted in the United States (US GAAP) differ from the accounting principles generally accepted in the UK (UK GAAP), which have been used in the preparation of the financial statements contained in the annual report. Therefore, companies whose shares are traded in the US may have a number of pages which convert some of the significant financial information according to US GAAP.

There is clearly a major public relations emphasis in the majority of reports and this is particularly evident in the amount of space given to illustrations in most annual reports. In order to make the document more attractive and to portray a positive image, the text is frequently interspersed with pictorial representations of various aspects of a company's activities.

Summary

Companies are obliged to produce a minimum of information in accordance with the demand placed upon them by the regulatory bodies described in Chapter 1, and in recent years there have been more moves to provide greater transparency in the affairs of companies on both a European and a world-wide basis. This puts pressure on companies to provide extensive, technical and detailed appraisals of their activities in order to comply with the demands placed upon them.

At the same time, however, many companies appear to chose to go beyond the minimum requirements with regard to the information which they supply. The annual report and accounts are regarded as a good opportunity to inform a large number of people about a company. Naturally companies want to keep in touch with their shareholders and other prospective investors. They also wish to appeal to potential creditors, clients and customers, and they may be increasingly concerned about maintaining the confidence of their own employees.

There is sometimes a clash between satisfying the requirements of the regulatory bodies, on the one hand, and providing user friendly information in an easily digestible form for a broader public, on the other. In recognition of this an increasing number of companies are having recourse to producing simplified and/or abridged documents for shareholders and/or employees. S&N, for example, produces a quarterly review for employees with comments on performance and trends, together with a video on its annual results, while Marks and Spencer provides an audio tape containing the highlights of its annual report for the benefit of visually impaired people. However, the traditional annual report and accounts document still remains as an essential source of information for those wishing to obtain a comprehensive picture of a company's past performance and an insight into its future development.

Exercises

These exercises are based on the extracts from the S&N 1997 annual report and accounts in Appendix 3.

1. What are the sources of authority for the following elements in the annual report?

   - report of the remuneration committee *codes of best practice*
   - balance sheet *company's act legal*
   - cash flow statement

2. What sort of information would you expect to find in the five-year record?

3. Where will you find details of the total number of shareholders? What was the closing price of S&N ordinary shares on 25 April 1997 and how does this compare with the price on 29 April 1996?

4. Where will you find reference to S&N's policy towards the environment? Who has responsibility for environmental matters?

5. To what extent, if any, do the contents of the S&N report as stated in Table 2.5 appear to differ from those of Bass? (You may need to refer to Chapter 3.)

Reports and reviews

Introduction

As seen in Chapter 2, in addition to financial statements, the annual report and accounts document contains a number of reports and reviews which provide important insights into the past performance and future prospects of the company concerned.

The S&N annual report and accounts document contains all the reports normally produced by major UK companies and these are listed in Table 3.1 in the order in which they appear in the S&N annual report. Reference is also made to whether their inclusion is based on the provisions of the Companies Act, a result of a code of best practice or a voluntary means of communicating with the various users of the accounts.

Table 3.1 Reports found within the S&N annual report

Report	Reason for inclusion
Chairman's statement	Voluntary
Chief executive's review	Voluntary
Financial review	Code of best practice
Report of the directors	Companies Act
Report of the remuneration committee	Code of best practice
Corporate governance	Code of best practice
Report by the auditors on corporate governance matters	Code of best practice
Statement of directors' responsibilities	Code of best practice
Report of the auditors	Companies Act

reports produced by major UK companies

At times these reports overlap and, on occasions, companies may choose to include items under one heading rather than another and to vary the order in which the reports appear. Here, however, we will consider these reports in the order in which they are found in the S&N 1997 annual report.

It is standard practice at the beginning of the annual report to find a statement from the company chairman. This sets the scene for the following pages and helps to bring the subsequent numbers to life. It gives the chairman an opportunity to reach out to a wide audience often beyond the readers of the report itself, as it will be hoped that some of the highlights of the statement will receive more general publicity. As a media conscious exercise the statement is usually relatively brief and straightforward.

However, as it is not required by law, some companies may not include a chairman's statement as such. Bass, for example, starts its 1997 annual report with the *Operating and Financial Review* and in the directors' report reference is made to the chairman's statement, which is to be found in a separate document entitled *Annual Review and Summary Financial Statement*. Likewise, the Weir Group dispenses with a chairman's statement and instead begins its 1996 annual report with a *Statement to Shareholders and Operating and Financial Review* which is attributed to both the chairman and the chief executive.

Nevertheless, most annual reports do have a chairman's statement. Where this is the case, because there is no statutory provision, there is no formal pattern and the format very much depends on the house style adopted by the individual company. This, in turn, will be influenced by the other components of the annual report and whether or not certain details can be sited more logically elsewhere. It would appear that with the increase in more specifically designated sections of the annual report in response to the recommendations of the Cadbury and Greenbury Committees' reports, the chairman's statement is now becoming somewhat shorter and more standardized.

As a general rule we can expect the chairman's statement to be cautiously optimistic. The chairman has to bear in mind the impact of the statement on shareholders and potential investors and therefore while stressing the (hopefully) good performance of the company during the past year he/she has to be careful not to overstate the prospects for the future. The statement usually begins with a summary of the principal results of the previous year, as with the S&N 1997 annual report, where the chairman states:

> Overall Group results have demonstrated that Scottish & Newcastle's strategic positioning as a major player . . . provides a platform for sustained profit growth.
>
> Pre-tax profits have again risen sharply . . . earnings per share increased by 17.4% . . . Your Directors recommended a final dividend of 14.17p per share, an increase of 10%.

Results need to be viewed within the context of the economy as a whole and the specific sector in particular. It is likely therefore that there will be reference to problems and prospects in regard to the particular industrial sector in which the company operates as well as to the general economic and political environment. In the case of S&N, the chairman refers to:

a modest pick up in consumer spending in those sectors upon which our Company relies for its sales and profit growth. By contrast, in continental Europe . . . structural uncompetitiveness and fiscal policies . . . have adversely affected both consumer markets and exchange rates.

Later on he draws attention to the 'value of the existing, limited maintenance of the brewery tie continuing into the future'. Here he is referring to the vertical integration of breweries and pub outlets, which continues to be the subject of scrutiny by the European Commission.

The closer integration of Europe in recent years has meant that European issues have become more prominent in many annual reports. The 1996 S&N chairman's statement, while stressing 'the Company's total belief in a single European Market', expresses concern about a single currency. This theme was picked up again in 1997 with reference to 'too early participation in the EMU', although the chairman still reiterates the hope of being 'good Europeans'.

The amount of space devoted to certain issues will, of course, vary from time to time, depending on the circumstances of the company concerned. Thus, for example, in the BT 1997 annual report, the chairman's statement was almost entirely about the global tele-communications industry, particularly in view of the intended merger, at that time, with MCI to form Concert.

This can also be the place in the annual report where reference may be made to any miscellaneous issues which arise in the annual accounts. Thus, for example, the S&N chairman makes reference to a change in policy regarding the political donations which the company had made up to and including 1997 as follows:

In April the Board agreed that it was inappropriate for the Company to make any contribution to any political party and consequently we would not expect to do so in the future.

A chairman may also wish to give a message to the government of the day in relation to its policies or its legislative programme. In the 1997 annual report, S&N chairman re-echoes the concern about Scottish devolution expressed in the previous year by his predecessor, who had pointed out that S&N was the 'largest industrial group headquartered in Scotland'. The chairman is now clearly anxious about the impact of tax levying powers on the competitiveness of Scottish goods and services.

It is customary in this section to thank the employees for their efforts during the past year, although an increasing number of companies now produce separate employee reports which go into greater deal about the achievements of staff.

The directors, too, are likely to be thanked at this point and any impending changes in the composition of the board will be commented upon. Considerable space in the S&N 1997 annual report was devoted to a tribute to the previous chairman who had retired earlier in the year. At the same time, this provided the opportunity for the new chairman to highlight the expansion and development of the company during his predecessor's long association with the group.

The chairman's statement normally concludes with a brief and generally optimistic reference to the future growth of the company and

S&N is no exception in this as its chairman concludes his 1997 statement as follows:

> Your Company is in an excellent position to maintain the sound progress that has been achieved in the year under review and to continue to invest in the people, brands and productive assets which will secure its sustained growth.

Chief executive's review

This, to a large extent, complements and supplements the chairman's statement. It covers some of the same ground, but in greater detail, and it can also be described as a 'business review'. The two reports together therefore often appear to fulfil the statutory requirements of the directors to supply a business review and an indication of likely future developments. It is common, therefore, in the directors' report to see cross-references to the chairman's statement and the chief executive's review.

At the same time, some companies, including, for example, Bass and Marks and Spencer, do not include a chief executive's report as such in their annual report. However, the type of ground covered in a chief executive's report is found elsewhere in the form of information about the operations of the company and the activities of its various divisions.

S&N follows the more standard pattern of including a specific chief executive's report, and its role, together with that of the chairman's statement, is made clear in the report of the directors under the title of *Business Review and Future Developments*, where it is stated that:

> The Report of the Directors should be read in conjunction with the Chairman's Statement, the Chief Executive's Review and the Financial Review on pages 2 to 25 which contain details of the Group's trading during the year and an indication of likely future developments.

In the S&N 1997 annual report, the chief executive summarizes the overall achievements of the company in two pages which are then followed by 14 pages dealing in greater detail with the three divisions of the company. These introductory pages are a summary of the achievements of the company over the past year, which is representative of the kind of approach found in the equivalent reviews of other companies. It is here that issues of particular significance to a company can be emphasized and where successes can be flagged with reminders of some of the problems which have to be tackled.

The remaining sections of the chief executive's report are entitled *Brand Building and Divisional Highlights, Retail Division, Beer Division, Leisure Division* and *In the Community*. These bear the hallmark of an operational review as they examine the results of each S&N division with reference to details of specific performances and prospects. It is here that flesh is given to the bare bones of the financial statements, which appear later in annual reports, and where interested parties can learn about the range of a company's activities.

The section *In the Community* contains reference to charitable donations given directly by the company, in addition to fund raising by individual teams of employees, together with reference to community and environment projects. With increasing concern being expressed generally about the environment, this has become a sensitive issue where more companies are seeking to make their stance known. S&N is no exception and it declares its position as follows:

> Scottish and Newcastle's commitment to protecting the environment is underlined with direct financial support for suitable projects and initiatives.
>
> The Company has made an annual donation . . . to fund a Chair in environment research.
>
> In summary our commitment to the environment encompasses every aspect of our operations and the Company continues to develop an active programme in this area.

Financial review

This is a relatively recent addition to the reports contained within the annual report. It sets out to summarize some of the key details and therefore to make them more accessible to the average reader. It also helps to provide explanations for the accounting treatments that have been adopted.

Again what may or may not feature in this section may vary from company to company, largely depending upon whether the company chooses to provide the information here or elsewhere. Thus, for example, Marks and Spencer have chosen to comment on segmental turnover and operating profit in this part of the annual report, while S&N dealt with them in the operational review section of the chief executive's review. Likewise Marks and Spencer include the Cadbury requirement for a reference to 'going concern' here, while S&N do this within the corporate governance section of the annual report (see below, Corporate governance).

There are clearly certain issues which are important at particular moments and which will therefore be more prominent within the financial review. Thus, the acquisition of Courage by S&N was an important theme throughout the 1996 S&N report and it figured prominently in the financial review. Subsequently, the 1997 financial review reflects the integration which has successfully taken place:

> The Courage beer business is now fully integrated with our own Beer business and, as such, it is no longer possible to identify separately the contribution made.

In 1997, in addition to a review of the financial results of each division, S&N provides information on the following:

- interest payable
- profit before taxation
- taxation
- earnings per share and dividends
- acquisitions and disposals

- property revaluation
- foreign exchange
- interest rate management
- treasury policy and capital structure
- accounting policies
- year 2000

Directors' report

A report disclosing certain information to the shareholders by the directors of the company is required by the Companies Act.

The Stock Exchange has also laid down a number of requirements with regard to the information which quoted companies must supply in their annual report in order to keep shareholders abreast of developments and so protect their interests. These requirements, however, largely overlap with those of the Companies Act. In recent years the need to comply with the code of best practice recommended by the Cadbury Report has led in most instances to the appearance of a separate report on corporate governance (see Corporate governance, page 32). To some extent, this has diminished the content of the directors' report. On the other hand, some companies, such as Bass, have incorporated corporate governance issues into the directors' report, which has resulted in a somewhat lengthier version.

The directors' report of most companies, including S&N, follows a similar pattern. The following list gives the items which are included in the S&N 1997 directors' report. These are discussed below.

- group results
- dividends
- business review and future developments
- AGM special business
- share capital
- payment of suppliers
- notifiable interests
- directors
- employee relations and involvement
- disabled persons
- political and charitable contributions
- auditors

Group results

This is a cross-reference to note 2 of the accounts section of the S&N annual report, which gives a segmental analysis of the group's principal activities of retailing, beer and leisure. Other companies, for example Marks and Spencer, supply a figure for group results at this point.

Dividends

Here S&N, like many companies, state the dividend which the directors are recommending for acceptance at the annual general meeting (AGM) of the company. Some companies, such as WH Smith, make reference to the dividend elsewhere within the directors' report, while others, such as BT, mention dividends in the financial review or another section of the annual report.

Business review and future developments

The Companies Act obliges the directors to present a 'business review' which should provide a fair review of the development of the company's business during the year in question, and give an indication of likely future developments.

As the fulfilment of this requirement can be seen as a substantial undertaking, it is now common practice among most of the major companies to cross-reference this to one or more of the earlier reports or reviews in the annual report, where a considerable number of pages can be devoted to describe the performance and likely developments of the business in question.

It is perhaps because of the interest in and usefulness of this section of the report that it has been transferred from the more arid directors' report to find greater prominence within the public relations-oriented areas of annual reports. Thus, readers of the S&N annual report are informed that:

> The Report of the Directors should be read in conjunction with the Chairman's statement, the Chief Executive's Review and the Financial Review.

AGM special business

To comply with Stock Exchange rules, companies need to include an explanation of any non-routine business which they intend to process at the AGM. In 1996 many companies, including S&N, notified shareholders of their intention to formalize the introduction of trading in the company's shares through the Crest system by modifying the Articles of Association of the company.

In 1997 S&N signalled its intention to take advantage of new regulations which will permit it to send summary financial statements to shareholders instead of the full annual report and accounts, unless these are specifically requested.

Another such example is provided by Scottish Television, which announced its intention to seek shareholders' agreement to a change of name to Scottish Media in this section of its 1997 annual report.

On the other hand, routine resolutions which are to be considered at the annual general meeting are included with details of the meeting sent to shareholders and/or included within the annual report (see Notice of Meeting in Appendix 3).

Share capital

The Companies Act requires disclosure of information about share capital in both the directors' report and the balance sheet. Some companies find it convenient to present the relevant details together in one place. Thus, for example, the S&N directors draw the reader's attention to note 21 in the notes to the accounts, where details can be found of:

shares issued during the year, including shares issued and options granted under the employee share schemes.

Payment of suppliers

In 1996 a number of mainly deregulatory changes were made to the Companies Act. At the same time an amendment was introduced requiring directors to explain the company's policy regarding the payment of suppliers.

Sometimes this merely takes the form of a short statement to the effect that it is, for example, 'the company's policy to agree terms and conditions in advance and to pay in accordance with these terms'. In their 1997 report the S&N directors went a little further by declaring that:

> the amount owed to trade creditors by the company was equivalent to 31 days of purchases from suppliers.

Marks and Spencer, on the other hand, in their 1996 report devoted several paragraphs to their policy, distinguishing between general merchandise, food, UK distribution suppliers and suppliers to overseas subsidiaries. Likewise, the 1997 BT annual report contains considerable detail of its policy on the payment of suppliers in this section of its directors' report.

Notifiable interests

Many companies use the heading *Substantial Interests* for this item. This is part of the directors' report which might provide a useful insight as to the possibilities of future bids or offers. The Stock Exchange requires directors to provide information on holdings, other than by the directors themselves, of 3% or more of any class of voting capital. In the case of S&N, the directors state that:

> As from 30 June 1997 the Company has been notified of the following interests representing 3% or more of the issued ordinary share capital of the Company:
> PDFM Ltd 11.5%
> Scottish Widows Fund and Life Assurance Society 3.5%.

Examining previous S&N annual reports, it can be seen that Scottish Widows is a new interest, while PDFM, which held 15.14% in 1995, has decreased its holding.

Directors

The Companies Act requires the disclosure of the names of the directors, whether they or any directors proposed for re-election at the AGM have a service contract with the company and what interests the directors have in shares or debentures of the company. Many users will be interested in studying the composition of the board of directors and noting the interests of board members in the company's shares. Trade union representatives may be looking for arguments to help pursue their claims for improved terms and conditions, while investors will cast a critical eye on any changes in the composition of the board.

This section of the S&N directors' report confines itself to listing changes in the composition of the board, stating the directors who have service contracts and confirming that:

> No director had, during or at the end of the year, any material interest in any contract of significance in relation to the Group's business.

On the other hand, information about the directors, non-executive directors and the interests of directors in the company's shares is found in other sections. S&N refers the reader for details of current directors to pages 26 and 27 of the annual report, where their responsibilities within the company are outlined, together with some biographical details. It also directs the reader to the report of the remuneration committee (see below, Remuneration committee report) for information about the interests of the directors in the shares of the company.

Employee relations and involvement

Practice varies considerably with regard to this section and to the treatment of information generally about employees. Many companies fulfil Companies Act requirements by giving a factual statement under this heading but comment elsewhere in the annual report on significant developments concerning staff involvement.

S&N adopt this approach in 1997 by simply declaring:

> The Company is firmly committed to the principles of employee involvement. A full range of briefing, consultation and bargaining arrangements have been developed in all parts of the Group and these are subject to continual review and improvement.

However, where there was something new to report, as was the case in 1996 for S&N with the adaptation of their Company Council into a Company Forum, then this was reported in the chairman's statement rather than in the directors' report.

On the other hand, BT makes no reference to employees in the 1997 directors' report, but does this within a separate business review section where details are also provided of the BT European Consultative Council. In contrast, Marks and Spencer provides details of employee involvement in the directors' report itself and in the 1996 report this includes the announcement of the setting up of its European Council.

Disabled persons

In compliance with the Companies Act, S&N state their policy for disabled persons, which is as follows:

> Full and fair consideration has been given to applications for employment made by disabled persons and appropriate training, career development and promotion have been provided in all cases.

In 1995 and 1996, unlike many other companies, they also offered additional information about the number of registered disabled people that they employed.

Political and charitable contributions

This has often been an area which has aroused curiosity, if not controversy, at least as far as political contributions were concerned. In

1997 S&N disclosed charitable contributions amounting to £525 000 which were also referred to in a section entitled *In the Community*, page 154. The company also disclosed that it made a contribution of £50 000 during the financial year to the Conservative Party. However, as we saw in the chairman's statement, this practice is to cease with effect from 1997, which now seems to reflect the trend among leading UK companies.

Auditors

Here the directors of S&N have followed what appears to be general practice among companies, although not a statutory requirement, by stating the resolution which will be put to the AGM recommending the reappointment of the existing auditors.

Other items often found in the directors' report

There are a number of other issues which the directors are obliged to refer to, where appropriate, and which are not in the current S&N directors' report either because they are not relevant or because they are found elsewhere in the annual report. These are:

- principal activities
- significant changes in fixed assets
- post-balance sheet events
- research and development
- the company's interest in its own shares
- non-executive directors

Principal activities

The Companies Act requires companies to refer to their 'principal activities' during the year and to disclose any significant changes in such activities. Some companies fulfil this requirement by means of an all-embracing statement such as that of HSBC Holdings which declares that 'the Group provides a comprehensive range of banking and related financial services'. Likewise, Hanson states that it 'is an industrial management company'. Both these companies, however, then go on to refer shareholders to other sections of the annual report which comment on recent developments. Bass provides a fuller picture which could be similarly appropriate for S&N, as shown in Example 3.1.

Example 3.1
Extract from Bass 1995
directors' report

Activities of the Group
The principal activities of the Group are in:

- **Hotels**, through franchising, management or ownership;
- **Leisure retailing**, through ownership, management or leasing of public houses, restaurants, bingo clubs, betting shops, bowling and other amusement centres; through the manufacture, supply and operation of amusement and gaming machines; and
- **Branded drinks**, primarily through the production and distribution of beer and soft drinks.

However, S&N itself makes no direct reference in the directors' report to 'principal activities' but, as discussed above, it refers under the heading *Group Results* to note 2, where an analysis of results in each class of business is presented. This, together with the sections devoted to the operations of its three divisions, makes clear what its principal activities are.

Significant changes in fixed assets

The Companies Act requires the directors to provide details of significant changes in fixed assets during the year and to indicate any substantial differences between the market value and the book value of interests in land and buildings. The 1997 S&N directors' report makes no reference to any changes, but in 1996 readers were referred, in the case of the fixed assets, to notes 12 and 13 of the accounts, which gave details of tangible assets and investments. At the same time it was stated that:

> In the opinion of the Directors, the carrying value of the Group's land and buildings is not more than their current market value.

Post-balance sheet events

The Companies Act requires that these are disclosed in the directors' report. However, the absence of any reference in the S&N directors' report implies that there have not been any important events which have affected the company between the end of the financial year and the date of the approval of the accounts. Where this was important, for example in the case of Hanson in 1995, readers were referred to note 29 of the accounts for details of 'material post-balance sheet events'.

Research and development

Companies have to give an indication of their activities, if any, in this field. Given the nature of S&N's business, it is not surprising that this item does not figure. However, it is more surprising to note that it does not feature in the directors' reports of companies such as GEC, ICI and Zeneca, to name but a few. It seems that the significance of the item is such that, where research and development does take place on a significant scale, companies draw attention to it elsewhere in their reports. Thus, for example, the three companies referred to include research and development within their financial reviews.

The company's interest in its own shares

The Companies Act obliges the directors to declare if the company has purchased any of its own shares during the year in question. Some companies keep their options open by acquiring authority from their shareholders to purchase shares should they subsequently wish to do so. GEC, for example, obtained authority from the AGM to make purchases of its own shares in previous years, and in the 1997 directors' report the directors state their desire to renew and extend this authority, as they consider that:

> further purchases by the Company of its ordinary shares for cancellation may in certain circumstances be advantageous to shareholders through resultant increased earnings per share.

This heading as such does not appear in the S&N directors' report. Instead, reference is made to obtaining such an authority under the heading *AGM Special Business*. This, once again, illustrates the fact that practice varies from company to company, and even from year to year, with regard to the presentation of some items of information.

Non-executive directors

S&N comply with the Stock Exchange Listing Rules to provide biographical details of any directors who are not full-time employees of the company, by including information about their two non-executive directors, with the photographs and details of the full board of directors, see page 158 or pages 26 and 27 of the 1997 annual report. Reference is also made to the non-executive directors in the report of the remuneration committee (see below, Remuneration committee report).

Users of the annual report will be interested to see to what extent non-executive directors may bring further expertise and useful business connections to a company.

Remuneration committee report

In recent years there has been increased interest in the remuneration received by company directors, whether in the form of emoluments (salaries, fees, bonus payments and 'golden handshakes', etc.), or through the receipt of shares in share option schemes or by means of pension arrangements.

Reference to directors' remuneration was normally found in the notes to the accounts, but nowadays in order to forestall criticism most companies adhere very strictly to the best practice provisions annexed to the London Stock Exchange Listing Rules. Companies generally comply with these provisions by including a separate report from their remuneration (or compensation) committee, although a few prefer to disclose this information within the directors' report, as for example in the P&O 1996 annual report and accounts. Since 1996, S&N have adopted the practice of setting out all the details in the remuneration committee report, which is cross-referenced from the notes to the accounts, as shown in Example 3.2.

Example 3.2
Extract from S&N 1997 notes to the accounts

6 DIRECTORS' REMUNERATION
Information concerning directors' emoluments, shareholdings and options is shown in the Report of the Remuneration Committee on pages 30 to 34.

As the presentation of this separate report is still a relatively new practice most companies preface the report with an explanation of the role of the committee and a statement of policy. Hanson, in the 1996 report of its committee, states:

> The role of the compensation committee is to consider and approve on behalf of the board and the shareholders the conditions of

service of the chairman and executive directors. Fees payable to non-executive directors are determined by the full board.

S&N set out the composition, role and policy of this committee at the beginning, as illustrated in Example 3.3, taken from the 1997 report of the remuneration committee.

The Remuneration Committee . . . meets at least three times a year and is responsible for setting all elements of Executive Directors' remuneration packages . . . for establishing the annual targets for the Company's Results Related Bonus Scheme and granting options under the Company's Share Option Schemes, as well as approving participation in, and the operation of, the Company's Long-Term Incentive Package.

In setting the remuneration package for Executive Directors, the Committee aims to ensure that the total package including benefits is competitive with companies of a similar size, activity and complexity.

Because leading companies are adhering to a clear code of best practice the format of remuneration committee reports is virtually the same in all cases. Therefore, interest lies more in analysing the differences in the terms under which directors are employed.

The report of the S&N remuneration committee, for example, provides details of the remuneration package for directors under a series of headings as follows:

- base salary
- results-related bonus scheme
- pensions and life assurance
- other benefits
- long-term plan
- share schemes
- service contracts
- directors' remuneration and interests

The information disclosed in the section on remuneration and interests is similar to that formerly contained in the notes to the accounts, with a breakdown under various headings (with comparative figures for the previous year where appropriate) of the following items:

- total remuneration
- individual remuneration
- pension entitlements
- shares
- executive and savings related share options
- long-term incentive plan

The S&N 1997 remuneration committee report concludes with reference to external appointments, non-executive chairman and non-executive directors as described below.

External appointments

Here we learn that directors are encouraged to become non-executive directors of other leading companies because of the benefit this knowledge and experience can bring:

The company encourages its Executive Directors to become Non-Executive Directors of other leading companies as it believes that the exposure to other companies and the wider knowledge and experience gained benefits the Company.

Non-executive chairman

This section discloses a limitation on the chairman's total package of emoluments:

The Chairman does not participate in the Company's share schemes, Bonus Scheme, Long-Term Incentive Plan or Pension Scheme, but receives life and medical insurance and the provision of a car.

Non-executive directors

This contains reference to the nature of the remuneration received by non-executive directors as follows:

Non-Executive Directors receive a fee only plus their expenses for attending Board and other Company meetings. A small additional fee is paid where a Non-Executive Director chairs a Board Committee. They do not receive any other benefits from the Company and their fees are set by the Board (excluding Non-Executive Directors) within the aggregate limit agreed by share-holders.

Corporate governance

Following the code of best practice issued by the Cadbury Committee and the subsequent Auditing Practices Board Bulletin 1995/1, *Disclosures Relating to Corporate Governance*, companies are expected to report on:

- their audit committee structure
- their internal financial control mechanisms
- their position regarding the ability to continue to operate as a going concern

The company's auditors are required to review compliance with certain aspects of the code of best practice in this connection, as specified by the London Stock Exchange rules (see page 34, Report by the auditors on corporate governance matters).

Practice varies in regard to the form in which companies comply with these requirements. In general, they supply similar information but it is sometimes located in different sections of the annual report. As often as not, directors simply acknowledge their responsibilities by means of a policy declaration confirming that, in fact, they have complied with the provisions of the code.

ICI, for example, in its 1996 annual report makes reference to compliance with corporate governance within the directors' report:

The Company is in full compliance with the Code of Best Practice published in December 1992 by the Committee on the Financial Aspects of Corporate Governance.

There then follows a description of the key elements of internal control which outlines the responsibilities and procedures for internal financial reporting.

On the other hand, the 1996 Marks and Spencer annual report provides a separate corporate governance report with details of the membership of the board of directors and the principal board committees, together with a description of the system of internal financial control.

As if to make the aim abundantly clear, WH Smith in its 1997 annual report presents a statement to reflect its policy on these issues under the lengthy title *Directors' Statement on Responsibilities, Internal Financial Control, Basis of Preparation of the Financial Statements and Corporate Governance.*

Prior to the 1995/6 financial year, when the provisions regarding internal financial control came into effect, S&N referred to corporate governance within the directors' report. However, since then it has produced a separate corporate governance section. This contains three headings which reflect the requirements of the code of best practice:

- corporate governance
- internal financial control
- going concern

The opening paragraph, entitled *corporate governance*, refers to membership of the audit committee and to the fact that since July 1997 that committee has operated with the three non-executive directors stipulated in the code. There is also a cross-reference to the report of the remuneration committee.

The section *internal financial controls* consists of a statement about responsibilities of the board of directors with an outline of five key procedures.

Finally, *going concern* contains a confirmation of the directors' view that the accounts have been rightly prepared on a going concern basis.

These three sections are illustrated in Example 3.4.

Example 3.4 Extract from S&N 1997 corporate governance	**CORPORATE GOVERNANCE** . . . Other than in respect of the periods referred to above when the audit committee operated with two Non-Executive Directors the Company has complied throughout the financial year with the Cadbury Committee's Code of Best Practice. The Report of the Remuneration Committee, arising out of the Greenbury Report on Directors' remuneration and in accordance with Stock Exchange Listing requirements, is set out on pages 30 to 34 following the Report of the Directors. **INTERNAL FINANCIAL CONTROL** The Board is responsible for the Group's system of internal financial control and has established a control structure to provide reasonable, but not absolute, assurance against material misstatement or loss. The key procedures within the control structure are . . . The Board has reviewed the appropriateness and the effectiveness of the system of internal control in operation during the financial year. No material weaknesses have been identified.

In general, these S&N statements regarding corporate governance issues reflect the approach and phraseology used by most leading companies.

Report by the auditors on corporate governance matters

In addition to their audit of the accounts (see below, Auditors' report) the auditors of a company are now required to review the directors' statement on the company's compliance with the code of best practice and to draw any attention to any non-compliance with the paragraphs of the code which have been specified by the Stock Exchange. This report may be found, as in the case of S&N, adjacent to the statement on corporate governance. On the other hand, in the case of other companies such as Bass it may be located together with the auditors' report on the accounts.

Here again we cannot expect to learn anything new about the company, unless there have been some very significant problems which the auditors have encountered and which they are obliged to indicate. In the absence of any need to qualify their statement, the auditors adopt the wording given in an Auditing Practices Board example. The form of words which is used in the 1997 S&N auditors' report on corporate governance matters, which is reproduced in Example 3.5, is therefore similar to that used by other companies.

Example 3.5
Extract from S&N 1997 report by the auditors on corporate governance matters

REPORT BY THE AUDITORS TO SCOTTISH & NEWCASTLE plc ON CORPORATE GOVERNANCE MATTERS
In addition to our audit of the accounts we have reviewed the Directors' statement above on the Company's compliance with the paragraphs of the Code of Best Practice specified for our review by the London Stock Exchange . . .

We carried out our review in accordance with [guidance] issued by the Auditing Practices Board, and assessed whether the Directors' statements on going concern and internal financial control are consistent with the information of which we are aware from our audit. That [guidance] does not require us to perform the additional work necessary to, and we do not, express any opinion on the effectiveness of either the Group's system of internal financial control or its corporate governance procedures nor on the ability of the Group to continue in operational existence.

Opinion
With respect to the Directors' statements on internal financial control above other than the opinion on effectiveness, which is outside the scope of our report, and going concern above, in our opinion the Directors have provided the disclosures required . . . and such statements are consistent with the information of which we are aware from our audit work on the accounts.

> Based on enquiry of certain Directors and officers of the Company, and examination of relevant documents, in our opinion the Directors' statement above appropriately reflects the Company's compliance with the other paragraphs of the Code specified for our review, [by Listing Rule 12.43(j)].

Statement of directors' responsibilities

All annual reports contain a more or less similar statement concerning the responsibilities of the directors in regard to the financial statements. An extract from the S&N statement of directors' responsibilities is reproduced in Example 3.6.

Example 3.6
Extract from S&N 1997 statement of directors' responsibilities

> The Directors are required by law to prepare accounts which give a true and fair view of the state of affairs of the Company and of the Group at the end of the financial year and of the profits for that year . . . that proper and adequate accounting records have been kept and that appropriate procedures have been followed . . . Appropriate accounting policies . . . have been applied consistently . . .

This statement should be read in conjunction with the auditors' report, which will be found in close juxtaposition.

Auditors' report

At their annual general meeting, all companies have to appoint auditors who are responsible for reporting to the shareholders on whether the accounts have been prepared in accordance with the Companies Act and the appropriate accounting standards, and whether the accounts give a 'true and fair view' of the state of affairs of the company (and of the group, if relevant) and of the profit. Also, as we have seen above, they are now expected to express an opinion on the directors' corporate governance report, although this is stated separately from what is normally recognized as the auditors' report, which is under consideration here.

In the annual report of S&N, in line with other companies, the respective responsibilities of the directors and the auditors are made clear by means of a paragraph entitled *Respective responsibilities of directors and auditors*. This also links with the statement of directors' responsibilities referred to immediately above. The respective responsibilities of directors and auditors are succinctly expressed as shown in Example 3.7.

Example 3.7
Extract from S&N 1997 report of the auditors

> As described above (i.e. in the *Statement of Directors' Responsibilities*) the Company's Directors are responsible for the preparation of the accounts. It is our responsibility to form an independent opinion, based on our audit, on those accounts and to report our opinion to you (i.e. the shareholders).

At first glance the auditors' report, in view of its importance, the amount of work involved and the size of the fees incurred, is extremely brief. However, this is because the report itself follows a set formula which does not describe in detail the work involved in reaching the opinion expressed. The 1997 S&N auditors' report, a further extract from which is reproduced in Example 3.8, is therefore typical in style and content of those found in the annual reports of other UK companies.

It should be noted that the report is addressed to the shareholders of the company, to whom the auditors are ultimately responsible. It is in fact the shareholders who appoint or reappoint the auditors at a company's annual general meeting. Most auditors' reports contain four sections with the following headings:

1 *to the members*, which spells out the areas audited or examined by the auditors
2 *respective responsibilities of directors and auditors*, which we referred to above
3 *basis of opinion*, which refers to how the audit was undertaken
4 *opinion*, which normally confirms that the accounts give a true and fair view of the state of affairs of the company (and the group, where applicable) and of the profit.

These headings are illustrated within the context of the S&N annual report as shown in Example 3.8.

Example 3.8
Extract from S&N 1997
Report of the Auditors

To the members of Scottish & Newcastle plc
We have audited the financial statements on pages . . .

Respective responsibilities of directors and auditors
As described above . . .

Basis of opinion
We conducted our audit in accordance with Auditing Standards issued by the Auditing Practices Board. An audit includes examination, on a test basis, of evidence relevant to the amounts and disclosures in the accounts. It also includes assessment of the significant estimates and judgements made by the Directors in the preparation of the accounts . . .

We planned and performed our audit so as to obtain all the information and explanations . . . in forming our opinion we also evaluated the overall adequacy of the presentation of information in the accounts.

Opinion
In our opinion the accounts give a true and fair view of the state of affairs of the Company and of the Group as at 27 April 1997 and of the profit of the Group for the 52 weeks then ended and have been properly prepared in accordance with the Companies Act 1985.

If, for some reason, the auditors were not satisfied with the financial statements because, for example, of lack of evidence on which to form their opinion, or because they disagreed with the way a particular item had been treated in the accounts, then they would issue a 'qualified opinion'. There is a set way in which the auditors express their reservations about the accounts and in such cases the wording in their report would follow a recommended pattern. Thus, at one extreme, if the auditors were in fundamental disagreement, they would state that the accounts 'do not give a true and fair view'. On the other hand, if it were a question of uncertainty about a particular matter, then they would state that their opinion was 'subject to . . .' and then refer, for example, to clarification of a specific matter in the accounts.

Summary

In addition to the financial statements and notes to accounts which are discussed in Chapters 4 to 10 of this book, there are two reports which have to be included by law within the annual report. These are the directors' report and the auditors' report.

There are also a number of further reports which appear as a result of the rules of the Stock Exchange and codes of best practice. These include a financial review, a report on corporate governance and a report by the remuneration committee.

We will not necessarily find disclosure of information in an identical manner in every company annual report. Companies sometimes chose to locate information in different sections of their annual reports and there are often cross-references within the documentation to indicate how a company has complied with its obligations.

Annual reports provide a good opportunity for companies to publicize their achievements and to enhance their images. The chairman's statement and chief executive's report and/or the operational review are generally used for these purposes.

The reports and reviews in the annual report help users to gain a wider appreciation of the activities and performance of a particular company. They provide the flesh to the bare bones of the financial statements which follow. However, they need to be studied with caution, bearing in mind the different goals the preparers are aiming at.

Exercises

These exercises are based on the extracts from the S&N 1997 annual report and accounts in Appendix 3.

1 Where would you find the business review and information about future developments?

2 The chairman's statement refers to a recommended final dividend of 14.17p per share. Where will you find details of the total ordinary dividend for 1997 and what is it?

3 S&N executive directors and selected managers may benefit from a long-term incentive plan. Where would you expect to find details of this? What criterion is used to determine the group's performance in relation to the allocation of shares under this plan?

4 Who are S&N's auditors? Is it proposed to reappoint them at the 1997 AGM? Have they presented a qualified or unqualified report in respect of the 1997 accounts?

5 What is meant by 'going concern'? Where do S&N's directors confirm that this is the case?

The balance sheet: formats, headings and totals

The balance sheet is a statement which shows the financial position of a person or an organization at a particular moment in time. Anyone's financial position is represented by what they own less what they owe. We often refer to what a person owns as *assets* and what that person owes as *liabilities*.

As an example, if, at 1 January 1997, John owns assets of £78 000 and has liabilities of £28 000, we might summarize this by saying that John is worth £50 000 (i.e. £78 000 – £28 000). We can present this information in the form of a statement as shown in Example 4.1.

Example 4.1	
John's financial position at	Assets	78 000
1 January 1997	Liabilities	28 000
	John's worth	50 000

Example 4.1	Assets	78 000
John's financial position at 1 January 1997	Liabilities	28 000
	John's worth	50 000

The above statement is John's balance sheet, i.e. it is a statement of John's financial position at a particular moment in time. If we had more details about what his individual assets and liabilities are we could present a more detailed version of his balance sheet. For example, if he has very recently bought a house and a car, and assuming that we have obtained details of his liabilities, his balance sheet could be as shown in Example 4.2.

Example 4.2	**Assets**		
John: balance sheet at 1 January 1997	House	70 000	
	Car	5 000	
	Cash	3 000	78 000
	Liabilities		
	Money owed to building society	27 000	
	Money owed on credit card	1 000	28 000
	John's worth		50 000

Instead of presenting the balance sheet in this way (i.e. vertically), we could use a horizontal presentation as in Example 4.3.

Example 4.3
John: balance sheet at 1
January 1997 (horizontal
format)

Assets	£	Liabilities	£
House	70 000	Money owed to building society	27 000
Car	5 000	Money owed on credit card	1 000
Cash	3 000		
			28 000
		John's worth	50 000
	78 000		78 000

We have been careful to say that the house and car were bought 'very recently' in order to avoid becoming involved in a debate about how we put a value on the house and any other assets and, consequently, what impact this has on John's 'worth'. The problem of the valuation of balance sheet items is an important accounting issue and we will need to discuss this later. For the moment, we will follow the fairly conventional approach, which is to bring assets into the balance sheet at their cost price.

The balance sheet of a business organization is based on the same relationship between assets and liabilities as the balance sheet of an individual person and it contains the same sort of information. However, a business balance sheet usually includes much more detail as well as having subtotals for various classes of assets and liabilities. In addition, there is likely to be a certain amount of accounting jargon, one example being that the difference between what is owned by the business (i.e. its assets) and what the business owes to outsiders (its liabilities to outsiders) is usually called *capital*.

For the moment, if we can accept the notion of headings and subtotals (which we will come back to), we can consider the business balance sheet in Example 4.4, which has been drawn up for the retail fruit business of Mary.

Example 4.4
Mary: balance sheet at 31
January 1997

	£			£
Fixed assets				
Premises	58 000		Creditors: amounts falling due after more than one year	
			Loan	38 000
Equipment	11 000		Creditors: amounts falling due within one year	
Delivery van	5 000	74 000	Trade creditors (i.e. amounts owed to suppliers)	1 500
Current assets				
Stock (i.e. of fruit)	150		**Capital**	37 180
Trade debtors (i.e. amounts owed by customers)	620			
Cash at bank and in hand	1 910	2 680		
		76 680		76 680

There is much more detail in the above example than in John's balance sheet but the underlying relationship remains, i.e:

Assets	(74 000 + 2680)	76 680
Liabilities	(38 000 + 1500)	39 500
Capital		37 180

We can express this relationship as follows:

Assets – Liabilities = Capital

or as:

Assets = Liabilities + Capital

Just one point to notice here: we are implicitly defining liabilities as liabilities to outsiders. It is necessary to draw attention to this now because the term *liabilities* is sometimes used in a broader sense to incorporate the liability of the business to the proprietor. Although this is not of great significance, we might come across balance sheets, for example from some European countries, where this more inclusive meaning is used. Provided we are careful to define what we mean when we use these terms this will not present any problem.

The balance sheet of a major public limited company will probably contain more detail and jargon than the examples we have considered so far, but the underlying relationship remains. Remember that public limited companies will usually present two balance sheets, a group balance sheet and a company balance sheet. In any discussion we have we must, therefore, be careful to identify to which balance sheet we are referring.

From the S&N 1997 group balance sheet (see Appendix 3: Extracts from S&N annual report and accounts) we can identify this basic underlying relationship as shown in Example 4.5.

Example 4.5
Extract from S&N 1997
group balance sheet

Assets – Liabilities	£2207.7 million
Capital (called *Capital and Reserves* in this example)	£2207.7 million

The figure for Assets – Liabilities (£2207.7 million) is arrived at by adding together the two asset figures (fixed assets £3192.9 million and current assets £673.4 million) and deducting the three liability figures (creditors falling due within one year £1166.5 million, creditors falling due after more than one year £409.2 million and provisions for liabilities and charges £82.9 million). We will need to look at these items and the subtotals in the balance sheet in more detail later but, for now, the main point is that the underlying balance sheet relationship is the same for a public limited company as it is in the above examples for John and Mary.

Balance sheet formats

There are several different ways in which a balance sheet may be set out. In the UK, limited companies must use one of two formats prescribed in the Companies Act. These are reproduced in Appendix 1.

Most UK companies, including S&N, use Format 1, which focuses on the shareholders' interest in the company. For S&N, as we have seen, this is £2207.7 million.

The S&N 1997 group balance sheet, adapted from the annual report and accounts, is set out below in Example 4.6. We have inserted (1) and (2), to identify the totals which make up the balance sheet relationship (i.e. Assets – Liabilities = Capital).

Example 4.6

S&N 1997 group balance
sheet (Format 1 balance
sheet)

	£million
Fixed assets	
Tangible assets	2966.9
Investments	226.0
	3192.9
Current assets	
Stocks	149.6
Debtors	450.8
Cash and short-term deposits	73.0
	673.4
Creditors: amounts falling due within one year	1166.5
Net current liabilities	(493.1)
Total assets less current liabilities	2699.8
Less:	
Creditors: amounts falling due after more than one year	409.2
Provisions for liabilities and charges	82.9
(1)	**2207.7**
Capital and reserves	
Equity share capital	183.6
Non-equity share capital	12.4
Called up share capital	196.0
Equity reserves	
Share premium account	831.3
Revaluation reserve	312.8
Other reserves	(433.3)
Profit and loss account	1300.9
(2)	**2207.7**

(1) Assets – Liabilities
(2) Capital

In Example 4.7 the figures from the S&N 1997 group balance sheet have been rearranged to provide an example of a Format 2 balance sheet. Again, we have identified the items making up the balance sheet equation (expressed as assets = liabilities + capital) this time by inserting (A) and (B).

Example 4.7

Format 2 balance sheet
(using S&N figures for
illustration)

	£million
Fixed assets	
Tangible assets	2966.9
Investments	226.0
	3192.9
Current assets	
Stocks	149.6
Debtors	450.8
Cash and short-term deposits	73.0
	673.4
(A)	**3866.3**
Capital and reserves	
Called up share capital	196.0
Share premium account	831.3
Revaluation reserve	312.8
Other reserves	(433.3)
Profit and loss account	1300.9
	2207.7
Provisions for liabilities and charges	82.9
Creditors	1575.7
(B)	**3866.3**

(A) Assets
(B) Liabilities + capital
The figure for creditors in the Format 2 balance sheet is shown as one figure, 1575.7 In the above example it is arrived at by adding the two creditors figures, i.e. 1166.5 + 409.2 in Example 4.6.

Making comparisons between companies can be facilitated by the use of prescribed formats, but we must allow for the fact that, even with such formats, there might be differences in presentations used by companies. Companies will only use the format headings to the extent that they are relevant; for example, a company which does not have any fixed assets will omit the heading *fixed assets* from its balance sheet. In addition, there is a limited amount of flexibility within the formats with regard to the positioning of certain items.

There may be other, more important, differences between two companies' balance sheets: first, between the amount of detailed information that is included, and second, because of possible differences in the ways in which companies arrive at the values of balance sheet items. Accountants refer to the former as *disclosure differences* and to the latter as *measurement differences*.

As we have seen in Chapter 1, the form and contents of a public company's annual accounts are governed by the Companies Act, accounting standards, the Stock Exchange and codes of best practice. However, some companies may choose to give more details for some items than is strictly necessary. Moreover, the general prescriptive rules set out by the authoritative sources still leave room for companies to chose from a number of possible accounting methods in respect of certain transactions or asset valuation methods. Hence, it is important to look at a company's statement of accounting policies to ascertain the accounting treatment chosen by the company for any particular item in which we are interested.

Balance sheet headings and subtotals

Having considered what a balance sheet is and how it might be laid out, we can now examine in more detail the contents of the balance sheet. We will need to discuss both the balance sheet headings and subtotals, as well as the individual items. In this chapter we will consider the balance sheet headings and subtotals and how they relate to each other. The individual items which appear under the main headings are considered in Chapters 5 and 6.

The following headings and subtotals are those shown in bold in Example 4.6.

Fixed assets

These are defined in the Companies Act as assets 'intended for use on a continuing basis in the company's activities' (Sch 4, 77). Such assets are not acquired for resale. They include tangible assets such as land and machinery, intangible assets such as patents and brand names, and investments such as shares held in other companies. These individual items are discussed below (see Chapter 5).

Current assets

These are assets which a company possesses but which it does not intend to hold long term, i.e. they are held by a company on a short-term basis. The definition of short term for this purpose is usually taken as one year.

The main items found under this heading are stock, debtors and cash. An alternative term which used to be employed instead of *current assets* is *circulating assets*. This is a useful term in that it underlines the basic relationship between the various types of current assets which are used up in the generation of cash during the company's operating activities. Broadly speaking:

> a company hopes to make sales to its customers from its holding of items in *stock*; customers who owe money for *stock* they have bought will be called *debtors*; when the *debtors* pay their bills this will increase the company's balance of *cash*; the company can use this *cash* to buy more *stock*; and so on . . . and so on.

Of course, in the same way that a company might need to grant credit to its customers, the same company would look to obtaining credit from its own suppliers. Hence, the amount of cash needed at any one time will be reduced by the credit the company receives from suppliers. Any sums owed to suppliers and which are due within the next year will be included under the heading *creditors: amounts falling due within one year*.

Creditors: amounts falling due within one year

Creditors are other companies or individuals to whom a company owes sums of money. Any sums which are due for payment within one year are included under this heading. Items found here include amounts owed for goods or services supplied, taxes due and amounts due under short-term loans including bank overdrafts (see Chapter 6). In addition, any part of a long-term loan which is due for payment within the next year will be classified under this heading.

We might come across an alternative term, *current liabilities*, being used instead of the term *creditors: amounts falling due within one year*.

Net current liabilities

This is one of two terms which is used to describe the relationship between the items *current assets* and *creditors: amounts falling due within one year*. These two terms are *net current assets* (where the figure for *current assets* is greater than the figure for *creditors: amounts falling due within one year*) and *net current liabilities* (where the figure for *creditors: amounts falling due within one year* is greater than the figure for *current assets*).

For S&N, the relationship results in a figure entitled *net current liabilities*, as can be seen in Example 4.8.

Example 4.8
Extract from S&N 1997
group balance sheet

	£million
Current assets	673.4
less	
Creditors: amounts falling due within one year	1166.5
gives	
Net current liabilities	(493.1)

(The figure for net current liabilities is shown in brackets to indicate that it is a negative figure, i.e. liabilities are greater than assets.)

The relationship between the items *current assets* and *creditors: amounts falling due within one year* is an important one. In order to be able to pay the items which are included under the heading *creditors: amounts falling due within one year*, we need to have cash available and the cash needs to be available within the next 12 months. The sort of assets which will produce the cash for us are current assets. If we do not have sufficient money available from current assets we will have to find it in other ways, for example by borrowing more.

Another term which is used to describe this relationship, when the current assets exceed the *creditors: amounts falling due within one year* is *working capital*. It is rarely found as a description within a balance sheet, but it is often used in discussions about company finance.

Total assets less current liabilities

This subtotal is made up of the total assets less the current liabilities.

The Format 1 balance sheet (see Appendix 1) does not require a separate figure to be shown for total assets. Total assets is the sum of the fixed assets and the current assets. We know that *current liabilities* is an alternative term for *creditors: amounts falling due within one year*.

Hence, the three items which make up this subtotal are: *fixed assets, current assets* and *creditors: amounts falling due within one year*. We already have a subtotal for *current assets* less *creditors: amounts falling due within one year* (i.e. the net current liabilities, 493.1). For the S&N 1997 group balance sheet the figures are as shown in Example 4.9.

Example 4.9 Extract from S&N 1997 group balance sheet		£million
	Fixed assets	3192.9
	Net current liabilities	(493.1)
	Total assets less current liabilities	2699.8

This item represents the total amount invested by a company in its fixed assets and working capital.

If an individual approached his bank manager with a view to borrowing some money to start a business, the manager would want to know what the total financial requirement was. The total required would be made up of the amount needed to buy fixed assets together with the amount needed to run the business on a day-to-day basis, i.e. the working capital. The latter would include cash, to pay wages and other expenses, and adequate stock to meet customers' demands. Having ascertained the total requirement for finance, the bank manager might suggest that the business should be financed partly from the individual's own funds and partly from a loan from the bank. Many businesses are financed in this way, i.e. in part from funds supplied by the owners and in part from borrowings. The next item in the balance sheet identifies the loans which have been borrowed on a long-term basis.

Creditors: amounts falling due after more than one year

This heading covers the amounts due to creditors where the settlement is not due until after one year. The most usual items included under this heading are various forms of loans which are due to be repaid after one year (see Chapter 6). Alternative terms for *creditors: amounts falling due after more than one year* which we might come across, sometimes in translations of foreign company accounts, are *long-term creditors* and *long-term liabilities*.

The items included under the heading *creditors: amounts falling due after more than one year* consist, in the main, of loans which have arisen from contractual arrangements. Other possible long-term liabilities are dealt with under the heading which now follows.

Provisions for liabilities and charges

We saw in the immediately preceding section that any long-term amounts owing to creditors as a result of a contractual arrangement, for example a long-term loan, are included under the heading *creditors: amounts falling due after more than one year*. We also have to think about other possible liabilities and losses. Broadly speaking, there are two reasons which give rise to such items. First, there might be liabilities or losses which are certain to be incurred, but where we are uncertain as to the amount or as to the date on which they will be incurred; second, we might have liabilities or losses which are likely to be incurred. The Companies Act requires that these items are included in the balance sheet. Examples are reorganization costs and pension costs. These and similar items are shown under the heading *provisions for liabilities and charges* (for individual items, see Chapter 6).

Balance sheet total (1) Assets − liabilities £2207.7 million

In order to arrive at the figure for assets less liabilities, we have to take the figure for total assets less current liabilities and deduct the two long-term liability amounts, i.e. creditors: amounts falling due after one year and provisions for liabilities and charges. This is illustrated by the S&N 1997 group balance sheet in Example 4.10.

Example 4.10
Extract from S&N 1997
group balance sheet

	£million
Total assets less current liabilities	2699.8
less:	
Creditors: amounts falling due after more than one year	409.2
Provisions for liabilities and charges	82.9
	2207.7

We have now arrived at a total for assets less liabilities. In order to complete our balance sheet equation, i.e. assets − liabilities = capital, we need a figure for capital. This is the final item in our discussion of balance sheet headings and subtotals.

Capital and reserves

This item represents the stake of the owners in the business. In terms of the balance sheet equation it is the difference between the assets and the liabilities to outsiders.

When any firm is set up the owners need to find the necessary money to acquire fixed assets and to provide an adequate amount of working capital. As we have seen, the total financial requirement might be provided partly by the owners and partly from loans. We have already shown in the balance sheet the amount of loans (long-term loans are included under the heading *creditors: amounts falling due after more than one year*). Here, under this heading of *capital and reserves*, we find the amount provided by the owners. The individual items under this heading are discussed in Chapter 6.

Balance sheet total (2) Capital £2207.7 million

This is the sum of the individual items which appear under the *capital and reserves* heading.

Summary

There is an underlying relationship in the balance sheet which can be expressed as: assets − liabilities = capital.

In the UK, company balance sheets have to comply with one of the standard formats set out in the Companies Act. These formats include standard headings which have been discussed in this chapter. The individual items which appear under these headings are examined in the following two chapters.

These exercises are based on the extracts from the S&N 1997 annual report and accounts in Appendix 3.

1 What is the total amount of assets for the company at 27 April 1997?
2 What is the total amount of liabilities of the group, including amounts provided for, at 27 April 1997?
3 Complete the following table for the S&N company for 1996

£million

Fixed assets	-----------------------
Net current liabilities	-----------------------
Total assets less current liabilities	-----------------------

4 What is the difference between fixed assets and current assets?
5 In all business balance sheets there is an underlying relationship which may be expressed as assets – liabilities = capital. With appropriate figures, show this relationship for the company at 27 April 1997.

The balance sheet: fixed assets and current assets

Introduction

Now that we have examined the balance sheet headings and subtotals we can consider the individual items which are found under these headings:

- fixed assets
- current assets
- creditors: amounts falling due within one year
- creditors: amounts falling due after more than one year
- provisions for liabilities and charges
- capital and reserves

In this chapter we will deal with the first two of these headings; the remaining four will be discussed in Chapter 6.

In our discussion on the individual items, we will make reference to information found on the face of the balance sheet, as well as information to be found in the notes to the accounts section.

As a general point, we need to remember that companies have to set out their important accounting policies in a separate statement (often note 1 of the notes to the accounts) and readers of sets of accounts should also refer to that statement.

Fixed assets

This heading includes three types of fixed assets:

1 intangible assets
2 tangible assets
3 investments

Where appropriate, a balance sheet will include all three types of fixed assets, as can be seen in the Boots 1997 group balance sheet, shown in Example 5.1.

Example 5.1
Extract from Boots 1997 group balance sheet

	Notes	£million
Fixed assets		
Intangible assets	10	33.8
Tangible assets	11	1769.7
Investments	12	0.5

S&N, on the other hand, in common with most UK companies, does not include intangible assets. For example, the S&N 1997 group balance sheet, as shown in Example 5.2, includes only two of the three fixed asset items.

Example 5.2
Extract from S&N 1997 group balance sheet

	Notes	£million
Fixed assets		
Tangible assets	12	2966.9
Investments	13	226.0

Intangible fixed assets

The intangible assets which Boots includes in its balance sheet (Example 5.1) are, according to the relevant note to the accounts, 'Patents, trademarks and other product rights accrued'. The Companies Act lists the following examples of intangible assets in the standard balance sheet formats:

- development costs
- concessions, patents, trademarks and similar rights and assets
- goodwill
- payments on account

It is a Companies Act requirement that fixed assets, including intangible assets, with a limited useful economic life are to be reduced to their residual value (often this means the 'scrap value') over such life, i.e. over the time that they will be used by the company. Example 5.3 illustrates the meaning of the terms *depreciation* and *amortization*, which are used to describe the spreading of costs.

Example 5.3
Amortization and depreciation

A company purchases for £100 000 a patent to manufacture a certain product; the patent has five years to run. The company will need to spread the cost of the patent over the next five years by charging an appropriate amount against its profits. In this example the company can divide the cost, £100 000, by the remaining useful life, 5 years, to arrive at an amount of £20 000, to be charged against its profits for each of the next five years. We usually use the term 'depreciation' for spreading the costs of tangible assets and 'amortization' when referring to intangible assets. At the end of the first year the asset will have a balance sheet value of £80 000, i.e. cost £100 000 less amortization £20 000.

The treatment of various intangible assets in balance sheets has been debated by accountants for several years. Two intangible assets, research and development and goodwill, are each covered by a separate SSAP. A recent exposure draft, FRED 12: Goodwill and intangible assets, covers intangible assets in general, including brands which have appeared in some company balance sheets in recent years.

The following types of intangible assets are discussed below:

- research and development
- goodwill
- brands

Research and development

S&N is not engaged in operations where research and development is of major concern. However, in other companies it is a significant item and is the subject of a separate accounting standard, SSAP 13: Accounting for research and development.

SSAP 13 requires that:

- the cost of fixed assets which provide facilities for research and development be shown as fixed assets and depreciated over their useful lives by charges to the profit and loss account;
- research expenditure, on both pure and applied research, be charged to the profit and loss account in the year of expenditure;
- development expenditure be written off to the profit and loss account in the year of expenditure.

Provided certain criteria (including the ultimate profitability of the project being developed) are met, it is possible for a company to treat some development expenditure as an tangible fixed asset. In such a case the value included as an asset will have to be amortized over its useful life.

The following extract from the accounting policies statement of Smith Kline Beecham in 1995, shown in Example 5.4, is a fairly typical example from a company engaged in research and development.

Example 5.4	**Research and development expenditure**
Extract from Smith Kline Beecham 1995 annual report	Laboratory buildings and equipment used for research and development are included as tangible fixed assets and written off in accordance with the Group's depreciation policy. Other research and development expenditure is written off in the year in which it is incurred.

Goodwill

At present, the accounting treatment of goodwill is covered by SSAP 22. However, the accounting treatment currently applied is likely to change because goodwill is the subject of an exposure draft (FRED 12). As the exposure draft points out, 'Accounting for goodwill has been a contentious issue in the UK for many years'.

Goodwill is an intangible asset which arises when the value of the business as a whole exceeds the sum of the values of the identifiable net assets. This is illustrated in Example 5.5.

Example 5.5	The balance sheet of company B at 1 January 1998 is as follows:	
Identifiable net assets		£million
	Fixed assets	100
	Net current assets	70
		170
	Creditors: amounts due after more than one year	20
		150*

Capital and reserves	
Share capital	60
Reserves	90
	150

*This is the sum of the values of the assets less liabilities which have been identified and included in the balance sheet.

Assuming that in this example the balance sheet values approximate to the market values, we can say that the business is worth £150 million. However, if a prospective buyer is willing to pay £175 million for the business, the extra £25 million represents a payment for an asset not identified in the balance sheet, i.e. a payment for the goodwill of the business.

The existence of goodwill might arise from a number of factors, including an especially good location, possession of well-known brand names, a highly skilled workforce, management expertise or other attributes associated with a company.

From an accounting standpoint, there are two types of goodwill:

- internally generated goodwill
- purchased goodwill

Internally generated goodwill can exist but the only occasion when a verifiable value can be attributed to it is when a business is sold. Hence, internally generated goodwill is not included in a company's balance sheet. This is the accounting treatment (or lack of treatment!) specified in both the existing accounting standard (SSAP 22) and the proposed standard contained in FRED 12.

Purchased goodwill arises when a purchaser of an individual company pays more than the fair (i.e. market) values of the identified net assets, as in the above example (Example 5.5).

The vast majority of cases where purchased goodwill arises are acquisitions (takeovers) of one company by another. When this occurs the excess price paid to acquire control, sometimes referred to as *goodwill arising on consolidation*, has to be accounted for in the group accounts. This is illustrated in Example 5.6.

Example 5.6
Goodwill arising on consolidation

Company B (from Example 5.5) is taken over by company A on 1 January 1998. The balance sheets of company A and company B immediately after the takeover are shown below.

Company A and company B balance sheets at 1 January 1998

	A £million	B £million
Fixed assets	220	100
Investment in B	175	
Net current assets	195	70
	590	170
Creditors: amounts due after one year	90	20
	500	150

Capital and reserves		
Share capital	200	60
Reserves	300	90
	500	150

Company A has paid £175 million to obtain control of company B, which has a balance sheet capital (called *capital and reserves*) of £150 million, the difference being the goodwill.

When the figures are consolidated into a group balance sheet, the assets and liabilities of both companies are added together. The cost of the investment in B (in A's balance sheet) is then compared with what B is worth according to its balance sheet (i.e. B's capital and reserves). The group balance sheet will be as follows:

Group balance sheet at 1 January 1998

	£million
Goodwill	25 (175 − (60 + 90))
Fixed assets	320 (220 + 100)
Net current assets	265 (195 + 70)
	610
Creditors: amounts due after one year	110 (90 + 20)
	500
Capital and reserves	
Share capital	200
Reserves	300
	500

The overall result is that the investment in B (from A's balance sheet) has been replaced by the assets and liabilities of B, and the premium paid by A, over and above the balance sheet worth of B, has been shown as goodwill.

In Example 5.6 the goodwill is included as an asset in the group balance sheet. There are, in fact, two ways in which goodwill can be dealt with in the group accounts.

Before discussing these different treatments, it is interesting to compare the balance sheet of the individual company (company A) which is now the owner of company B with the group balance sheet. This will be as shown in Example 5.7.

Example 5.7
Group and company
balance sheets

Balance sheets at 1 January 1998

	Group	Company (i.e. company A)
	£million	£million
Goodwill	25	
Fixed assets	320	220
Investment		175
Net current assets	265	195
	610	590
Creditors: amounts after more than one year	110	90
	500	500
Capital and reserves		
Share capital	200	200
Reserves	300	300
	500	500

FIXED ASSETS

In a real-world balance sheet the goodwill would be included under the heading *intangible assets* but it has been shown as a separate item in this example in order to emphasize that goodwill appears in the group balance sheet only. At the same time it can be observed that the investment (£175 million) in the company balance sheet is not included in the group balance sheet; this is because, in the group accounts, the investment has been replaced by the underlying assets and liabilities of the investee company (company B).

There are two methods by which goodwill can be treated in the accounts:

1 Include the goodwill as an asset and amortize it over its useful life.
2 Write off the value attributed to goodwill immediately against existing reserves.

These alternatives are illustrated in Example 5.8 below (using the group balance sheet from Example 5.7).

Example 5.8
Alternative accounting treatments for goodwill

Group balance sheet at 1 January 1998	Method (1) £million	Method (2) £million
Goodwill	25	
Fixed assets	320	320
Net current assets	265	265
	610	585
Creditors: amounts due after one year	110	110
	500	475
Capital and reserves		
Share capital	200	200
Reserves	300	275 (300 – 25)
	500	475

Under method (1) the value of the goodwill, £25 million, will be written off over future years, i.e. against future profits. The act of bringing goodwill into the balance sheet as an asset can be referred to as *capitalization of goodwill*.

Under method (2), the value of the goodwill, £25 million, has been written off over existing reserves, i.e. against profits which have been built up in previous years.

Most UK companies follow (2), which is the treatment stipulated in SSAP 22 for 'normal' circumstances ('Purchased goodwill should normally be eliminated from the accounts immediately on acquisition against reserves', SSAP 22). S&N adopts this treatment, as can be seen in the extract from the notes to the accounts shown in Example 5.9.

Example 5.9
Extract from S&N 1997 notes to the accounts

1 ACCOUNTING POLICIES
(b) Basis of consolidation
(ii) On the acquisition of subsidiary undertakings or businesses, fair values are attributed to the underlying net tangible assets acquired. Goodwill, being the excess of the consideration over the fair values, is taken to reserves.

By adopting this treatment, i.e. deducting the goodwill from the reserves, companies are protecting future profits from goodwill amortization. However, it is the alternative method (1) which is proposed in the new draft standard (FRED 12). Adoption of this proposal would bring UK accounting into line with practice in many foreign countries; most overseas companies capitalize goodwill. The possibility of different accounting treatments being used needs to be taken into account when comparisons are being made between the financial statements of companies from different countries. The effects of different accounting treatments for goodwill is highlighted in Example 5.10, which has been adapted from the Hanson annual report for 1995.

Hanson plc is a UK company and therefore prepares its accounts in accordance with UK accounting rules and standards (UK GAAP). However, because of its US involvement, it includes, voluntarily, in its annual report a statement showing the effects of preparing the accounts in accordance with US GAAP compared with UK GAAP.

Example 5.10
Extract from Hanson 1995
annual report

		£million
Profit available for appropriation as reported in the consolidated profit and loss account (i.e. based on UK GAAP)		1015
Significant adjustments:		
Goodwill amortization	(106)	
Other adjustments	(37)	
		(143)
Estimated profit available for appropriation as adjusted to accord with US GAAP		872
Ordinary shareholders' interest as reported in the consolidated balance sheet		3623
Significant adjustments:		
Goodwill	5055	
Other adjustments	(727)	
		4328
Estimated ordinary shareholders' interest as adjusted to accord with US GAAP		7951

The profit computed in accordance with US GAAP is less than that computed in accordance with UK GAAP by £143 million, of which £106 million arises because of goodwill amortization during this year. On the other hand, the shareholders' interest when computed using US GAAP is higher than it is using UK GAAP because in the UK the shareholders' interest would have been reduced by the immediate write-off to existing reserves when goodwill arose.

Brands
Unlike research and development and goodwill, there is currently no accounting standard on brands. However, the exposure draft previously referred to in the discussion on goodwill, FRED12, as its title

'Goodwill and intangible assets' implies, does include brands within its scope, but only generically.

Over the last twenty years or so there has been an ongoing debate concerning the valuation of brands and their possible inclusion in the balance sheet. A major factor contributing to this debate was the decision by some large food and drinks companies to put a value on their brands and to include them as assets in their balance sheets. Companies do this in order to boost their total asset value, hence giving possible protection against hostile takeovers, impacting favourably on the share price and increasing their borrowing capacity. The inclusion of brands as a separate intangible asset in a takeover situation means that the acquiring company can include the asset in the group accounts without needing to amortize the asset, which would have been required (against either past or future profits) if the asset had been treated as goodwill. One company which adopts this policy is Grand Metropolitan; the relevant accounting policy is shown in Example 5.11.

Example 5.11
Extract from Grand Metropolitan 1995 annual report

Accounting policies

Intangible assets

Significant owned brands, acquired since 1st January 1985, the value of which is not expected to diminish in the foreseeable future, are recorded at cost, less appropriate provisions, as fixed intangible assets. No annual amortization is provided on these assets but their value is reviewed annually by the directors and the cost written down as an exceptional item where permanent diminution in value has occurred.

In the notes accompanying the accounts, details of the amounts involved are set out and further details are given as shown in Example 5.12.

Example 5.12
Extract from Grand Metropolitan 1995 notes to the accounts

Fixed assets – intangible assets

	Brand £million
Cost	
At 30th September 1994	2782
Exchange adjustments	(9)
New subsidiaries	1067
At 30th September 1995	3840

The brands are stated at fair value on acquisition, denominated in the currencies of their principal markets. An annual review is carried out by the directors to consider whether any brand has suffered permanent diminution in value. Although the current aggregate value significantly exceeds the book value, no increase is made to the original value. The principal brands included above are Smirnoff, Pillsbury, Green Giant, Burger King, Häagen-Dazs and, acquired during the year, Old El Paso and Progresso.

Many companies possess valuable 'home-grown' brands, akin to internally generated goodwill, but, with a few exceptions, do not include them in the balance sheet. FRED 12 proposes that internally generated goodwill should not be recognized as an asset in the balance sheet and that internally developed intangible assets (including brands) should be recognized only where they have a readily ascertainable market value.

In practice, there are several methods by which brands are accounted for. It is recognized by the accounting profession that accounting for brands is inextricably linked with the valuation of goodwill. One possible reason for the build-up of a company's goodwill is the company's ownership of well-known brand names. Undoubtedly, the price an acquiring company is prepared to offer for another company is affected by the value of any brands possessed by the latter. However, in the absence of a specific accounting standard, making meaningful comparisons between different companies, particularly in the food and drinks industry, will remain a problem.

Tangible fixed assets

The tangible fixed assets in the S&N 1997 group balance sheet are as shown in Example 5.13.

<table>
<tr><td rowspan="3">**Example 5.13**
Extract from S&N 1997
group balance sheet</td><td></td><td>Notes</td><td>£million</td></tr>
<tr><td>Fixed assets</td><td></td><td></td></tr>
<tr><td>Tangible assets</td><td>12</td><td>2966.9</td></tr>
</table>

Details of the make-up of this figure are set out in note 12. There is a considerable amount of information in this note; however, we can summarize this for the group by looking at the total column and identifying the two main figures which make up the £2966.9 million. This is shown in Example 5.14.

<table>
<tr><td rowspan="8">**Example 5.14**
Summary of S&N group
tangible assets at 27 April
1997</td><td></td><td>Total
£million</td></tr>
<tr><td>GROUP</td><td></td></tr>
<tr><td>Cost or valuation of tangible assets</td><td></td></tr>
<tr><td>At 27 April 1997</td><td>3895.2</td></tr>
<tr><td>Depreciation of tangible assets</td><td></td></tr>
<tr><td>At 27 April 1997</td><td>928.3</td></tr>
<tr><td>Net book value at 27 April 1997</td><td>2966.9</td></tr>
</table>

If we want to know the corresponding figure for the previous year, this is £2901.9 million, which is shown in note 12 between the £928.3 million and the £2966.9 million, as shown in Example 5.15.

<table>
<tr><td rowspan="7">**Example 5.15**
Extract from S&N 1997
notes to the accounts</td><td>TANGIBLE ASSETS</td><td>Total</td></tr>
<tr><td>GROUP</td><td>£million</td></tr>
<tr><td>At 27 April 1997</td><td>3895.2</td></tr>
<tr><td>Depreciation</td><td></td></tr>
<tr><td>At 27 April 1997</td><td>928.3</td></tr>
<tr><td>Net book value at 28 April 1996</td><td>2901.9</td></tr>
<tr><td>Net book value at 27 April 1997</td><td>2966.9</td></tr>
</table>

The Companies Act balance sheet formats require disclosure of the following tangible fixed assets:

- land and buildings
- plant and machinery
- fixtures, fittings, tools and equipment
- payments on account and assets in the course of construction

In practice, and subject to the materiality of the amounts involved, companies fulfil these requirements within an overall presentation of tangible fixed assets classified in a manner appropriate to the company's business activities. The classification adopted by S&N (found in note 12) is shown in Example 5.16.

Example 5.16
Extract from S&N 1997
notes to the accounts

12 TANGIBLE ASSETS

- Licensed and related properties
- Breweries, warehouses and other properties
- Leisure properties
- Vehicles, plant and equipment

In contrast the power generating company Powergen adopts the classification shown in Example 5.17.

Example 5.17
Extract from Powergen
1996 notes to the
accounts

Tangible fixed assets

- Generating assets
- Oil and gas assets
- Assets in the course of construction
- Other assets

The Companies Act and accounting standards require disclosure of the movements in tangible fixed assets (i.e. additions, disposals, etc.) as well as an analysis of the basis of ownership of land and buildings (freehold, leasehold, etc.). In addition, where assets are included in the balance sheet at revalued amounts details of the valuations and the valuers are to be disclosed.

S&N complies with these requirements by presenting the relevant details in note 12. The first part of note 12 (see Appendix 3) gives details of movements in the various classes of tangible fixed assets in respect of the two headings: *cost or valuation* and *depreciation*. This is illustrated in Example 5.18 in respect of the heading *licensed and related properties*. In the second part (see Appendix 3) details of freehold and leasehold properties, including details of valuations and valuers, are given.

Example 5.18
Extract from S&N 1997
notes to the accounts

12 TANGIBLE ASSETS

	Licensed and related properties £million
GROUP	
Cost or valuation	
At 28 April 1996	1404.1
Transfers	(7.5)
Additions	109.9
Disposals	(33.1)
Revaluation	125.8
Exchange adjustment	—
At 27 April 1997	1599.2
Depreciation	
At 27 April 1996	265.9
Transfers	—
Provided during the year	32.0
Disposals	(17.7)
Exchange adjustments	—
At 27 April 1997	280.2
Net book value at 28 April 1996	1138.2
Net book value at 27 April 1997	1319.0

However, information about tangible fixed assets is not confined to note 12. We can find further details in note 1: *Accounting policies*, which contains four sections which refer to tangible fixed assets:

- note 1 (a) gives the basis of preparation of the accounts, which is that accounts are prepared under the historical cost convention except that certain properties are included at valuation, revaluation surpluses being taken directly to a revaluation reserve.
- note 1 (c) sets out details concerning depreciation methods and rates.
- note 1 (d) on interest capitalization informs us that 'The cost of the development of holiday villages includes interest on construction up to the time of opening'.
- note 1 (i) states the policy in respect of operating lease rentals.

The four issues covered in the note can lead to difficulties in practice, particularly for users of accounts who are making comparisons between different companies. The issues, which are discussed below, are:

- revaluations
- depreciation
- capitalization of interest
- leased assets

Revaluations
Revaluations of assets are particularly relevant to properties. A distinction can be made between properties occupied by a company as part of its business activities, called *operating properties*, and properties held for their investment potential, called *investment properties*.

Tangible fixed assets, including properties, can be included in the balance sheet at their cost less a provision for depreciation. The concept of depreciation, discussed above in relation to intangible assets, applies equally to tangible assets, i.e. spreading the value of the asset over its expected life by periodic charges against profits. However, many UK companies take advantage of the alternative accounting rules permitted by the Companies Act to revalue certain of their assets, usually properties, and to include the revalued amounts in the balance sheet. In a recent discussion paper (*Measurement of Tangible Assets*, Accounting Standards Board, October 1996), it was pointed out that recent independent research (*Company Reporting*, October 1995) indicated that 60% of a sample of 510 listed companies had incorporated valuations of operating properties in their accounts. Hence, while some companies use pure historical cost, others use *historical cost modified* for the balance sheet valuation of their operating properties.

Whether or not revalued amounts are incorporated into the accounts, where there are substantial differences between the market and book values of properties these must be reported by the directors in their report.

Investment properties must be included in the balance sheet at their market value, i.e. they are revalued each year, and are not to be subject to periodic depreciation charges. This is an accounting standards requirement (SSAP 19: Accounting for investment properties). However, the distinction between operating properties and investment properties has been questioned and is raised in the Accounting Standards Board discussion paper *Measurement of Tangible Assets*, referred to above.

When assets are revalued and the revalued amounts are brought into the balance sheet, then, bearing in mind the balance sheet equation, i.e. assets − liabilities = capital, a surplus on revaluation which is incorporated into the asset's value must also be included in the capital. This is illustrated in Example 5.19.

Example 5.19 The effect of asset revaluation on the balance sheet		Assets − liabilities £million	Capital £million
	Balance sheet before revaluation	2000	2000
	Surplus on revaluation of property	100	100
	Balance sheet after revaluation	2100	2100
	Individual balance sheet items affected: Tangible fixed assets	+100	Revaluation reserve +100

If, on a subsequent revaluation, there is a fall in the property values, this would cause a reduction in the revaluation reserve. However, if the value fell below original cost, the deficit below cost would be charged to the profit and loss account.

In the 1997 S&N accounts, it is explained in note 12 that the difference between valuations carried out in 1993 and the balance sheet date 27 April 1997 disclosed a total net surplus of £105.6 million and that there were surpluses of £107.6 million on some properties and 'permanent diminutions in value below historic cost' in others. In terms of the balance sheet equation these amounts have been dealt with as shown in Example 5.20.

Example 5.20

S&N balance sheet items
affected by revaluations

	Assets – liabilities £million	Capital £million
Tangible fixed assets	+105.6	
		Revaluation reserve +107.6
		Profit and loss a/c – 2.0

Revaluation surpluses are not a permanent feature of the UK economy, as many companies found out in the era of depressed property values in the early 1990s, when revaluation deficits had to be dealt with. Several major companies, including retailers, had to charge deficits to their profit and loss accounts.

In order for a company to be able to pay dividends it must have made a profit, but the surplus arising on a revaluation of properties cannot be used for this purpose. The surplus has not been realized, i.e. the properties have not been sold but merely revalued. Another way of expressing this is to say that the revaluation reserve cannot be used for dividends, it is not a distributable reserve. On the other hand, the company's balance sheet is strengthened, i.e. its worth as measured by balance sheet values has increased. Overall, the issue of revaluation of tangible fixed assets continues to present challenges to accounting standard-setters and to create uncertainties for accounts users.

Depreciation

Depreciation is defined in accounting standard SSAP 12: Accounting for depreciation as 'The measure of the wearing out, consumption or other reduction in the useful economic life of a fixed asset whether arising from use, effuxion of time or obsolescence through technological or market changes'. SSAP 12 applies to all fixed assets except for those dealt with under their own specific standards (i.e. investment properties, goodwill and development costs). The standard recognizes that depreciation will not normally be relevant for freehold land but, that apart, the requirement is that all fixed assets will be subject to periodic depreciation charges.

The application of depreciation of an intangible asset, patents, is illustrated in Example 5.3 above. The method adopted in the example, i.e. spreading the cost of the asset in equal instalments over the asset's useful life, is known as the fixed instalment method or the straight line method. Other methods are used to arrive at the periodic charge to be made against the company's profits. One alternative is the reducing balance method, whereby depreciation charges are calculated for each year on the basis of the cost less depreciation already charged. This is illustrated in Example 5.21.

Example 5.21

Reducing balance method
of depreciation

On 1 January 1996 a company buys a motor vehicle for £20 000 and decides to apply the reducing balance method of depreciation at a rate of 25% per year. The financial year end of the company is 31 December. The yearly depreciation charges and the balance sheet values for the first two years are shown below.

	Depreciation charge		Balance sheet value	
Year 31 Dec. 1996	(25% x 20 000)	5000	Cost	20 000
			Depreciation	5 000
				15 000

Companies must disclose:

- the depreciation methods used
- the useful economic lives or the depreciation rates used
- the total depreciation charged for the period
- the gross amount of depreciable assets and the related accumulated depreciation

Capitalization of interest

The balance sheet cost of a fixed asset built by or for a company may include interest on capital borrowed to finance the production of that asset. Note 1(d) in the S&N 1997 notes to the accounts states that this policy is adopted by S&N in respect of the development of holiday villages. Not all companies choose to capitalize interest in this way. Those doing so must show the amount of the interest in a note to the accounts. S&N show the relevant amount (for 1996 in this case) in note 7.

The inconsistency in financial reporting between companies has been recognized and the recent Accounting Standards Board discussion paper *Measurement of tangible assets*, mentioned earlier, addresses the issue by suggesting that capitalization of interest should be either mandatory or prohibited.

Leased assets

When a company leases an asset (such as a property, a machine or a motor vehicle) from the asset's owner, the company is acquiring the right to use the asset in return for a payment called a lease rental. The owner of the asset is the lessor and the company leasing the asset from the owner is the lessee. From the accounting standpoint, two types of lease are recognized: finance leases and operating leases. A finance lease is similar to a hire purchase contract. A simple hire purchase contract is illustrated in Example 5.22.

Example 5.22
Hire purchase contract

A company acquires an asset under a hire purchase contract. The cash price of the asset is £300, the interest (or 'finance') charge is 10% per year and settlement is to be in three equal annual instalments. These details can be summarized as follows:

	£
Cash price	300
Interest (3 x 10%)	90
Total price	390

Payable in 3 instalments of £130 = £390

Each instalment represents a part repayment of the £300 and a payment of the interest due to date.

Under the terms of a hire purchase contract, the asset becomes the property of the hirer at the end of the hire term on payment of a nominal fee. Conventionally, the accounting treatment for such a contract is to bring the asset into the balance sheet and show the amount owing (excluding the finance charge) as a liability, i.e. both the assets and the liabilities in the balance sheet are increased (by £300 in the above example), the interest being charged to the profit and loss account as it becomes due over the life of the contract.

SSAP 21: Accounting for leases and hire purchase contracts is the main authoritative source for accounting for leases and hire purchase contracts. The publication of the standard in 1984 was necessary as a consequence of the growth of leasing as a major source of finance in the UK.

The standard indicates that under a finance lease substantially all of the benefits of using the asset and substantially all of the risks associated with ownership are taken over by the company concerned. It states: 'In economic substance it is similar to the purchase of an asset even though the legal title to the asset remains with the lessor'. In order to achieve comparability between companies, the standard requires a company which acquires an asset under a finance lease to bring the asset on to the balance sheet, in the same way it would do if it had purchased the asset outright. This is considered in Example 5.23.

Example 5.23
Acquisition of assets
	The balance sheet of a company is as follows:
	
	               £million
	Assets 1000
	Capital 1000
	
	The company borrows £200 million, which it uses to purchase an asset. Both the asset and the loan taken out to finance its acquisition will be included in the balance sheet, which will now be:
	
	               £million
	Assets 1200
	Liability (loan) 200
	Capital 1000
	               1200

If the company had chosen to acquire the asset by means of a finance lease, then without the application of the SSAP 21 requirement neither the asset nor the finance would appear on the balance sheet; we would have an example of off-balance sheet finance. Companies have engaged in off-balance sheet finance for a number of reasons, one being to increase their borrowing capacity by not showing a liability on the balance sheet. The application of the accounting standard results in both the asset and the related finance being included in the balance sheet, which will then be in line with the second balance sheet shown in Example 5.23 above. There are rules relating to the calculation of the relevant amounts but, broadly speaking, the cash price of the asset (i.e. what the company would have paid if it had made a straightforward purchase of the asset) often gives the required figure, the mechanics of the exercise being similar to the conventional treatment of assets acquired on hire purchase.

Operating leases are usually of short duration and do not transfer substantially all of the risks and rewards of ownership to the company using the asset. Unlike finance leases, they are not brought into the balance sheet. The accounting treatment is to charge the rentals on a straight line basis to the profit and loss account over the lease term.

Example 5.24 shows the accounting policy of British Airways in respect of leased and hire purchased assets. To set the note in context, a summary of the group's assets in current use at 31 March 1997 is shown in Example 5.25.

<table>
<tr><td>

Example 5.24
Extract from British
Airways 1996/97
accounting policy for
leased and hire purchased
assets

</td><td>

Where assets are financed through finance leases or hire purchase arrangements, under which substantially all the risks and rewards of ownership are transferred to the Group, the assets are treated as if they had been purchased outright. The amount included in the cost of tangible fixed assets represents the aggregate of the capital elements payable during the lease or hire purchase term. The corresponding obligation, reduced by the appropriate proportion of lease or hire purchase payments made, is included in creditors. The amount included in the cost of tangible fixed assets is depreciated on the basis described in the preceding paragraphs. The interest element of lease or hire purchase payments made is included in interest payable in the profit and loss account.

</td></tr>
</table>

<table>
<tr><td>

Example 5.25
Extract from British
Airways 1996/97 notes to
the accounts

</td><td>

British Airways at 31 March 1997

Tangible assets (fleet, property, equipment)	£million
Net book amounts	7588
including fleet	6337
Analysis of fleet	
Owned	2248
Finance leased	1266
Hire purchase arrangements	1968
Progress payments	851
Assets held for resale	4

</td></tr>
</table>

The fleet is the only British Airways asset subject to finance lease and hire purchase arrangements.

Payments under all other lease arrangements, known as *operating leases*, are charged to the profit and loss account in equal annual amounts over the period of the lease.

The 'substance over form' approach used in SSAP 21 has been formally extended by the publication, in April 1994, of FRS 5: Reporting the substance of transactions, which is of much wider application. Its preamble states: 'It will mainly affect those more complex transactions whose substance may not be readily apparent'. The range and complexity of transactions continues to grow, but the rules and guidelines of FRS 5 are aimed at achieving a greater level of consistency between companies in this area.

Investments

Investments, the third type of fixed asset, in common with intangible and tangible fixed assets, will be included in the balance sheet at cost or valuation less depreciation, where appropriate, together with a schedule showing movements during the year. For investments which are listed on a stock exchange, the market value must be shown.

S&N has the fixed asset investments shown in Example 5.26.

	Note	Group £million	Company £million
Investments	13	226.0	1196.3

We saw in Example 5.7 that any investments held by the parent company in its subsidiaries will not be included in the group balance sheet because, in the group balance sheet, the investment in the investee companies has been replaced by the underlying assets and liabilities of the investee companies.

If we turn to note 13 in the S&N 1997 annual report we can obtain an analysis of the investments, which fall into the following categories:

- shares in subsidiary undertakings
- associated undertakings
- other investments
- trade loans

Items falling within the *trade loans* heading include loans to customers to assist with updating premises and bars, which are a feature of brewing and similar industries. The other three headings are discussed below.

Shares in subsidiary undertakings

When one company holds a majority of the voting shares in a second company the first company is called the *parent company* and the second company can be referred to as the *subsidiary*. This is illustrated in Example 1.1 in Chapter 1. In that example, company A (the *parent*) holds 70% of the voting shares of company B (the *subsidiary*). In situations such as that, i.e. where the parent company holds less than 100% of the subsidiary's shares, the relevant proportion of the subsidiary's worth (represented by its share capital and reserves) would be shown in the group's balance sheet and called a *minority interest*.

In the example only 70% of the shares in company B are held by the parent company (company A), the remaining 30% being held by other outside shareholders. It is the interest of these other shareholders which is referred to as the *minority interest*. This concept is also discussed in Chapter 7.

Associated undertakings

Where one company holds less than a majority of the voting shares in another company the accounting treatment in the group accounts is determined largely by the extent to which the company holding the shares is able to exert significant influence over the other company. Significant influence is deemed to be present if the holding is at least 20% and there is nothing to suggest otherwise. The company in which the shares are held is termed an *associated undertaking*.

In the balance sheet of the individual company which holds the shares the investment in the associated undertaking is shown at its cost. However, in the group balance sheet the value of the shares will include the relevant proportion of the associated company's profits and losses since it was acquired. This is illustrated in Example 5.27.

Example 5.27
Associated companies

On 1 January 1996 company Z, which is the parent company of a number of subsidiaries, acquired 25% of the shares of company A for £10 million. Company A is deemed to be an associated undertaking of company Z. The financial year end of the companies is 31 December. For the year ended 31 December 1996 company A made a profit of £1 million, i.e. the associated undertaking has made profits of £1 million since it was acquired. The balance sheet amounts for the investment in the associated undertaking will appear as shown below:

	Group £million	Company £million
Investments		
Shares in associated undertakings	10.25	10.00

It can be seen that the value in the group balance sheet is higher by £0.25 million (i.e. 25% of £1 million). The group's reserves will include the increase of £0.25 million.

Note 1(b) (iii) in the S&N 1997 notes to the accounts explains that certain investments have been treated as associated undertakings. Note 13 adds that the principal associated undertaking is a 50% holding in one company. It has to be realized that 50% is less than a majority and therefore the company concerned is not a subsidiary company.

Other investments

If a company holds less than a majority of the shares in another company but the holding is not deemed to be an associated undertaking, the cost of the investment will be included under the heading *other investments*. Where such a holding is deemed to be significant (which for this purpose is defined as either more than 10% of the nominal value of the investee company's shares or more than 10% of the group's or the company's total assets) certain further information has to be disclosed.

It is possible that a company will hold certain investments which it classifies as current rather than fixed assets. For example, the company might invest, temporarily, surplus funds which it has available. On the other hand, where the intention is that an investment will be held long term it will be classified as a fixed asset.

Current assets

It was noted in Chapter 4 that the main items found in this category are stocks, debtors and cash, using the term *cash* generically to include bank balances. The S&N current assets from the group balance sheet are shown in Example 5.28.

Example 5.28
Extract from S&N 1997
group balance sheet

	Notes	£million
Current assets		
Stocks	14	149.6
Debtors	15	450.8
Cash and short-term deposits	16	73.0
		673.4

Detailed analyses of these figures are supplied in the accompanying notes to the accounts.

The types of items included under the heading *stocks* will vary from company to company dependent upon the nature of a company's business. Under the heading *debtors* there will usually be more similarities, but companies might include items specific to them or the figure for debtors can be affected if the company has engaged in factoring. The two items are discussed below.

Stocks

It can be seen from note 14 in the accounts that S&N stocks consist of:

- raw materials and consumables
- work in progress
- finished goods and goods for resale

The valuation of these items, set out in note 1(e), follows the basic accounting standard rule of the lower of cost or net realizable value.

As would be expected for a company like S&N, the figure for work in progress represents only a small part of the total current assets. This would not necessarily be the case for a different type of company. As an illustration, the group stocks figure for the electronic and electrical equipment company GEC is shown in Example 5.29.

Example 5.29
Extract from GEC 1997
notes to the accounts

Stocks and contracts in progress	£million
Raw materials and bought-out components	179
Work in progress	292
Payments on account	(87)
Long-term contract work in progress	1177
Payments on account	(734)
Finished goods	287
	1114

The item *long-term contract work in progress* has been valued in accordance with the relevant accounting standard, SSAP 9: Stocks and long-term contracts, the standard's aim being the reflection in accounts of the profits that can fairly be said to have been earned in the period under review. The amount concerned is therefore included in the valuation of the long-term contract work in progress and is also included in the profit for the year. Details of the accounting policy included in GEC's accounting policies statement are shown in Example 5.30.

Example 5.30
Extract from GEC 1997
notes to the accounts

Stocks and contracts in progress
Stocks and contracts in progress are valued at the lower of cost, inclusive of appropriate overheads, and estimated net realizable value. Provisions are made for any losses incurred or expected to be incurred on uncompleted contracts. Profit on long-term contracts in progress is taken when a sale is recorded on part-delivery of products or part-performance of services, provided that the outcome of the contract can be assessed with reasonable certainty. Advance payments received from customers are shown as creditors until there is a right of set-off against the value of work undertaken. Progress payments received are deducted from the value of work carried out, any excess being included with payments received in advance.

CURRENT ASSETS

In some types of businesses there can be difficulties in deciding at what specific time an asset or liability should be recognized for inclusion in the balance sheet. An example is consignment stock which is held by a dealer with the right to sell the stock or to return it unsold to the legal owner. We are again in the 'substance over form' arena and FRS 5, Reporting the substance of transactions, gives advice on this and similar transactions.

Debtors

The figure included for debtors represents what the debtors are worth at the balance sheet date. Where appropriate, the amounts due from debtors will have been reduced if there is uncertainty that the company will receive these amounts in full, i.e. the company will have made a provision for bad debts. The amount of such provision will reduce the profits and reduce the value of the debtors figure in the balance sheet.

In order to release funds tied up in amounts owing from debtors, companies can enter into a factoring agreement whereby the debtors' balances are sold to a factor, often a bank, who remits a proportion of the amounts due immediately and collects the amounts direct from the debtors. These agreements take a variety of forms and can present difficulties in deciding when debtors (i.e. customers' balances) should be included in a company's balance sheet. Guidance on this is given in FRS 5: Reporting the substance of transactions.

Summary

The balance sheet is part of a set of financial statements and must be set out in accordance with one of the prescribed formats laid down in the Companies Act.

UK companies need to comply with a number of authoritative sources when preparing a balance sheet for presentation to the shareholders. A great deal of detailed information is required either on the balance sheet or in the accompanying notes to the accounts.

In this chapter we have looked in detail at the balance sheet headings fixed assets and current assets. The other headings are covered in Chapter 6.

Exercises

These exercises are based on the extracts from the S&N 1997 annual report and accounts in Appendix 3.

1 Why are there no intangible assets in the balance sheets?
2 In the balance sheet, where would you expect to find vehicles?
3 Complete the following table by inserting the relevant figures in the spaces marked x:

Company: tangible assets

	Cost or valuation £million	Depreciation £million	Net book value £million
At 28 April 1996	x	x	x
Additions/disposals during the year	49.5*	(57.6)*	107.1
At 27 April 1997	x	x	x

* These are summaries of the items shown in the total column for the company shown in note 12, tangible assets, i.e.

Cost or valuation	£million
Additions	161.8
Transfers	5.8
Disposals	(156.1)
Revaluation	38.0
	49.5
Depreciation provided during the year	82.8
Transfer	0.5
Disposals	(140.9)
	(57.6)

4 Identify the items which account for the differences between the amounts shown for investments in the group and company balance sheets at 27 April 1997. You will need to use the information in the notes to the accounts to find the relevant figures.

5 In the group balance sheet, where would you expect to find short-term deposits which had been made by group undertakings?

The balance sheet: creditors, provisions for liabilities and charges, and capital and reserves

Introduction

Chapter 5 was concerned with the detailed items under the headings *fixed assets* and *current assets*. In this chapter we will discuss the individual items which appear under the following headings:

- creditors: amounts falling due within one year
- creditors: amounts falling due after more than one year
- provisions for liabilities and charges
- capital and reserves

As previously, in our discussion on the individual items, we shall make reference to information found on the face of the balance sheet, as well as to information to be found in the notes to the accounts section.

Once again, as a general point, we need to remember that companies have to set out their important accounting policies in a separate statement (often note 1 of the notes to the accounts), and readers of sets of accounts should also refer to that statement.

Creditors: amounts falling due within one year

Items to be separately disclosed under the heading *creditors: amounts falling due within one year* are set out in the Format 1 balance sheet (see Appendix 1).

The figure for S&N *creditors: amounts falling due within one year* is £1166.5 million and the details of this are set out in note 17, as shown in Example 6.1. Some companies similarly present all the detailed information in a supporting note; others show more detail on the face of the balance sheet and less in the note.

Example 6.1
Extract from S&N 1997
notes to the accounts

17 CREDITORS: AMOUNTS FALLING DUE WITHIN ONE YEAR	Group 1997 £million
Loan Capital (note 19)	29.3
Bank overdraft	331.0
Trade creditors	169.4

Current taxation	105.8
Other taxes and social security costs	137.3
Dividends	87.5
Other creditors	128.0
Accruals and deferred income	178.2
Amounts owing to associated undertakings	–
Amounts owing to subsidiary undertakings	–
	1166.5

In the main, the items which S&N includes under this heading are self-explanatory. Two items, *current taxation* and *accruals and deferred income*, together with a third item *bills of exchange* (which does not appear in S&N but which is in the Format 1 list), are discussed below. The item *loan capital* is discussed under *creditors: amounts falling due after more than one year*.

Current taxation

A company's liability for UK corporation tax will usually appear under the heading *creditors: amounts falling due within one year* because the tax on the profits of a particular year is due for payment within the next nine months. S&N has a current tax liability of £105.8 million included under that heading.

The application of the tax rules sometimes results in a payment becoming due only after one year and such a liability is classified in the balance sheet under the heading *creditors: amounts falling due after more than one year*, as is the case with the S&N liability of £0.4 million (see Example 6.3).

Accruals and deferred income

Accruals are amounts which relate to one accounting period but which are not paid until a subsequent period. An example is wages which have been earned by employees before the balance sheet date but which are not due to be paid until after that date.

Deferred income relates to receipts coming into a company in one accounting period but which relate to a subsequent period. An example is a government grant which has been received in respect of a fixed asset bought by the company. The grant might be received in year 1 but the benefit has to be spread over the life of the asset, which could extend over years 1–5.

Both accruals and deferred income are classified according to whether the subsequent period only is affected, i.e. as *creditors: amounts due within one year*, or whether further periods are affected, in which case the relevant amounts are classified as *creditors: amounts falling due after more than one year*.

Bills of exchange

The only other item in the Format 1 list which is not in the S&N note is *bills of exchange payable*, which are a form of financing and can be considered together with the item *bills of exchange receivable*, from the current assets section of a balance sheet. The legal definition of a bill of exchange is:

> an unconditional order in writing addressed by one person to another signed by the person giving it, requiring the person to whom it is addressed to pay on demand, or at a fixed or determinable future time, a sum certain in money to, or to the order of, a specified person or to the bearer.

A cheque is a form of bill which is payable on demand. The incorporation of a 'future period' into bills of exchange other than cheques results in bills being used as a form of financing because they are a negotiable instrument, which means they can be sold to other parties. In the UK, bills of exchange are most often used in the settlement of import and export contracts. In some countries, for example Spain, they are a common means of effecting settlement of domestic transactions. The creditworthiness of the parties concerned is an important feature of this form of financing. The accounting effects are illustrated in Example 6.2.

Example 6.2 Bills of exchange	On 1 December 1997 Smith plc sells goods to Brown plc for £10 000, payment being due on 28 February 1998. Smith plc draws up a bill of exchange, a document stating that Brown plc will pay £10 000 on 28 February 1998 to Smith (or whoever possesses the bill on that date). Brown signs the bill to signify acceptance. In the event of Brown failing to settle on 28 February 1998, it is agreed that Smith will pay the amount due. Smith sells the bill to a bank, Big Bank plc, and receives £10 000 less a discounting charge. All parties concerned have an accounting year ending on 31 December. On 31 December 1997: Brown plc includes a liability of £10 000 in its balance sheet under the heading *bill of exchange payable* or *bill payable*. Big Bank plc (or whoever holds the bill) includes an asset of £10 000 in its balance sheet under the heading *bill of exchange receivable* or *bill receivable*. Smith plc states, in a note to the accounts, that it has a contingent liability in respect of a bill of exchange (the contingency being that Brown does not pay).

For companies adopting the Format 2 balance sheet, which has only one heading for creditors (Item E), each item must be split into those *falling due within one year* and those *falling due after more than one year*. However, many companies, including S&N, use Format 1, which has separate headings for *creditors* according to duration. We will now examine the second of these headings.

Items to be separately disclosed under the heading *creditors: amounts falling due after more than one year* are set out in the Format 1 balance sheet. These items are the same as those for the heading *creditors: amounts falling due within one year*, discussed above. The S&N figures are shown in Example 6.3.

18 CREDITORS: AMOUNTS FALLING DUE AFTER MORE THAN ONE YEAR

	Group 1997 £million
Loan Capital (note 19)	400.8
Corporation tax	0.4
Other creditors	4.5
Accruals and deferred income	3.5
	409.2

Other companies may use a slightly different layout in presenting the information under this heading. Examples 6.4 and 6.5 show how Coats Viyella give the required details.

Example 6.4
Extract from Coats Viyella
1996 group balance sheet

		Group 1996 £million
Creditors – amounts falling due after more than one year		
Other creditors	18	(294.4)
Convertible debt	18	(67.0)
		(361.4)

Example 6.5
Extract from Coats Viyella
1996 notes to the
accounts

	Group 1996 £million
18 Creditors – amounts falling due after more than one year	
Other creditors	
Trade creditors	0.9
Debentures, loans and loan stock (note 19)	217.4
Amounts owed to subsidiaries	—
Corporation tax	—
Other creditors	1.4
Accruals and deferred income	33.3
Finance lease obligations	41.4
	294.4

The most important item appearing under this heading is *loan capital*, which is discussed below under the following headings:

- loan capital: presentation of information
- loan capital: types of loan capital

Loan capital: presentation of information

There are two main sources from which a company can finance its activities, i.e. from its shareholders or by borrowing externally. To distinguish between these, we can use the terms *equity capital* (borrowing from shareholders in the form of ordinary shares) and *loan capital* (borrowing from external sources in the form of loans and bonds, etc., and classed as debt). These are not Companies Act terms but they are useful in helping us to focus on these important sources of company finance.

In Example 6.3 the major part of the creditors' figure is the loan capital of £400.8 million, representing debts owed by the company in the form of a variety of long-term loans. There are requirements for additional information to be disclosed for each item shown under either creditors heading (*creditors: amounts falling due within one year* and *creditors: amounts falling due after more than one year*). Broadly speaking, the requirements are to show:

- the amount of loans not wholly repayable within five years (split between those payable by instalments and others)
- terms of repayment and interest rates
- for each item for which security has been given, an indication of the nature of the security
- for bank loans and for other borrowings, an analysis of the periods of repayments into those due:
  - in one year or less or on demand
  - between one and two years
  - between two and five years, and
  - in five years or more

The details in S&N note 19 provide an illustration of how these requirements are complied with, as shown in Example 6.6.

<table>
<tr><td align="right">**Example 6.6**
Extract from S&N 1997
notes to the accounts</td><td>**19 LOAN CAPITAL**</td><td align="right">Group
1997
£million</td></tr>
<tr><td></td><td>Not wholly repayable within five years</td><td></td></tr>
<tr><td></td><td>   Repayable by instalments</td><td align="right">15.3</td></tr>
<tr><td></td><td>   Repayable otherwise than by instalments</td><td align="right">82.3</td></tr>
<tr><td></td><td>Wholly repayable within five years</td><td align="right">332.5</td></tr>
<tr><td></td><td></td><td align="right">430.1</td></tr>
<tr><td></td><td>Instalments not due within five years</td><td align="right">5.2</td></tr>
<tr><td></td><td>Amounts due are repayable as follows:</td><td></td></tr>
<tr><td></td><td>Bank loans</td><td></td></tr>
<tr><td></td><td>   More than five years</td><td align="right">24.9</td></tr>
<tr><td></td><td>   Between two and five years</td><td align="right">298.6</td></tr>
<tr><td></td><td>   Between one and two years</td><td align="right">13.3</td></tr>
<tr><td></td><td>   Less than one year (note 17)</td><td align="right">28.8</td></tr>
<tr><td></td><td></td><td align="right">365.6</td></tr>
<tr><td></td><td>Other loans</td><td></td></tr>
<tr><td></td><td>   More than five years</td><td align="right">60.3</td></tr>
<tr><td></td><td>   Between two and five years</td><td align="right">3.3</td></tr>
<tr><td></td><td>   Between one and two years</td><td align="right">0.4</td></tr>
<tr><td></td><td>   Less than one year (note 17)</td><td align="right">0.5</td></tr>
<tr><td></td><td></td><td align="right">64.5</td></tr>
<tr><td></td><td>Loan capital – more than one year (note 18)</td><td align="right">400.8</td></tr>
</table>

Notice that the group total for loan capital, £430.1 million, shown in the first section of note 19's analysis is the combined figure for the loan capital items included in both creditors' headings (i.e. *creditors: amounts falling due within one year* and *creditors: amounts falling due after more than one year*). The relevant figures are summarized in Example 6.7.

Loan capital:	£million
due within one year (from note 17)	29.3
due after more than one year (from Note 18)	400.8
Total (shown in note 19)	430.1

From note 19 we can also see that the total for loan capital of £430.1 million consists of *bank loans* £365.6 million and *other loans* £64.5 million. Details of the *other loans* are shown in Example 6.8.

	Group 1997 £million
Other loans comprise	
9.75% unsecured bonds 2006	15.1
6.9% private placements	15.9
7.9% redeemable debenture stock 2008	28.2
Others	5.3
	64.5

Loan capital: types of loan capital

From the S&N and Coats Viyella extracts we can identify a number of types of loan capital, i.e., from S&N:

- unsecured bonds
- private placements
- redeemable debenture stock

and from Coats Viyella:

- convertible debt
- loan stock
- finance lease obligations

These various types are discussed in the following paragraphs (with the terms above in italics to facilitate recognition).

From the legal standpoint, a debenture is a document issued to acknowledge a loan. *Debenture stock* is the total amount of a debenture, split into units which can be traded on a stock exchange, e.g. instead of having one debenture of £10 000 we could have 10 000 units of £1 each.

Loan stock and *bonds* are effectively the same as debenture stock. Usually, all three:

- carry a fixed rate of interest
- are issued to the general public, for subsequent trading on a stock exchange

They may be:

- secured or unsecured (*secured* means that the loan has been guaranteed by something valuable being deposited with the lender; *unsecured* means that this form of guarantee has not been provided)
- redeemable or irredeemable (*redeemable* means that the loan can be repaid at some date in the future; *irredeemable* means the loan is of a permanent nature)
- identified with a ranking for priority for repayment and/or payment of interest (e.g. 'senior', 'subordinated')

Where a loan is *secured*, the security can take the form of a charge against a specific asset, such a charge being termed a *fixed charge*. An alternative is to attach the charge to all assets or to all assets in one class (for example all fixed assets or all stocks and work in progress). Such a charge is termed a *floating charge*. A floating charge relates to the assets which exist at any given moment, which means that the company is not prohibited from selling any particular asset.

One particular type of bond is called a *eurobond*. This is a bond which is denominated in a currency other than that of the country where it is issued. The 'euro' prefix is misleading; it is not restricted to Europe but relates to all foreign issues: for example, a UK company might issue US dollar bonds. Instead of being issued to a named holder, such bonds are bearer bonds, i.e. the person who holds the bonds claims the interest and eventual repayment.

Some of the S&N loan capital has been obtained by *private placements* rather than being offered to the general public.

Convertible debt is a generic name for loan capital, of whatever type, which carries the right to be converted into ordinary shares (discussed under capital and reserves below), thus being transferred from the loan capital figure into equity capital.

Other types of loan capital are continually being developed and there are many variations on the types discussed above. With some of these new capital instruments it can be difficult to decide whether they are truly loan capital or de facto part of equity capital. An accounting standard, FRS 4: Capital instruments, addresses this issue. The application of this standard can also result in a reclassification of equity capital into loan capital. This is illustrated in Example 6.9.

Example 6.9
Extract from Coats Viyella
1996 notes to the
accounts

Under loans repayable after one year the following is included
Coats Viyella Finance Co. Limited
Redeemable Preference Shares due 1998*

* In accordance with FRS4 this amount is classified as debt in the Group accounts as the obligations are guaranteed by the parent company.

Finance lease obligations is the amount owed at the balance sheet date in respect of assets leased by the company under finance leases. From the earlier discussion in Chapter 5, under tangible fixed assets, we know that, applying the substance over form argument, such assets are brought into the balance sheet (usually at a value approximating to their cash price), with an equivalent amount being brought in as a liability to the lessor and called *finance lease obligations*.

As indicated in Chapter 4, this heading covers possible liabilities and losses which have to be taken into account but which are not classified under the *creditors* heading. A provision for liabilities and charges is defined in the Companies Act as an amount retained as reasonably necessary for the purpose of providing for any liability or loss which is either likely to be incurred, or certain to be incurred but uncertain as to the amount or as to the date on which it will arise. The standard formats (see Appendix 1) identify three categories which must be separately disclosed:

1 pensions and similar obligations
2 taxation, including deferred taxation
3 other provisions

Companies are required to show the movements in each category of provision during the financial year. Example 6.10 shows the categories and their movements for the S&N Group.

Example 6.10
Extract from S&N 1997
notes to the accounts

20 PROVISIONS FOR LIABILITIES AND CHARGES

	Acquisition £million	Reorganization £million	Pensions £million	Deferred Tax £million	Total £million
GROUP					
At 28 April 1996	10.6	71.3	60.9	—	142.8
Transfer from debtors	—	—	—	(19.5)	(19.5)
Profit and loss account	—	—	—	2.8	2.8
Utilized during the year	(8.1)	(41.3)	(10.5)	—	(59.9)
Exchange adjustment	—	—	—	(1.9)	(1.9)
Transfer to debtors	—	—	—	18.6	18.6
At 27 April 1997	2.5	30.0	50.4	—	82.9

Apart from provisions in respect of pensions and deferred taxation, S&N has presented two 'other' provisions, one for costs involved in the acquisition of other businesses, and one for costs of reorganizations. In previous years costs to be incurred in respect of acquisitions and reorganizations were recognized (of £10.6 million and £71.3 million, respectively). It might be recalled from Chapter 1 that the application of the prudence principle requires that companies recognize liabilities for expenses or losses as soon as they are aware of them. By 'recognize' we mean taking them into account by reducing profits. The expenditure on these two provisions during the year has been £8.1 million and £41.3 million, respectively.

Where the 'other' provision category is used by a company, it will be appropriate for the company concerned. Example 6.11 shows how the information is presented by Cable and Wireless in its balance sheet and Example 6.12 identifies the company's other provisions.

Example 6.11	**Provisions for liabilities and charges**	Note	£million
Extract from Cable and	Deferred taxation	23	161
Wireless 1997 group	Other provisions	24	59
balance sheet			

Example 6.12		1997
Extract from Cable and		£million
Wireless 1997 notes to the	Other provisions comprise	
accounts	Pension, redundancy payments and unfunded gratuities	15
	Ships' periodic overhauls	3
	Reorganization	41
		59

These items which make up provisions for liabilities and charges all have an effect on the profit and loss account and are discussed in further detail in Chapter 7.

Capital and reserves

This heading represents, at balance sheet values, the stake of the owners in the business, i.e. the owners' capital.

There are two elements which make up the owners' capital. First, there are the actual sums contributed by owners by way of investment in the company either when the company is set up or at any time subsequently; this is called the *share capital.* Second, there is an item called *reserves.* Reserves can be built up in a number of ways. One extremely important source is from profits made by the company which have not been distributed to the shareholders as dividends; in other words, those which have been left in the company for use in its business activities. The share capital and the reserves are discussed below.

Share capital

If the prospective owners of a business decide to set up the business as a limited company they will contribute their capital in the form of shares. For example, if the initial requirement for funds was £15 million, and £5 million was borrowed, then the prospective owners would be asked for £10 million. This amount would be divided up into shares. It could be 10 million shares of £1 each or 20 million shares of 50p each or some other convenient subdivision. Each share has a face value (e.g. of £1, 50p), known as its nominal value. Hence we refer to the *share capital* of the company.

Shareholders buy shares in a company in the expectation that the company will make profits. The shareholders are prepared to take a risk (that their shares will lose value) in order to make a return on their shares. The return will take the form of a rise in the value of their shares, and/or the receipt of dividends paid by the company to its shareholders.

Different classes of shares may be issued. Each class carries different entitlements. Examples of different types of shares are:

- preference shares
- ordinary shares
- deferred shares

Preference shares

Preference shares carry rights giving them preference over other classes of shares. Normally, preference shares are non-voting but they give their holders the right to receive a fixed rate of dividend, and to receive repayment in the event of a liquidation, before dividends and repayments are paid to other classes. Preference shares may be *cumulative* or *non-cumulative*. *Cumulative* means that in the event of a preference dividend being missed in one or more years no dividends can be paid to the ordinary shareholders until the arrears of preference dividends have been paid. *Convertible* preference shares carry the right to convert the preference shares into ordinary shares in accordance with specified times and conditions. Preference shares which are issued with a finite life are called *redeemable*, i.e. shareholders will receive back the nominal value of their shares at a predetermined time.

Ordinary shares

Ordinary shares carry rights to the profits remaining after payment of preferential dividends. Normally ordinary shares have voting rights but in the event of the company going into liquidation the ordinary shareholders will receive repayment of their capital after the claims of creditors and preference shareholders have been settled.

Deferred shares

Deferred shares carry deferred rights such as receiving a dividend only after ordinary shareholders have received a predetermined level of dividend, or receiving a dividend after an agreed future date.

When the term *equity share capital* is used it refers to the shares which carry the main risk and which are entitled to the balance of the profits after preferential dividends have been paid, i.e. usually the ordinary shares.

A company's statutes must stipulate an amount of share capital which the company is authorized to issue; this is called its *authorized share capital*. When a company decides to issue some of these shares it does so by requesting payments of agreed amounts (possibly by way of instalments) from its prospective shareholders. The jargon employed here is that the company is 'calling up' the amounts due; hence we can refer to *called-up share capital*. The Companies Act requires the authorized share capital and the called-up share capital to be disclosed in the accounts.

S&N discloses the called-up share capital, distinguishing equity share capital from non-equity share capital, on the face of the balance sheet, as shown in Example 6.13.

Example 6.13

Extract from S&N 1997
group balance sheet

	Note	£million
Equity share capital	21	183.6
Non-equity share capital	21	12.4
Called up share capital		196.0

Analyses of both the authorized share capital and the called-up share capital are included in note 21, where S&N describes the latter as *issued and fully paid*, as shown in Example 6.14.

Example 6.14

Extract from S&N 1997
notes to the accounts

21 SHARE CAPITAL

	Authorized 1997 £million	Issued and fully paid 1997 £million
Equity share capital		
Ordinary shares of 20p each	141.5	123.5
Special deferred shares of 20p each	60.1	60.1
	201.6	183.6
Non-Equity share capital		
Cumulative preference shares of £1 each		
4.6% + tax credit	3.9	3.9
6.425% + tax credit	7.0	7.0
7% convertible	1.5	1.5
	12.4	12.4

When a newly formed company issues shares, the issue price is normally the *nominal value*. The nominal value of a share represents the limit of a shareholder's liability (hence 'limited liability' company). It is the nominal value which has to be included in the figures for authorized share capital and called-up share capital in the balance sheet. However, for a company which has been in existence several years, it is almost certain that the market value of the shares will be different from the nominal value (higher or lower depending on the company's performance). If the market value of the existing shares is higher than the nominal value, the company will expect that any new shares it decides to issue will be issued at around the market value of the existing shares, otherwise the existing shareholders would be at a disadvantage. The difference between the nominal value and the issue price is the share premium and this must be shown separately under a balance sheet heading called *share premium account*. This is illustrated in Example 6.15.

Example 6.15

Issue of shares at a
premium

The called-up share capital of a company is 100 million ordinary shares. The nominal value of a share is £1. The company decides to issue 10 million ordinary shares. At the time of the issue the market price is £1.50 per share and the company decides to issue the new shares at this figure. The entries in the capital and reserves section at the date of the next balance sheet will be:

Capital and reserves

	£million
Called-up share capital	
110 million ordinary shares of £1 each	110
Share premium account	5

Reserves

Reserves constitute the second element making up the owners' capital of a limited company. Example 6.16 shows the reserves in the S&N group balance sheet.

Example 6.16
Extract from S&N 1997
group balance sheet

Share premium account	22	831.3
Revaluation reserve	23	312.8
Other reserves	24	(433.3)
Profit and loss account	25	1300.9

The four S&N headings for *reserves* are shown separately as laid down in the Companies Act, which also requires an analysis of the movement on reserves during the year. These four reserves are discussed below.

Share premium account

As noted above, a share premium account has to be opened when shares are issued at a price above their nominal value. The Companies Act restricts the uses to which the balance on the share premium account can be put, so that in effect the share premium account is almost the same as share capital. A share premium account can be used:

- to issue bonus shares (as shown in Example 6.17)
- to write off preliminary expenses or underwriting commission (i.e. instead of reducing the profit and loss account by these amounts)
- to provide a premium to be used on the redemption of debentures

Example 6.17
Issue of bonus shares

A company's balance sheet includes the following:

	£million
Ordinary share capital (shares of £1 each)	50
Share premium account	10

The company decides to issue, at no cost, 10 million £1 shares to its existing shareholders on the basis of one new share for every five shares held and to use the balance on the share premium account for this purpose.

The number of new shares is $\frac{50}{5}$ million = 10 million

After the issue of the new shares the share premium account will be removed from the balance sheet, which will now show:

	£million
Ordinary share capital (shares of £1)	60

Such an issue is called a *bonus issue*, or alternatively a *capitalization issue*.

Relief from these restricted uses of a share premium account is possible under Section 131 of the Companies Act. Broadly speaking, this applies when a company has acquired at least 90% of the shares of another company, with the first company issuing its shares, at a premium, in settlement. The share premium account that would otherwise be created can be used to write off any goodwill arising on consolidation.

Revaluation reserve

This is created when a company revalues any of its assets. The use of this reserve has been discussed under tangible fixed assets.

Other reserves

The balance sheet formats (see Appendix 1), under the heading *other reserves*, require the following reserves to be identified:

- capital redemption reserve
- reserve for own shares
- reserves provided for by the articles of association
- other reserves

The item *capital redemption reserve* is created following the redemption of shares, for example redeemable preference shares. In effect, the redeemed shares in the balance sheet are replaced by the capital redemption reserve. This is for creditor protection, to avoid what would otherwise be a reduction in share capital. The balance on the capital redemption reserve may only be used for a bonus issue of new shares.

We are unlikely to come across *reserve for own shares*, which is incorporated into UK legislation as part of European Union harmonization. It is possible for UK companies to buy their own shares, in certain carefully controlled situations, but they must be cancelled after purchase and the question of a reserve for own shares does not arise.

Reserves provided for by the articles of association are the reserves stipulated in the company's own internal regulations.

The fourth heading, *other reserves*, will cover all reserves that do not have their own headings in the balance sheet formats. Any such reserves which are significant should be separately identified. In the case of S&N, the movements in the other reserves are found in note 24, as shown in Example 6.18.

<table>
<tr><td>Example 6.18
Extract from S&N 1997
notes to the accounts</td><td colspan="2">24 OTHER RESERVES</td></tr>
<tr><td></td><td></td><td>Group
£million</td></tr>
<tr><td></td><td>At 28 April 1996</td><td>(352.1)</td></tr>
<tr><td></td><td>Contribution to employee share trust</td><td>(3.7)</td></tr>
<tr><td></td><td>Goodwill on acquisition</td><td>0.9</td></tr>
<tr><td></td><td>Goodwill on disposals</td><td>2.4</td></tr>
<tr><td></td><td>Exchange adjustments – on assets</td><td>(121.0)</td></tr>
<tr><td></td><td>– on borrowings</td><td>40.2</td></tr>
<tr><td></td><td>At 27 April 1997</td><td>(433.3)</td></tr>
</table>

Notice that the total figure (£433.3 million) is shown in brackets because this is deducted from the other items shown under the heading *equity reserves* in the balance sheet. From the analysis in note 24 we can see that £352.1 million is brought forward from last year, and £121.0 million represents foreign exchange adjustments on assets, i.e. assets designated in foreign currency have decreased in value as a result of exchange rate movements. The £352.1 million could be traced back in previous years' accounts and doing so would show that the bulk is represented by amounts of goodwill. The cumulative total of goodwill written off (i.e. included as a negative figure in the reserves) is shown to be £583.8 million.

Profit and loss account

The figure that appears in the balance sheet under the heading *profit and loss account* is the accumulated balance of profits (or losses). It is made up of the accumulated balance brought forward from the previous year, to which is added the current year's balance. For S&N, the make-up is as in note 25, shown in Example 6.19. The profit and loss account itself is a separate financial statement found in a company's annual report and accounts and is discussed in Chapter 7.

Example 6.19
Extract from S&N 1997
notes to the accounts

25 PROFIT AND LOSS ACCOUNT	Group £million
At 28 April 1996	1157.8
Profit/(loss) for year retained	154.1
Transferred from revaluation reserve (note 23)	(2.2)
Exchange adjustment	(8.8)
At 27 April 1997	1300.9

The totals of the two items *called-up share capital* and *reserves* are added together to arrive at one figure, called *capital and reserves*. For S&N the total is £2207.7 million, as shown in Example 6.20.

Example 6.20
Extract from S&N 1997
group balance sheet

		£million
Capital and reserves		
Equity share capital	21	183.6
Non-equity share capital	21	12.4
Called-up share capital		196.0
Equity reserves		
Share premium account	22	831.3
Revaluation reserve	23	312.8
Other reserves	24	(433.3)
Profit and loss account	25	1300.9
		2207.7

The £2207.7 million is made up of *called-up share capital* of £196.0 million and *equity reserves*, which themselves total £2011.7 million (i.e. £831 million + £312.8 million − £433.3 million + £1300.9 million).

We might find the equivalent figure in the balance sheet of other companies described as *shareholders' funds*. This is illustrated in the case of Tomkins in Example 6.21.

CAPITAL AND RESERVES

Example 6.21

Extract from Tomkins
1997 balance sheet

Capital and reserves	Note	£million
CALLED-UP SHARE CAPITAL		
Ordinary shares		59.8
Convertible cumulative preference shares		338.0
Redeemable convertible cumulative preference shares		391.4
	19	789.2
Share premium account	20	90.1
Capital reserve	20	––
Profit and loss account	20	558.0
Equity shareholders' funds	707.9	
Non-equity shareholders' funds	729.4	
SHAREHOLDERS' FUNDS		1437.3
Minority interest – equity		18.0
		1455.3

There are three further things to notice in Example 6.21. First, there have been issues of two classes of preference shares (convertible cumulative preference shares £338.0 million and redeemable convertible cumulative preference shares £391.4 million). We can expect to find further details concerning these share issues in the relevant notes, which have been cross-referenced in the balance sheet. In addition, details might be available elsewhere. In this case an explanation is set out in the financial review as shown in Example 6.22.

Example 6.22

Extract from Tomkins
1997 financial review

Acquisitions and disposals

The major event of the year was the consummation of the acquisition of the Gates Corporation with effect from 29 July 1996 for a total consideration of £752.9 million (including costs of £8.4 million) plus the inheritance of £129.7 million ($202.1 million) of net debt. The consideration for the Gates shares of £744.5 million ($1160.0 million) was satisfied by the issue of two types of Tomkins preference shares:

- $633.4 million (£406.5 million)* of redeemable convertible cumulative preference shares
- $526.6 million (£338.0 million) of convertible cumulative preference shares

*Author note: the £406.5 million is offset by a foreign exchange difference of £15.1 million in order to arrive at the balance sheet figure of £391.4 million.

Second, after the figure for shareholders' funds £1437.3 million there is a figure for minority interest – equity of £18.0 million. The minority interest is the interest in a subsidiary's net assets attributable to outside shareholders. This was discussed earlier under *investments* (see Chapter 5).

Third, notice that the subtotal, in the main column, of £1437.3 million is analysed in the inner column with reference to equity shareholders' funds £707.9 million and non-equity shareholders' funds £729.4 million.

Summary

The balance sheet is part of a set of financial statements and must be set out in accordance with one of the prescribed formats laid down in the Companies Act.

UK companies need to comply with rules set out in a number of authoritative sources when preparing a balance sheet for presentation to the shareholders. A great deal of detailed information is required either on the balance sheet or in the notes to the accounts.

In Chapter 5 we discussed the information required in respect of fixed assets and current assets. In this chapter we have covered the balance sheet headings of *creditors: amounts falling due within one year; creditors: amounts falling due after more than one year; provisions for liabilities and charges; capital and reserves.*

Exercises

These exercises are based on the extracts from the S&N 1997 annual report and accounts in Appendix 3.

1 Give an example of deferred income.
2 What are the amounts for the item *accruals and deferred income* at 27 April 1997.
3 In note 21: share capital, under the heading *During the year*, it is stated that '2.7 million ordinary shares of £0.5 million nominal value were issued at a consideration of £13.5 million'. Where, under the heading *capital and reserves*, would the £13.5 million be located?
4 How is the profit retained, £154.1 million, which is shown in the group profit and loss account, incorporated into the group balance sheet?
5 What is the effect on the underlying relationship in the balance sheet when the profit of £154.1 million is incorporated into the balance sheet?

The profit and loss account

Introduction

The profit and loss account is a financial statement which shows whether a company has made a profit or a loss for a particular period and how the profit or loss has been arrived at. A company will make a profit if the revenue from selling goods and/or services is more than the expenses incurred to achieve its sales. If the expenses are more than its revenues, the company will make a loss.

Companies derive revenues from the activities in which they are engaged. These might include selling goods, providing services and investing. If in a particular period a company has revenues from the sale of goods of £100 000 and has incurred expenses of £80 000, we can say that the company has made a profit of £20 000. Example 7.1 shows how this information might be set out in a profit and loss account.

Example 7.1
Profit and loss account

A–Z Co. Ltd	
Profit and loss account for the year ended 31 December 1997	
	£
Turnover	100 000
Expenses	80 000
Profit for the year	20 000

From the example it can be seen that the following have been included:

- the name of the company
- the period covered
- turnover (i.e. proceeds from the sale of goods in this example)
- expenses
- profit

All profit and loss accounts are built around this framework but will usually contain much more detail than in the example above.

The term *turnover* is defined in the authoritative sources as:

> the amount derived from the provision of goods and services falling within the company's ordinary activities after deduction of trade discounts, value added tax and any other taxes based on the amounts so derived.

There is no definition of the item *expenses* in the authoritative sources. Moreover, in this context we have to be careful, even with a standard dictionary definition such as 'spending of money'. This is because accountants recognize two types of money spent: money spent on capital items (called *capital expenditure*) and money spent on revenue items (called either *revenue expenditure* or *revenue expenses*). The purchase of a car would be classified as capital expenditure, whereas the purchase of petrol to run the car would be classified as revenue expenditure.

Capital expenditure is included in the balance sheet. For example, the car would be included as a fixed asset in the company's balance sheet at the end of its financial year. As we saw in Example 5.3, it is then necessary to spread the cost of the asset over the years which derive benefit from its use by means of annual charges for depreciation.

Revenue expenses are included in the profit and loss account. They are items that relate to the financial year concerned, for example the petrol used up in that year.

In the main, there is no difficulty in identifying an item as being either capital expenditure or revenue expenditure. However, there are cases where the distinction might not be clear.

The final figure in the profit and loss account in Example 7.1 is the profit for the year. For a real-world company we have to go beyond this to consider how much of the profit will go to the government by way of taxation and to the shareholders by way of dividends. Before discussing these and other issues in detail, it is useful to reiterate that there is a link between the balance sheet and the profit and loss account. This relationship is illustrated in Example 7.2.

Example 7.2 Relationship between the balance sheet and the profit and loss account	The ZZZ Co. Ltd was set up on 1 January 1997 by the issue of 100 000 ordinary shares of £1 each. The company's balance sheet at 1 January 1997 will be as follows:

ZZZ Co. Ltd balance sheet at 1 January 1997

	£
Asset	
Bank	100 000
Capital	
Share capital	100 000

The business activity of ZZZ Co. Ltd is the purchase and sale of stationery. It was decided that the company's financial year end would be 31 December. During the financial year ended 31 December 1997 the company bought stationery for £80 000, which it sold for £140 000, incurring general expenses of £10 000. All transactions were settled through the bank immediately, i.e. no credit was given or received. The profit and loss account for the year will show a profit of £50 000, as follows:

ZZZ Co. Ltd profit and loss account for the year ended 31 December 1997

	£
Turnover	140 000
Expenses (£80 000 cost of stationery and £10 000 general expenses)	90 000
Profit for the year	50 000

The company's balance sheet at the year end will be as follows:

ZZZ Co. Ltd balance sheet at 31 December 1997

	£
Asset	
Bank (£100 000 − £80 000 + £140 000 − £10 000)	150 000
Capital and reserves	
Share capital	100 000
Profit and loss account	50 000
	150 000

The balance sheet at 31 December 1997 in Example 7.2 shows that the shareholders' interest in the company at that date, as reflected in the capital and reserves, was £150 000. This is £50 000 more than the position at the beginning of the year because the company has made a profit of £50 000, the make-up of the profit being set out in the profit and loss account. In the example it was assumed that all transactions were settled immediately through the bank. Hence, the profit of £50 000 has resulted in an increase in the assets (specifically the bank balance in this example) of £50 000. The profit is not just an entry on a statement called the *profit and loss account*. The fact that the company has made a profit has resulted in an increase in the company's assets. It is better off at the end of the year by £50 000. In practice, it is unlikely that, at the balance sheet date, the increase will be wholly represented by an increase in the company's bank balance. For example, if credit terms had been allowed to customers the company might not have received all the amounts due to it. In addition, some monies which have been received might already have been spent, for example on the acquisition of fixed assets.

We have discussed the framework for a profit and loss account (revenues − expenses = profit) and how the profit figure links in with the balance sheet. We can now consider ways in which profit and loss accounts can be presented.

Profit and loss account formats

There are several different ways in which a profit and loss account may be set out. In the UK, limited companies must use one of the four formats prescribed in the Companies Act. These are reproduced in Appendix 2.

Formats 1 and 2, with a vertical presentation, are the formats used by the vast majority of UK companies. Formats 3 and 4 are alternatives to Formats 1 and 2, respectively. These are used by many companies in continental Europe, where the preference is for the horizontal layout for which Formats 3 and 4 are designed.

Formats 1 and 2 both start with the figure for turnover. Thereafter the distinction between them arises from their respective methods for analysing expenses; Format 1 analyses expenses by function (e.g. cost of sales, distribution costs, administration expenses), whereas Format 2 analyses by types of expenses (e.g. raw materials, consumables, staff costs). The Companies Act does not provide definitions for the Format 1 functional headings (cost of sales, etc.); hence, comparisons between companies might not be possible because one company's definition can be different from that of another.

In addition to the items specified in the prescribed formats, the Companies Act requires that profit and loss accounts must show:

- profit or loss on ordinary activities before taxation
- transfers to and withdrawals from reserves
- dividends paid and proposed

Some departure from the prescribed formats is permitted (e.g. combining headings to facilitate the assessment of the company's profit or loss). Furthermore, the way in which the items are arranged and the headings and subheadings used is to be adapted where the special nature of the company's business requires such adaptation. As a result, there is some variation between companies in the formats presented in practice.

One way in which the accounts of a particular year might be used is to assess how the company will perform in the future. It is important when comparing one year with another to compare like with like. If a company has discontinued any of its operations during the year, the person doing the assessment needs to be able to identify and eliminate these results because only continuing operations will have an effect on the future. Similarly, when the forecast results for a particular year are compared with the actual results, the latter should exclude any profit contributions from recent acquisitions which were not included in the forecast.

Since 1993, FRS 3: Reporting financial performance has required companies to analyse all profit and loss account figures down to operating profit, between results from continuing operations, acquisitions (as a component of continuing operations) and discontinued operations. Example 7.3 illustrates an analysis where there are no discontinued operations.

Consolidated Profit and Loss Account
for the year ended 31 December 1996

	Note	1996 Acquired activities £million	1996 Continuing activities £million	1996 Total £million
Turnover	1	16.0	504.4	520.4
Cost of sales		(14.6)	(392.8)	(407.4)
Gross profit		1.4	111.6	113.0
Sales and distribution costs		(0.4)	(31.8)	(32.2)
Administration expenses		(0.5)	(26.0)	(26.5)
Other operating income		—	1.1	1.1
Operating profit		0.5	54.9	55.4
Interest	2			(1.9)
Profit on ordinary activities before taxation	3			53.5
Taxation	6			(16.0)

Profit for the year		37.5
Dividends	7	(13.2)
Retained profit for the year	20	24.3

In Example 7.3 the TT group uses, and sticks closely to, a Format 1 presentation. All items down to operating profit have been analysed as required. For example, we can see that, of the total turnover of £520.4 million, £16.0 million is attributable to businesses acquired during the year, leaving £504.4 million attributable to existing continuing activities.

Other companies choose to present the required information partly on the face of the profit and loss account and partly in the notes to the accounts. Example 7.4 illustrates this in respect of a company with continuing and discontinued operations.

Example 7.4
Extract from Laird Group 1996 annual report and accounts

Group Profit and Loss Account
for the year to 31 December

	1996
Note	£million
1 Turnover	
continuing operations	973.9
discontinued operations	18.7
	992.6
2 Operating profit	
continuing operations	74.3
discontinued operations	(1.6)
	72.7
Loss on disposal of business	(1.0)
Profit on ordinary activities before taxation	71.7

NOTES TO THE ACCOUNTS
2 Operating profit

	1996		
	Discontinued operations £million	Continuing operations £million	Total £million
Turnover	18.7	973.9	992.6
Cost of sales	(16.4)	(818.5)	(834.9)
Gross profit	2.3	155.4	157.7
Administrative expenses	(3.9)	(81.1)	(85.0)
Operating profit	(1.6)	74.3	72.7

The Laird group shows analysed figures for turnover and operating profit on the face of the profit and loss account and presents an analysis which incorporates the expenses figure (cost of sales and administrative expenses).

This type of analysis did not apply to S&N's 1997 profit and loss account but was required in the 1996 profit and loss account as a result of the Courage acquisition. The figures for turnover and net operating profit are shown in Example 7.5.

Example 7.5
Extract from S&N 1996
group profit and loss
account

Group Profit and Loss Account

	Notes	1996 £million	£million
Turnover	2		
Continuing operations		2083.6	
Acquisition		885.3	
			2968.9
Net operating costs	4		(2604.5)
Operating profit	2		
Continuing operations		327.7	
Acquisition		36.7	
			364.4
Loss on disposal of fixed assets	3		(0.5)
Reorganization costs	3		(150.8)
Profit on ordinary activities before interest			213.1

The Companies Act, together with other authoritative sources (accounting standards, Stock Exchange requirements and codes of best practice on corporate governance), also contains provisions for the disclosure of other details. Some companies may give additional information, going beyond the minimum disclosure requirements.

Another factor to bear in mind is the necessity to look at a company's statement of accounting policies to ascertain the accounting treatment chosen by the company for any particular item in which we are interested. In addition to the accounting policies explicitly described in the statement, it is assumed, unless otherwise stated, that a company's accounts are based on certain fundamental accounting principles. In Chapter 1 we looked briefly at these principles as set out in the Companies Act. Four are singled out for special mention in SSAP 2: Disclosure of accounting policies, and these are considered below.

Fundamental accounting principles

In SSAP 2 (which refers to 'concepts' rather than 'principles') these are defined as 'broad basic assumptions which underlie the periodic financial accounts of business enterprises'. The four basic assumptions covered in SSAP 2 are:

1 going concern
2 accruals
3 consistency
4 prudence

These are considered below.

Going concern principle
The going concern principle assumes that 'the enterprise will continue in operational existence for the foreseeable future'. As an example of its

application, consider stock valuation. It can be assumed that if we buy goods for resale during one year and some of these goods are still in stock at the end of that year, the stock can be valued at cost price for the balance sheet and profit and loss account. This is because we assume that the enterprise will be carrying on, that the goods will be sold during the next year and, in the normal course of events, will be sold for more than their cost.

Another example is the purchase of a fixed asset, such as a car or a machine. If a company buys a machine which it expects to use over three years, the company can spread the cost over three years. At the end of the first year (and for simplicity assuming the machine has no ultimate scrap value) the company can value the machine at two-thirds of its original cost, again because the assumption is that the enterprise will carry on business, i.e. it is a going concern.

Accruals principle

This implies that all items of *revenues* and *expenses* are recognized in the profit and loss account when they are earned or incurred and not when money is received or paid.

For example, if goods are sold in a company's financial year ended 31 December 1997 but are not paid for until 1998, their sale is included in the turnover figure in the 1997 profit and loss account because the sale was made in that year. It is then necessary to match this sale with the cost of the goods (as part of the expenses figure).

The application of the principle gives rise to items of *accruals* and *prepayments*. For example, if the company has used electricity during 1997 but does not receive an invoice until February 1998 covering the period November 1997 until January 1998, then it is only the electricity consumed to 31 December 1997 which will be included in the 1997 profit and loss account. At 31 December 1997 it will be necessary to make an estimate of the consumption to the end of the financial year; this is referred to as an *accrual*. The effect is that the profit will decrease by the amount of the accrual and the balance sheet will include a liability for the (estimated) amount due.

The opposite is called a *prepayment*. As an example, if a company on 1 August 1997 has paid an insurance premium covering the next twelve months, to 31 July 1998, the insurance item included in the expenses in the 1997 profit and loss account would be reduced by $\frac{7}{12}$ of the premium because that proportion relates to the 1998 financial year. In the balance sheet at 31 December 1997 a figure would be included in respect of this prepayment.

Summing up, the accruals principle requires that revenues and expenses are recognized in the profit and loss account, when they are earned and incurred, respectively, and, most importantly, expenses items are matched with the revenues to which they relate.

Consistency principle

The requirement here is that 'there is consistency of accounting treatment of like items within each accounting period and from one period to the next'. As a result, anyone using the accounts of the company is able to make comparisons between years on a like-for-like basis.

Prudence principle

The application of this principle means that a company does not bring anticipated profits into its profit and loss account but it must bring in anticipated losses.

With regard to profits, they are only to be recognized for inclusion in the profit and loss account when they are realized, in the form of either cash or another asset which the company is reasonably certain will be converted into cash. For example, if a company with a financial year end of 31 December sells goods for £10 000 on 1 December 1997 to a customer who is allowed two months' credit, the £10 000 will be included in the profit and loss account for the year ended 31 December 1997; the company knows with reasonable certainty that its customer will settle the £10 000 by the end of January 1998. In the profit and loss account the £10 000 revenue will be included in the turnover figure and it will be matched with the expenses incurred to earn this revenue.

With regard to losses, these must be included in the profit and loss account as soon as they are recognized. For example, if at its financial year end of 31 March 1998 a company is owed £500 by customers but is uncertain as to whether the customers will pay in full, the company will be prudent and make a provision for doubtful debts. If we assume the amount of the provision is £100, the effect will be that profits will be reduced by £100 and the value of the debtors in the balance sheet will be £400 (i.e. the £500 owed, less provision for doubtful debts of £100).

Another example would be where, at its financial year end of 31 December 1997, a company recognizes that it is going to make a loss on a long-term project that will not be completed until its next financial year, 1998. The application of the prudence principle means that the company must reduce its 1997 profits by the amount, or estimated amount, of this loss. In accounting jargon the company is 'making provision for a foreseeable loss'. As a further illustration, in Example 7.6, GEC has shown that it has provided for anticipated losses.

Example 7.6 Extract from GEC 1997 notes to the accounts	**1997** **£million**
3 Exceptional items	
Losses less gains on disposals of subsidiaries and other fixed asset investments	
Realized net losses/gains	25
Anticipated losses on future disposals	75
	100

Contents of a profit and loss account

Having considered what a profit and loss account is, how it might be laid out and the fundamental accounting principles on which it is based, we can now examine in more detail the contents of the profit and loss account.

CONTENTS OF A PROFIT AND LOSS ACCOUNT

The headings found in a typical Format 2 presentation are illustrated by reference to the S&N 1997 profit and loss account, which is reproduced in Example 7.7. There are no acquisitions or discontinued operations and the corresponding figures for the previous year have been omitted so we can concentrate on just one column of figures. Each heading and subtotal on the face of the profit and loss account, together with selected items from the supporting notes, is discussed in the order in which it appears in the profit and loss account.

Example 7.7
Extract from S&N 1997
group profit and loss
account

Group Profit and Loss Account
52 weeks ended 27 April 1997

	Notes	1997 £million
Turnover	2	3349.2
Net operating costs	4	(2924.1)
Operating profit	2	425.1
Loss on disposal of fixed assets	3	(2.1)
Reorganization costs	3	—
Profit on ordinary activities before interest		423.0
Interest payable	7	(51.0)
Profit on ordinary activities before taxation		372.0
Taxation on profit on ordinary activities	8	(85.8)
Profit on ordinary activities after taxation	9	286.2
Preference dividends on non-equity shares		(0.8)
Profit attributable to ordinary shareholders		285.4
Ordinary dividends on equity shares	10	(131.3)
Profit/(loss) retained		154.1
		Pence
Basic earnings per ordinary share	11	46.5
Dilution effect of options and convertible cumulative preference shares		(0.7)
Fully diluted earnings per ordinary share excluding exceptional items		45.8

Turnover

This is the starting point for any profit and loss account. S&N defines turnover in its accounting policy statement, found in note 1 of the notes to the accounts, as shown in Example 7.8.

Example 7.8
Extract from S&N 1997
notes to the accounts

1 Accounting policies

(j) Turnover
Turnover is sales, including recovery of duty where appropriate, rents receivable and other trading income of the Group, after eliminating intra-Group transactions and excluding VAT and property disposals.

Net operating costs

This figure represents the total of the ordinary costs which have been incurred in order to achieve the 1997 turnover figure. In other words, they are the costs which need to be matched with the turnover in order to ascertain the operating profit. The accompanying note (note 4) giving the analysis of the company's figures is shown in Example 7.9.

4 NET OPERATING COSTS	1997
	£million
Change in stocks of finished goods and work in progress	7.8
Own work capitalized	(6.0)
Raw materials and consumables	911.8
Custom and excise duties	758.0
Employee costs (note 5)	535.7
Depreciation	123.7
Operating lease rentals – plant and machinery	8.7
– land and buildings	35.1
Income from investments	(8.8)
Share of profit of associated undertakings	(7.4)
Other operating charges	565.5
	2924.1

Own work capitalized represents the cost which the company has incurred in building or developing a fixed asset (for example an extension to a building). The elements which make up the cost, e.g. *raw materials and consumables, employee costs,* are included in the first instance under their appropriate headings, and then taken out as one total (£6.0 million), which is identified in the analysis of net operating costs.

Notice that in the list of items under net operating costs S&N have also included two items representing revenue into the company, i.e. *income from investments* (£8.8 million) and *share of profit of associated undertakings* (£7.4 million). (This latter item is discussed below.) In this example, these amounts are relatively insignificant and they have been disclosed here for convenience. However, S&N in consequence have incorporated 'net' into the heading *net operating costs.* Bass use the self-explanatory heading *costs and overheads, less other income,* but other companies, for example BT, prefer *operating costs* (i.e. without the term *net*), although the heading includes revenue items which have similarly been deducted from the final total.

As pointed out above, because *share of profits of associated undertakings* is not a significant item in the context of S&N's total figures, the company has chosen to include the amount (£7.4 million) in note 4. In other cases, where it is significant, it can be shown on the face of a company's profit and loss account. This item represents the group's share of the net profits of a company which is not a subsidiary, but in which the group has a holding (20%+) that enables the group to exercise significant influence. The increase in the group's profit as a result of bringing in this figure is equalled by an increase in the balance sheet value of the associated company. The impact on the balance sheet was illustrated in Example 5.27.

Operating profit

This is the difference between the turnover and the operating costs. The term *operating profit* is a useful way to describe this difference, although it is not used in the prescribed formats. It represents the profit made from a company's operating activities – for example, for S&N, brewing, running pubs and hotels and leisure parks; for BT, the supply of telecommunication services and equipment.

Loss on disposal of fixed assets: reorganization costs

These two items appear on the face of the S&N 1997 profit and loss account under the subtotal *operating profit*. In each case there is a cross-reference to note 3, the heading of which is *exceptional items*.

Exceptional items

FRS 3 refers to these as 'material items which derive from events or transactions that fall within the ordinary activities of the reporting entity'. They are part of the company's normal activities but, 'because of their exceptional size or incidence, require separate disclosure to explain the performance of a period'. Such items are to be included under the appropriate heading, with further details in supporting notes, with the exception of three situations, which are to be shown on the face of the profit and loss account. Two of these, as already indicated above, are reflected in the S&N profit and loss account, namely:

- profits or losses on the disposal of fixed assets
- costs of a fundamental reorganization or restructuring having a material effect on the nature and focus of the reporting entity's operations

Reference to these is made on the face of the profit and loss account, as shown in Example 7.7 above, and in note 3, as shown in Example 7.10 below.

The third situation where exceptional items are to be shown on the face of the profit and loss account is in the case of:

- profits or losses on the sale or termination of an operation.

This does not appear in the S&N accounts under consideration and so reference is made in this instance to the BT 1997 profit and loss account (see Example 7.11 below).

Profit or loss on disposal of fixed assets

In carrying out their operating activities, companies are quite likely to dispose of fixed assets which have come to the end of their useful lives. Profits or losses arising from these disposals are to be reported in the profit and loss account.

The S&N profit and loss account includes the item *loss on disposal of fixed assets* (£2.1 million) and details are given in note 3, as shown in Example 7.10. As we saw earlier in Examples 5.3 and 5.21, the balance sheet value of a fixed asset is its cost less depreciation. (We sometimes use the terms *book value* and *carrying value* as alternatives to *balance sheet value*.) If a company sells an asset for more than its book value, the company makes a profit on the disposal.

Example 7.10
Extract from S&N 1997
notes to the accounts

3 EXCEPTIONAL ITEMS

During the year there was a loss on disposal of fixed assets of £2.1 million (1996 – £0.5 million). Taxation on the loss was a credit of £2.1 million (1996 – £nil).

The reorganization costs in 1996 of £150.8 million related to the Beer Division. Tax relief on the reorganization costs was £25.2 million.

Costs of a fundamental reorganization or restructuring having a material effect on the nature and focus of the reporting entity's operations

S&N does not show a figure for this type of cost in the profit and loss account for 1997, but the 1996 corresponding column shows a figure of £150.8 million under the heading *reorganization costs*. This is commented on in note 3, reproduced in Example 7.10.

Profits or losses on the sale or termination of an operation

The BT 1997 profit and loss account includes the term *profit on sale of group undertakings*. Group undertakings are subsidiary companies. In the accompanying note 3, as shown in Example 7.11, BT explains that the transaction has negligible effects on the group's figures.

Example 7.11
Extract from BT 1997
notes to the financial
statements

3 Profit on sale of group undertakings

In the years ended 31 March 1996 and 31 March 1997 the subsidiary undertakings disposed of had a negligible effect on the group's operating profit and cash flows and their net assets were immaterial to the group's financial position.

In other cases where the effects are not negligible, an analysis of the profit or loss is to be given.

In Chapter 5, we discussed the treatment of goodwill on the acquisition of a subsidiary. When a subsidiary is acquired any goodwill arising will usually be written off against existing reserves and this can have an impact on profit if the subsidiary is subsequently sold. This is illustrated in Example 7.12, which we start with by using figures borrowed from Example 5.6.

Example 7.12
Profit/loss on disposal of a
subsidiary

Company A paid £175 million to obtain control of company B, which had net assets of £150 million. Hence a payment of £25 million was made for goodwill which was written off against reserves in the group balance sheet. The subsidiary's net assets are only worth £150 million in the group's balance sheet. The interest in company B is now sold for £166 million. In this case the loss is to be calculated as £175 million less £166 million = £9 million. This loss would be included as an exceptional expenses item in the group profit and loss account. This has been required accounting treatment since 1992. Previously some companies would have compared the £166 million with the book value of £150 million to produce a £16 million profit.

The Companies Act distinguishes between exceptional items and extraordinary items. Extraordinary items are not defined. FRS 3 recognizes the term *extraordinary items* but says, 'In view of the extreme rarity of such items no examples are provided'. Hence, it is extremely unlikely that UK companies will include extraordinary items in their accounts and this is no longer a contentious issue for UK companies.

Profit on ordinary activities before interest

FRS 3: Reporting financial performance includes the subtotal *profit on ordinary activities before interest* in its illustrative examples. The provision of this subtotal enables users of the accounts to see how much profit is available to cover the interest payable. Thus, in the case of the S&N 1997 profit and loss account, as we can see from Example 7.7, this is £423.0 million, from which the interest of £51.0 million is subsequently deducted.

Interest receivable; Interest payable

Both of these items have to be shown and the standard format provides separate headings for them. Detailed information is required and this will normally be given in a supporting note.

S&N show interest payable on the face of the profit and loss account, supported by the required detailed information in note 7. Note 7 includes a deduction of interest receivable, £4.7 million. As we have already seen in Example 7.9, S&N has included other income receivable, in the form of income from investments of £8.8 million, as a deduction from operating costs in note 4, on net operating costs. Where both amounts are material, other companies may show both interest receivable and interest payable as separate items on the face of the profit and loss account (see Example 7.14), while others may indicate net interest receivable.

Companies can borrow funds in a number of ways, for example, by issuing loan stock, debentures or bonds (see Chapter 6). Depending on market conditions it might be decided to make the issue at nominal value, at a discount or at a premium This is illustrated in Example 7.13.

Example 7.13
Issue of £100 debenture stock

	Amount received £
Issued at nominal value	100
Issued at 5% discount	95
Issued at 3% premium	103

The discount of £5 is really a form of interest payable which the issuing company has to bear and the £3 premium is a form of interest receivable. Stock might be issued on terms that it would be repayable at a premium. Such a premium is akin to interest payable. In practice there can be complexities associated with different types of capital instruments (i.e. instruments used as a means of raising finance) and these are dealt with in an accounting standard, FRS 4: Capital instruments.

The BT 1997 group profit and loss account includes the item *premium on repurchase of bonds* (£60 million). Because this item is akin to *interest payable* it is included alongside the items *interest receivable* and *interest payable* in the profit and loss account, as shown in Example 7.14.

Example 7.14
Extract from BT 1997
group profit and loss
account

	Notes	1997
		£million
Operating profit		3245
Group's share of profits of associated undertakings		139
Profit on sale of group undertakings	3	8
Interest receivable	4	206
Interest payable	4	(335)
Premium on repurchase of bonds	4	(60)
Profit on ordinary activities before taxation		3203

Profit on ordinary activities before taxation

The subtotal *profit on ordinary activities before taxation* is not one of the items in the standard format but it is used by most companies. It features in the illustrative examples in FRS 3: Reporting financial performance and it does provide symmetry with the subsequent subtotal, *profit on ordinary activities after taxation*.

Up to this point there can be some variation between the ways in which different companies present their profit and loss accounts. However, from this item onwards little variation is found in the published accounts of most UK companies.

Taxation on profit on ordinary activities

The tax charged is based on the profits of the year. Companies have to distinguish between UK tax and overseas tax. Broadly speaking, the taxes shown in Table 7.1 must be disclosed.

Example 7.15 shows how the S&N tax charge is analysed in note 8 of the 1997 notes to the accounts. At the same time this illustrates some of the headings found in Table 7.1.

Example 7.15
Extract from S&N 1997
notes to the accounts

8 TAXATION ON PROFIT ON ORDINARY ACTIVITIES

	1997
	£million
Based on profit for the year	
Corporation tax at 33%	77.3
Deferred taxation	2.8
Overseas taxation	4.2
Taxation on the share of profit in associated undertakings	1.5
	85.8

Table 7.1 UK and overseas tax

UK taxes	corporation tax – tax on group's profit – tax on share of profits of associated undertakings deferred tax income tax irrecoverable advance corporation tax (ACT)
Overseas taxes	tax on group's profits tax on share of profits of associated undertakings

We will now look at each of the elements of taxation shown in Table 7.1.

UK taxes
Corporation tax
The basis of the charge, usually 'the profits of the year', and any special circumstances that affect the tax liability are to be shown. Good practice includes disclosure of the rate. As can be seen from Example 7.14, the corporation tax on S&N group profits of £77.3 million and the taxation of S&N's share of profit in associated undertakings of £1.5 million are shown in note 8.

Deferred tax
If we assume a corporation tax rate of 30%, it would not be unreasonable to expect a tax charge based on the year's profits to be 30% of those profits. For example, if a company's profits were £1 000 000 we might expect to see a corporation tax charge of 30% of £1 000 000, i.e. £300 000. This is not always the case. In the UK there are differences between the way in which companies calculate their profits and the way in which the Inland Revenue calculates profit for tax purposes.

Differences arise for two main reasons. First, some expenses which are included as such in a company's profit and loss account are not allowable for tax purposes. These are called *permanent differences*; an example is entertainment expenses. Second, some items are included in different financial periods in the taxation computation for the Inland Revenue from the periods in which they are incurred in the company's financial statements. These are called *timing differences*, the most common example being the difference between a company's depreciation charge and the Inland Revenue figure, which is called a *capital allowance*. This type of 'timing difference' is illustrated in Example 7.16.

Example 7.16
Timing differences

A company buys a machine for £100 000 in Year 1. It is estimated that the machine will last for five years and will have no value at the end of its life.

It is decided to apply a charge for depreciation each year of £100 000/5 = £20 000.

For tax purposes the machine attracts a capital allowance of 25%, applied on a reducing balance basis, i.e. in Year 1, 25% x £100 000 = £25 000; in Year 2, 25% x (£100 000 – £25 000) = £18 750, and so on.

The company's profit on ordinary activities before taxation is £90 000 and the corporation tax rate is 30%. In arriving at £90 000, depreciation of £20 000 has been charged in the profit and loss account. If we go back to the position before depreciation we have a figure of £110 000. We now have:

Published accounts	£
Profit for year before tax	90 000

Taxation computations:	£	
Profits per accounts	90 000	
Add: depreciation	20 000	
	110 000	
Less capital allowance	25 000	85 000

The corporation tax charge in the profit and loss account will be 30% of £85 000 = £25 500 instead of an estimated charge of 30% x £90 000 = £27 000.

SSAP 15: Deferred tax requires that companies account for the tax effects of timing differences by opening a deferred tax account. The object is to smooth out the effects of timing differences in the profit and loss account.

Using the figures from Example 7.15:

In Year 1 the tax charge will be made up of:

		£	
Corporation tax	(30% x 85 000)	25 500	
Deferred tax	(30% x 5000)	1 500	(i.e. 30% x (90 000 – 85 000))
		27 000	(i.e. 30% x 90 000)

The creation of the deferred tax provision involves an increase in the tax charge in the profit and loss account, with a consequential reduction in profit. The balance is the deferred tax provision and this is included under the heading *provisions for liabilities and charges*.

In subsequent years the corporation tax amount will be reduced by appropriate transfers from the provision for deferred tax.

The topic presents many controversial issues and is currently the subject of an Accounting Standards Board discussion paper.

Income tax

Companies are liable for corporation tax on their profits and it is unlikely that UK companies will bear any income tax charges. If a group includes an undertaking subject to income tax, the amount of income tax will be disclosed in the group accounts.

When one UK company receives a dividend from another UK company paid out of profits which have borne corporation tax, the dividend is termed *franked investment income* in the hands of the recipient company. The recipient company is required to add to the actual amount received a notional credit to produce a 'grossed-up' figure. SSAP 8 requires the grossed up amount to be included as investment income in the profits of the company. The equivalent tax is included as an element of the tax charge in the profit and loss account.

There is no income tax element in the taxation charge in the S&N accounts.

Irrecoverable advance corporation tax (ACT)

When a company pays a dividend, this triggers off a liability to pay the associated tax charge on behalf of its shareholders. From the company's standpoint the payment is a payment on account of the ultimate corporation tax liability. A situation can arise whereby a company cannot set the ACT against a corporation tax bill (perhaps because profits come mostly from overseas and little UK corporation tax is payable). The ACT is then termed *irrecoverable ACT*, in the sense that it is not recoverable in the year in question. If the recovery is not 'reasonably certain and foreseeable' SSAP 8: Treatment of taxation requires that it be written off to the profit and loss account. The accounting treatment of irrecoverable ACT is the subject of a current Accounting Standards Board discussion paper. This type of item does not feature in the S&N accounts.

Overseas taxes

The amount of overseas taxes borne by a UK company on its profits for the year is to be disclosed. Where the company's UK tax liability is reduced as a result of relief given under a double tax agreement, the amount of this relief is also to be disclosed.

Example 7.17 illustrates how BT presents the required figures for UK and overseas taxes.

Example 7.17
Extract from BT 1997
notes to the financial
statements

5 TAX ON PROFIT ON ORDINARY ACTIVITIES

	1997 £million
United Kingdom	
Corporation tax at 33%	1135
Deferred taxation credit at 33%	(100)
Taxation on the group's share of results of associated undertakings	—
Prior year adjustments	1
Total UK taxation	1036
Overseas taxation:	
Current	17
Taxation on the group's share of results of associated undertakings	49
Total tax on profit on ordinary activities	1102

Profit on ordinary activities after taxation

This subtotal is a required heading in the standard format and represents the amount of profit 'belonging to' the shareholders. Companies which publish group accounts and comply with certain conditions in the Companies Act need not publish the profit and loss account of the parent company. The main condition is that the group profit and loss account must show how much of the consolidated profit or loss is dealt with in the companies' individual accounts. S&N shows the required details in note 9 (see Example 7.18).

Example 7.18
Extract from S&N 1997
notes to the accounts

9 PROFIT ON ORDINARY ACTIVITIES AFTER TAXATION

	1997 £million
Parent company	112.3
Subsidiary undertakings	169.5
Associated undertakings	4.4
	286.2

Minority interests

These are the interests of shareholders who own shares in those subsidiary companies not wholly owned by the parent company. When the group profit and loss account is prepared, we add together 100% of the revenues and 100% of the expenses of the parent company and all the subsidiaries to arrive at the group profit. If outsiders hold shares in one or more of the subsidiaries, the amount 'owned' by the minority interests is then deducted from the profit on ordinary activities after taxation to arrive at the amount available for parent company shareholders. A calculation of the profits due to minority interests is illustrated in Example 7.19.

Example 7.19

Minority interest share of group profit

At 31 December 1997, company P holds 100% of the voting shares of company S1 and 80% of the shares of company S2. For the year ended 31 December 1997 the profits of the three companies were:

	£million
Company P	10 000
Company S1	6 000
Company S2	5 000
The Group profit is	21 000
of which the minority interest is	1 000 (20% of 5000)
Leaving	20 000

This £20 000 is the amount available for the parent company shareholders

Preference dividends on non-equity shares

S&N has deducted dividends (£0.8 million) due to its preference shareholders in order to arrive at the next subtotal, labelled *profit attributable to ordinary shareholders*.

Profit attributable to ordinary shareholders

Having deducted the preference share dividends, one has the amount of profit which can be said to 'belong to' the holders of ordinary shares. For S&N ordinary shareholders in 1997 this was £285.4 million. This figure forms the basis for calculating the figure for earnings per share (EPS), which is discussed below.

Ordinary dividends on equity shares

S&N has deducted the dividends to ordinary shareholders in order to arrive at the amount of profit retained in the company. In the notes to the accounts companies give details of dividends in terms of pence per share as well as the total amounts. Example 7.20 shows this information as presented by S&N.

Example 7.20

Extract from S&N 1997 notes to the accounts

10 ORDINARY DIVIDENDS ON EQUITY SHARES

	1997
	£million
Interim 7.21p per share (1996 – 6.55p)	44.2
Proposed final 14.17p per share (1996 – 12.88p)	87.1
	131.3

Profit/(loss) retained

This is the figure which is derived from all the subtotals discussed above.

In the case of S&N in 1997 there is a profit of £154.1 million. This is the balance of profit 'ploughed back' into the company and this amount is added to reserves.

Basic earnings per share

Finally, as far as the profit and loss account is concerned, accounting standards require listed companies to state a figure for EPS. EPS is the earnings (i.e. the profits) available to the ordinary shareholders (£285.4 million for S&N) divided by the number of ordinary shares in issue. This has to be disclosed on the face of the profit and loss account, together with the basis for calculating the figure, which may alternatively be located in the notes section. To ensure consistency between companies and between one financial year and another, rules and definitions for the calculation of EPS are set out in SSAP 3: Earnings per share.

In appropriate circumstances, two figures are stated, the *basic earnings per share* and the *fully diluted earnings per share*. The latter takes into account that in circumstances where a company is contracted to make a further issue of shares the same amount of profit will have to be divided by a greater number of shares. An example is where a company has issued convertible loan stock, which gives holders the rights to convert the loan stock into ordinary shares.

The S&N 1997 profit and loss account, reproduced in Example 7.7, includes figures for basic earnings per share of 46.5p and 45.8p for fully diluted earnings per share. Note 11 then discloses how the amounts have been calculated, as shown in Example 7.21. EPS is discussed further in Chapter 11.

<table>
<tr><td>

Example 7.21

Extract from S&N 1997 notes to the accounts

</td><td>

11 EARNINGS PER SHARE

Basic earnings per share have been calculated on the average number of ordinary shares in issue during the year, namely 614.1 million (1996 – 585.6 million), and earnings of £285.4 million (1996 – £108.6 million).

Fully diluted earnings per share excluding exceptional items have also been calculated since, in the opinion of the Directors, this is a more representative indicator of the trading performance of the Group. Fully diluted earnings per share excluding exceptional items allow for the full exercise of all outstanding options and the conversion of convertible cumulative preference shares and are based on 629.4 million shares (1996 – 608.8 million) and adjusted earnings of £288.5 million (1996 – £237.5 million).

</td></tr>
</table>

SUMMARY

The profit and loss account is a financial statement which shows whether a company has made a profit or a loss for a particular period and how the profit or loss has been arrived at. If a company makes a profit for a period the amount of the profit is represented by an increase in the company's net assets. If a company makes a loss there will be a decrease in the net assets.

Prescribed formats for a company's profit and loss account are set out in the Companies Act. The Act also indicates the fundamental accounting principles underlying the preparation of the profit and loss account. The accounting policies applied by a company to the valuation of specific items in the account are disclosed in the notes to the accounts.

Items and subtotals contained in a profit and loss account were identified by reference to examples drawn from S&N and other companies. In many cases it is necessary to refer to the notes to the accounts to obtain analysis and further details for a particular item.

Exercises

These exercises are based on the extracts from the S&N 1997 annual report and accounts in Appendix 3.

1 How much is the group turnover for 1997?
2 How is the item 'turnover' defined?
3 Give an example to illustrate the application of the accruals principle in the preparation of a profit and loss account (not necessarily with reference to S&N).
4 What is the percentage increase in group turnover for 1997 compared with 1996?
5 What is the total amount of dividends which will be distributed to shareholders out of the 1997 profits?
6 What is the analysis of turnover for the year ended 28 April 1996?
7 How much of the 1997 operating profit of £425.1 million came from beer sales?
8 How much was provided for depreciation for 1997 and what effect has this on the accumulated depreciation figure in the balance sheet?
9 By how much did the net interest payable for 1997 exceed income from investments?
10 How much of the net operating costs for 1997 – £2924.1 million – was attributable to employee costs and how much of the employee costs was for directors' remuneration?

The cash flow statement

As we saw in Chapter 4, the balance sheet is a statement of a company's financial position at the end of its financial year. The profit and loss account, which shows whether a company has made a profit or loss (see Chapter 7), is linked to the balance sheet because any retained profit is included in the reserves in the balance sheet. These two statements are required by the Companies Act. For a number of years, to comply with accounting standards, companies have also been required to prepare a third statement which explains the changes in the financial position which have occurred during the year. Such a statement can be constructed in a number of ways but, since 1992, under FRS 1, Cash flow statements, UK companies have been required to prepare a statement which focuses on the impact of their activities on their cash position. This is in recognition of the vital importance to any company of being able to generate cash and to control its cash flow in such a way that it does not have short- or long-term liquidity problems. Not surprisingly, the statement is called a *cash flow statement.*

The statement highlights the impact on cash of various activities undertaken by a company. When a company prepares a profit and loss account it identifies an item called *profit on ordinary activities.* Ordinary activities mean the activities in which the company engages in seeking to make a profit: selling shoes, brewing beer, building ships or whatever. We can call these the *operating activities* of the company. This is to distinguish them from a company's other activities. Before a company can carry out its operating activities it will have to obtain the necessary finance (from shareholders or external lenders), i.e. it will be involved in financing activities, which we can refer to as *financing.*

Once a company has the necessary finance available, it can then make decisions to spend money by way of capital expenditure (e.g. buying a factory or machinery, etc.) and possibly consider making financial investments (e.g. buying shares in other companies or making loans to third parties). Hence, we can consider another activity, which we can call *capital expenditure and financial investment.* In addition to these activities, a company may chose to grow by means of taking over other businesses and/or disposing of a section of its own business. We can refer to these activities as *acquisitions and disposals*. The identification of these major areas of activity and their impact on cash flow, together with associated flows (interest, taxation, dividends), form the basis of the cash flow statement.

Format of the cash flow statement

FRS 1 does not prescribe a format but does provide examples of statements and accompanying notes applicable to various types of undertakings. However, FRS 1 requires cash flows to be classified under the following eight standard headings:

1 operating activities
2 returns on investment and servicing of finance
3 taxation
4 capital expenditure and financial investment
5 acquisitions and disposals
6 equity dividends paid
7 management of liquid resources
8 financing

Broadly speaking, companies present cash flow statements in one of two ways, (a) or (b):

(a) as a statement which contains only the main headings, with details being given in supporting notes;
(b) as a statement which presents the main headings, together with supporting details and amounts, on the face of the statement.

British Steel adopts the first of these (i.e. (a)), as shown in Example 8.1, which closely follows the illustrative example in FRS 1.

S&N adopts the second approach (i.e. (b)), as can be seen from Example 8.2.

In the two following examples numbers corresponding to the eight standard headings (see above) have been inserted for identification purposes. However, these numbers do not appear in the originals.

Example 8.1
Extract from British Steel
1996/97 consolidated
cash flow statement

	Note	1997 £million
1 Net cash flow income from operating activities	25	869
2 Returns on investment and servicing of finance	26	26
3 Tax paid	26	(281)
4 Capital expenditure and financial investment	26	(410)
5 Acquisitions and disposals	26	57
6 Equity dividends paid		(204)
Cash inflow before use of liquid resources and financing		57
7 Management of liquid resources		
Net purchase of short-term investments		(167)

8 Financing		
Issue of ordinary shares	26	1
Increase/reduction in debt	26	78
Net cash inflow/(outflow) from financing activities	26	79
(Decrease)/increase in cash in year		(31)

Example 8.2
Extract from S&N 1997 group cash flow statement

	Notes	1997 £million	£million
1 Net cash inflow from operating activities	30		475.0
2 Returns on investment and servicing of finance			
Interest received		5.8	
Interest paid		(52.0)	
Preference dividends paid		(0.8)	
Net cash outflow for returns on investments and servicing of finance			(47.0)
3 Taxation			(52.2)
4 Capital expenditure and financial investment			
Purchase of tangible fixed assets		(270.1)	
Purchase of investments		(42.0)	
Sale of tangible fixed assets		35.2	
Realization of investments		59.5	
Net cash outflow for capital expenditure and financial investment			(217.4)
5 Acquisitions and disposals			
Purchase of business		(20.2)	
Net cash acquired with business		—	
Purchase of investment in associated undertaking		—	
Net cash outflow for acquisitions and disposals			(20.2)
6 Equity dividends paid			(123.3)
Net cash inflow/(outflow) before use of liquid resources and financing			14.9
7 Management of liquid resources			
Movement in short-term deposits with banks			1.0
8 Financing			
Issues of ordinary share capital		9.8	
Proceeds of loan capital		194.0	
Repayment of loan capital		(185.0)	
Net cash inflow from financing			18.8
Increase in cash in the period	31		34.7
Liquid resources comprise term deposits of less than one year			

The number of supporting notes will vary from company to company depending on what information is shown on the face of the statement.

Using the S&N cash flow statement in Example 8.2 we can now discuss the individual items in the statement.

Net cash inflow from operating activities

This can be calculated by one of two methods: the direct method or the indirect method. The direct method involves going back to primary records and identifying the relevant constituent cash flows, in effect reproducing the company's cash book in summarized form. The indirect method, which is used by S&N and most other companies, starts with the operating profit which is found in the profit and loss account (£425.1 million for S&N in 1997), and then adjusts this for the effects of non-cash items to arrive at the cash generated as a result of the company's operating activities (£475.0 million for S&N in 1997).

FRS 1 requires companies to include a note to the accounts giving details of the necessary adjustments. The S&N note is shown in Example 8.3.

Example 8.3
Extract from S&N 1997 notes to the accounts

30 NET CASH INFLOW FROM OPERATING ACTIVITIES

	1997 £million
Operating profit	425.1
Share of profit of associated undertakings	(7.4)
Dividends from associated undertakings	1.5
Depreciation	123.7
Provisions against investments	1.6
(Increase)/decrease in stocks	7.9
Decrease in debtors	12.5
Decrease in creditors	(30.0)
Net cash inflow from ordinary operating activities	534.9
Reorganization costs	(41.3)
Utilization of acquisition and pension provisions	(18.6)
Net cash inflow from operating activities	475.0

Each of the items appearing in the list of figures shown in Example 8.3 represents an adjustment that has been made to the operating profit (£425.1 million) because the particular item does not reflect cash flowing into or out of the business. The point can be illustrated by reference to the decrease in debtors of £12.5 million. In Example 8.4, we have used hypothetical figures to show why this particular adjustment is necessary.

Example 8.4
Cash received from debtors

	£million
At the beginning of the financial year, a company's customers owed	42.50
During the financial year the company sells goods to its customers for	100.00
Also during the year, customers pay the company	(112.50)
Hence, at the end of the year the balance owed by customers is	
(42.50 + 100.00 – 112.50)	30.00
The only information that is shown on the profit and loss account is the sale of	100.00
We must make an addition in respect of the decrease in debtors (42.50 – 30.00) of	12.50
in order to arrive at the actual cash received of	112.50

The most common example of a non-cash item is depreciation. The amount charged for depreciation in a profit and loss account for a particular year does not represent a cash flow from the business but rather an estimate of the part of the asset's cost attributable to that year (see Example 5.3). Hence, a figure of £123.7 million is added to the £425.1 million in the S&N reconciliation.

From Example 8.2 we can see that this first item in the S&N cash flow statement, *net cash inflow from operating activities,* represents an *inflow* of cash to the S&N group of £475.0 million. The figures for the next five items in the statement (i.e. *returns on investment and servicing of finance, taxation, capital expenditure and financial investment, acquisitions and disposals* and *equity dividends paid*) are shown in brackets to indicate that they are *outflows* of cash from the group.

At this stage we reach a figure for *net cash inflow/(outflow) before use of liquid resources and financing.*

Net cash inflow/(outflow) before use of liquid resources and financing

This is a subtotal which is made up of the cash inflow of £475.0 million less the five cash outflows referred to above, i.e. (47.0 m) + (52.2 m) + (217.4 m) + (20.2 m) + (123.3 m).

	£million
Therefore the position is that there is a cash inflow of:	475.0
There are five outflows which together total:	460.1
The outflows deducted from the inflows leave a subtotal of:	14.9

This subtotal represents an inflow of cash. For this purpose the term *cash* means cash in hand and deposits which are repayable on demand less overdrafts.

Management of liquid resources

Apart from cash as defined above, most companies have assets which are very close to being cash, for example short-term deposits. In the context of a cash flow statement these sorts of asset are referred to as *liquid resources.*

S&N have identified their liquid resources as *short-term deposits with banks.* The amount involved, £1.0 million, represents an inflow and has to be added to the £14.9 million. If it was an outflow it would be shown in brackets and would have to be deducted.

Financing

The cash inflows and outflows from S&N's financing activities are now set out. In the current year they comprise inflows from the issue of ordinary share capital (£9.8 million) and further amounts borrowed: proceeds of loan capital £194.0 million; and an outflow arising from the repayment of loan capital (£185.0 million). These inflows and outflows taken together amount to a net cash inflow from financing of £18.8 million.

Increase in cash in the period

This is the final figure in the cash flow statement and is arrived at by adding to the net cash inflow before use of liquid resources and financing of £14.9 million the cash inflows from movement of liquid resources of £1.0 million and financing of £18.8 million, to give a figure for this item of £34.7 million.

FRS 1 requires that a note is included which shows how the final figure on the cash flow statement (for S&N, increase in cash for the period £34.7 million) links with the movement in net debt. Before looking at the relevant note in the S&N accounts (note 31), we need to discuss what is meant by the item *net debt*.

Companies obtain finance from shareholders and from borrowings from outside sources. The amounts borrowed may be referred to as *debt*. The total amount of debt for S&N at the end of the current year, in this instance 27 April 1997, is made up of the items *bank overdrafts* and *loan capital*. In note 32, part of which is reproduced in Example 8.5, these items are shown offset by the items *cash* and *short-term deposits* to produce a figure of net debt.

Example 8.5
Extract from S&N 1997
notes to the accounts

32 ANALYSIS OF NET DEBT

	At 27 April 1997 £million
Cash	55.7
Bank overdrafts	(331.0)
Net cash	(275.3)
Short-term deposits	17.3
Loan capital	(430.1)
Net debt	(688.1)

The presentation in Example 8.5 follows a conventional layout. Another way of expressing the message from the table is to say that, at the year end:

the *debt*: bank overdrafts (£331.0) + *loan capital* (£430.1 m) = (£761.1 m)
is offset by *cash* £55.7 m + *short-term deposits* £17.3 m, i.e. £73.0 m
giving a figure for *net debt* of (£688.1 m)

In addition to the data presented in the final column of note 32 (as shown in Example 8.5), the note also provides an analysis linking the items which make up the net debt to the cash flow during the year and showing the extent to which they were affected by exchange adjustments.

Having looked at the make-up of the net debt, we can now return to consider how the final figure on the cash flow statement (£34.7 million) links with the movement in net debt.

Reconciliation of net cash flow to movement in net debt
As mentioned above, FRS 1 requires that a note is included to show how the net cash flow is linked with the movement in net debt. The S&N note is shown in Example 8.6.

Example 8.6
Extract from S&N 1997
notes to the accounts

31 RECONCILIATION OF NET CASHFLOW TO MOVEMENT IN NET DEBT

	1997 £million
Increase in cash	34.7
Cash inflow from change in loan capital	(9.0)
Cash inflow from change in liquid reserves	(1.0)
Change in net debt resulting from cashflows	24.7
Loans acquired with business	—
Exchange	39.5
(Increase)/decrease in net debt	64.2
Net debt at 27 April 1996	(752.3)
Net debt at 27 April 1997	(688.1)

In looking at the details presented in note 31, we must remember that the total cash flow story is told in the cash flow statement. What note 31 is doing is identifying those parts of the story that enable us to see how the cash flow is linked with the movement in net debt.

£million

The last three figures in the note tell us that:

the net debt at the beginning of the year (28 April 1996) was:	752.3
and during the year there was an overall decrease of:	64.2
leaving a figure of net debt at the year end (27 April 1997) of:	688.1

With regard to the decrease of £64.2 million, this is made up as follows:

£million

the company has made an accounting adjustment for exchange differences of:	39.5
which together with the decrease in net debt resulting from cash flows of:	24.7
brings us back to the total for decrease in net debt of:	64.2

At the same time we are presented with the make-up of the change in net debt resulting from cash flows, i.e. the decrease of £24.7 million, as follows:

£million

the increase in cash (remember 'cash' = cash and bank balances and bank overdrafts) is:	34.7
of which loan capital is £9.0 million and short-term deposits £1.0 million, i.e. a total of:	(10.0)
giving us a change in net debt resulting from cash flows of:	24.7

Overall, note 31 links the increase in cash (the last item in the cash flow statement) of £34.7 million with the movement of net debt, to arrive at the net debt at the end of the year of £688.1 million.

Summary

The vital importance of the cash generating ability of a business is recognized by the accounting standard (FRS 3) requirement for the publication of a cash flow statement as part of the annual report and accounts of UK companies.

FRS 3 requires that cash flow statements highlight cash flow under the following headings:

1 operating activities
2 returns on investment and servicing of finance
3 taxation
4 capital expenditure and financial investment
5 acquisitions and disposals
6 equity dividends paid
7 management of liquid resources
8 financing

In addition to the cash flow statement itself, appropriate supporting notes are required.

In this chapter we have discussed the format and individual items found in a typical cash flow statement.

Exercises

These exercises are based on the extracts from the S&N 1997 annual report and accounts in Appendix 3.

1 Why does S&N produce a cash flow statement?
2 What items are found under the heading *capital expenditure and financial investment*?
3 How much interest did the group pay in 1997?
4 Did the group pay more or less tax in 1997 compared to 1996?
5 Why is the last figure in the cash flow statement for 1997, £34.7 million, not the same as the figure for cash shown in the group balance sheet?
6 In note 30, *net cash inflow from operating activities*, why is the profit and loss account charge for depreciation, £123.7 million, added back to the operating profit, £425.1 million?
7 In the group cash flow statement for 1997, the equity dividends paid (i.e. paid on ordinary shares) are £123.3 million. Why is this figure different from the figure for ordinary dividends on equity shares, £131.3 million, in the 1997 group profit and loss account?
8 For 1996 the figure for cash flow before use of liquid resources and financing was:

> net cash outflow £377.5 million

For 1997 the equivalent figure was:

> net cash inflow £14.9 million

i.e. a difference of £392.4 million

What was the main factor contributing to this difference?
9 How much of the cash spent on the purchase of tangible fixed assets, £270.1 million, was spent by each division?
10 The two main sources of finance for companies are shareholders and borrowing. How much net cash flow has been obtained from each of these sources for 1997?

Other financial statements

Introduction

The objective of FRS 3: Reporting financial performance, which was published in 1992, is:

> to require reporting entities falling within its scope to highlight a range of important components of financial performance to aid users in understanding the performance achieved by a reporting entity in a period and to assist them in forming a basis for their assessment of future results and cash flows.

We saw in Chapter 7 how the standard meets this objective with regard to the profit and loss account, for example by requiring an analysis of profits between discontinued and continuing operations, etc.

In addition, the standard requires companies to present three further statements:

- note on historical cost profits and losses
- statement of total recognized gains and losses
- reconciliation of movements in shareholders' funds

These are discussed below.

Note on historical cost profits and losses

Normally companies base their accounts on historical cost valuations (i.e. on the cost incurred when an asset was acquired or the amount incurred when a liability was created), but the Companies Act permits alternative accounting rules to be applied. The alternative rules enable companies to adopt a basis of valuation which reflects changes arising from general or specific price inflation.

As we saw in Chapter 5, in practice UK companies adopt either 'pure historical cost' or 'historical cost modified'. The latter basis means that companies have included some assets at historical cost but other assets, principally properties, at valuation. For example, if a property which had cost £10 million was found to have increased in value to £12 million, the company could choose to increase the value to £12 million. A company's statement of accounting policies will include reference to the valuation rules used by that company. Probably more than half of large public companies use a historical cost modified basis. The fact that companies use a variety of bases presents difficulties to users of accounts in making comparisons between companies.

To enable users to make more meaningful comparisons between companies, FRS 3 requires companies which have revalued assets to present an abbreviated re-statement of the profit and loss account. The object of this is to show a profit or loss figure as if no asset revaluations had been made. This re-statement is called *note on historical cost profits and losses* and is usually presented as illustrated in Example 9.1.

Example 9.1
Extract from P&O 1996
note on historical cost
profits and losses

Note of Group historical cost profits and losses for the year ended 31 December 1996	
	1996
	£million
Profit on ordinary activities before taxation	332.8
Realization of investment and property valuation movements of previous years	35.2
Historical cost profit on ordinary activities before taxation	368.0
Historical cost profit for the year retained after taxation, minority interests and dividends	92.7

The first figure in the note, *profit on ordinary activities before taxation* £332.8 million, comes from the profit and loss account and is the profit arrived at in accordance with the accounting rules and regulations in the UK. However, we have to remember that these rules require an amount to be charged for depreciation. For example, if a company buys an asset for £10 million and expects the asset to last for ten years, we could calculate an annual figure for depreciation of £10 million/ 10, i.e. £1 million per year. Suppose that the company decides to revalue the asset to £12 million, then the depreciation charge would be £12 million/10, i.e. £1.2 million per year. The annual charge to the profit and loss account for depreciation would be greater (by £0.2 million). In other words, the depreciation charge in the profit and loss account, based on the higher revaluation figures, will be higher than that based on historical cost and, consequently, the profit will be lower.

For P&O, current year profit is affected to the extent of £35.2 million in respect of this sort of adjustment. The description follows a fairly standard wording; in P&O's case the term used is *realization of investment and property valuation movements of previous years* £35.2 million.

When the £35.2 million is added back to the £332.8 million we arrive at a figure of £368 million in respect of the historical cost profit on ordinary activities for the year.

The corresponding note on historical cost profits and losses for S&N is shown in Example 9.2.

Example 9.2
Extract from S&N 1997
note on historical cost
profits and losses

Note on historical cost profits and losses
52 weeks ended 27 April 1997

	1997 £million
Reported profit on ordinary activities before taxation	372.0
Realization of property revaluation deficits of previous years	(2.2)
Historical cost profit on ordinary activities before taxation	369.8
Historical cost profit/(loss) for the year retained after taxation and dividends	151.9

The S&N note discloses property revaluation deficits, i.e. when revaluations were carried out the revalued amounts were lower than the original figure – in other words, the opposite to the P&O example. Hence, there is a consequential reduction in historical cost profits compared with reported profits. The figure for profit retained of £151.9 million which is also given, is derived from the figure of profit retained shown in the profit and loss account: £154.1 million, less the £2.2 million adjustment, to give £151.9 million. In other words, the last figure in the profit and loss account (£154.1 million) would have been £151.9 million if it had been calculated under pure historical cost rules.

FRS 3 states that the note on historical cost profits and losses is required whenever there is a material difference between the result as disclosed in the profit and loss account and the result on an unmodified historical cost basis (unless the historical cost information is unavailable). Wilson Connolly, the building and property development company, is an example of a company which presents its accounts on the basis of historical cost modified to include the revaluation of properties. As in Wilson Connolly's case there is no material difference between reported and historic cost profits, no note on historical cost profits and losses is given. Reference to this is made in a note accompanying the statement of total recognized gains and losses, as shown in Example 9.3.

Statement of total recognized gains and losses

As part of its objective of assisting users to understand a company's past performance and to assess future performance, FRS 3 requires companies to present a statement of total recognized gains and losses which are attributable to shareholders (i.e. the amount of profit which belongs to shareholders and from which dividends are paid).

In introducing the statement of total recognized gains and losses FRS 3 argues that the range of important components of financial performance which the FRS requires reporting entities to highlight would often be incomplete if it stopped short at the profit and loss account, since certain gains and losses are specifically permitted or required by law or an accounting standard to be taken directly to reserves, i.e. these figures do not appear in the profit and loss account itself, but will be found in the reserves figure in the balance sheet. (Remember that when an asset is revalued to a higher amount the surplus is added to the asset value and added to reserves.)

The reference to FRS 3 above mentions 'important components' and identifies two of these (i.e. the profit/loss for the year, shown in the profit and loss account, and a revaluation surplus included in reserves). For groups which have invested in foreign subsidiaries, a third component will be the gains/losses in the value of the investments as a result of currency movements (discussed in more detail in Chapter 10).

If there are no recognized gains or losses other than the profit and loss for the period, companies are to include a statement to this effect immediately below the profit and loss account. An example of a company where this is the case is shown in Example 9.3.

Example 9.3
Extract from Wilson
Connolly 1996 annual
report and accounts

GROUP STATEMENT OF TOTAL RECOGNIZED GAINS AND LOSSES
The group has no material recognized gains or losses other than the (loss)/profit stated above.
There is no material difference between the result as disclosed in the profit and loss account and the result on an historic cost basis.

For companies where a statement is required, the following components, if applicable, will be included:

- profit or loss before the deduction of dividends
- adjustments to the valuation of assets
- differences arising from changes in rates of exchange

All of these items are already shown somewhere in the accounts. What is new is the requirement that they are all brought together in one statement, thus enhancing the user's understanding of the information presented. A statement which includes all three components is shown in Example 9.4.

Example 9.4
Extract from S&N 1997
statement of total
recognized gains and
losses

Statement of Total Recognized Gains and Losses
52 weeks ended 27 April 1997

	1997 £million
Profit attributable to ordinary shareholders	285.4
Revaluations	109.1
Exchange adjustments	(107.0)
Total recognized gains and losses for financial year	287.5

In other words, S&N made profits on its ordinary activities of £285.4 million and had surpluses on revaluations of assets of £109.1 million. In addition, losses of £107.0 million occurred as a result of exchange rate movements. The net result of these three items is a total of £287.5 million.

FRS 3 also requires that the effect of any adjustments made to the accounts of previous years, known as *prior period adjustments*, should be shown at the foot of the statement of recognized gains and losses. Prior period adjustments are adjustments made as a result of changes in accounting policy or the correction of fundamental errors. The relevant figure is the amount by which the opening balance on the reserves has been adjusted. A presentation of this is shown in Example 9.5.

Example 9.5

Extract from Hanson 1996
statement of total
recognized gains and
losses

Statement of total recognized gains and losses
for the year ended 1 October 1996

	1996 £million
Profit on ordinary activities after taxation	1419
Currency translation differences on foreign net investments	27
Total recognized gains and losses relating to the year	1446
Prior year adjustment (changes in accounting policy) (note 19)	(3296)
Total gains and losses recognized since last annual report	(1850)

The massive prior year adjustment, £3296 million, has been deducted from Hanson's opening balance on the profit and loss account.

Reconciliation of movements in shareholders' funds

It has to be remembered that the statement of total recognized gains and losses relates to those recognized during the current year and which are part of shareholders' funds. The shareholders' funds figure can also be affected by other items, for example the issue of share capital. FRS 3 requires that all changes to shareholders' funds are brought together in a further statement called *reconciliation of movements in shareholders' funds.* The S&N statement is shown in Example 9.6.

Reconciliation of movements in shareholders' funds
52 weeks ended 27 April 1997

	1997 £million
Profit attributable to ordinary shareholders	285.4
Ordinary dividends	(131.3)
Other recognized gains and losses relating to the year (net)	2.1
New share capital issued	13.5
Contingent share capital	(21.1)
Contribution to employee share trust	(3.7)
Goodwill on acquisitions	0.9
Goodwill on disposals	2.4
Net additions to shareholders' funds	148.2
Shareholders' funds at 28 April 1996	2059.5
Shareholders' funds at 27 April 1997	2207.7

The statement starts with the figure from the profit and loss account for profit attributable to ordinary shareholders, of £285.4 million, from which dividends of £131.3 million are deducted.

The next figure, of £2.1 million for other recognized gains and losses, is made up of the net figure resulting from the gain (£109.1 million) and the loss (£107.0 million) identified in the statement of total recognized gains and losses (see Example 9.4).

The shareholders' funds have been increased by the issue of new share capital of £13.5 million during the year, but in turn this had been reduced by the removal of the contingent share capital (£21.1 million). The reason for the existence of this contingent share capital and its subsequent removal is explained in note 21 of the notes to the accounts as shown in Example 9.7. A further reduction (£3.7 million) resulted from the acquisition of shares by the employee share trust. Finally, two goodwill adjustments of £0.9 million and £2.4 million have been added to the shareholders' funds to arrive at the figure of £148.2 million for the net additions to shareholders' funds.

Overall the S&N 1997 reconciliation of movements in shareholders' funds statement shows that the capital and reserves figure in the balance sheet at 28 April 1996, £2059.5 million, has increased by £148.2 million to produce a figure of £2207.7 million at 27 April 1997.

Example 9.7
Extract from S&N 1997 notes to the accounts

21 SHARE CAPITAL
Contingent Share Capital
As part of the acquisition of the Courage business in 1995, Scottish and Newcastle plc agreed to pay to Foster's Brewing Group in either 1999 or 2000 a sum equal to the increase in value of ten million of the Company's shares over 537p per share. Scottish & Newcastle plc had the option of settling this consideration either by the issue of ordinary shares or in cash. At 28 April 1996 an estimate of the consideration (£21.1 million) was included in the balance sheet as contingent share capital. During the current financial year the Company's liability for the contingent consideration was assigned to a third party for a consideration of £20.2 million. Consequently, contingent share capital has been reduced to nil and a goodwill adjustment of £0.9 million has been made to reserves.

Summary

The annual report and accounts published by UK companies consist of a number of financial statements together with notes to the accounts. Three of the financial statements, the balance sheet, the profit and loss account and the cash flow statement, have been dealt with in earlier chapters.

A recent accounting standard, FRS 3: Reporting financial performance, has as its objective:

to require reporting entities falling within its scope to highlight a range of important components of financial performance to aid users in understanding the performance achieved by a reporting entity in a period and to assist them in forming a basis for their assessment of future results and cash flows.

To meet this objective, the FRS introduced changes in the way in which companies present the profit and loss account.

In addition, the FRS requires companies to present three further statements: note on historical cost profits and losses; statement of total recognized gains and losses; reconciliation of movements in shareholders' funds. These statements have been discussed in this chapter.

These exercises are based on the extracts from the S&N 1997 annual report and accounts in Appendix 3.

1 What is the aim of presenting a statement of total recognized gains and losses?

2 Where do the items in the statement of total recognized gains and losses appear elsewhere in the financial statements?

3 What is the main cause of a difference between a profit or loss shown in the profit and loss account and a profit or loss calculated on a purely historical cost basis?

4 Why have £21.1 million been deducted in the reconciliation of movements in shareholders' funds?

5 In the reconciliation of movements in shareholders' funds for 1996, what items make up the other recognized gains and losses relating to the year (£37.9 million net)?

Notes to the accounts

Introduction

Reference to *notes to the accounts* has been made in previous chapters and the term is found in the Companies Act. The notes provide additional details or supplementary information in a separate section of the annual report and accounts by means of cross-references from the face of the financial statements. This is done either because there is a Company's Act or accounting standard requirement to do so, or because the company chooses voluntarily to supply further details.

Notes to the accounts are an extremely important part of a company's annual report and accounts and they are considered to be an integral part of the financial statements. The auditors' report in the S&N 1997 annual report states that 'We have audited the financial statements on pages 38–57'. The fact that the notes are within these pages indicates that they are considered as part of the accounts.

As indicated in the Companies Act, the objectives of providing further details by way of notes are:

- to supplement the information given with respect to any particular item in the balance sheet and profit and loss account;
- to give information relevant to assessing the company's state of affairs, in the light of the information so given;
- to give details of circumstances affecting the items shown in the profit and loss account.

Items included in the notes to the accounts

Figure 10.1 provides a list of items for which detailed information is to be given in notes in accordance with requirements laid down in the authoritative sources. These apply to all companies but are subject to specific provision relating to investment companies and small and medium-sized companies. Some of the information in respect of directors may, alternatively, be presented in the directors' report.

Corresponding amounts for the previous year are to be given in respect of each item shown in the notes to the accounts, with the exception of:

- directors' loans and transactions
- fixed asset cost and depreciation analysis
- movements on reserves
- provisions for liabilities and charges
- subsidiaries and significant shareholdings

- accounting policies
- alternative accounting rules
- auditors' remuneration
- called-up share capital
- capital commitments
- contingent liabilities
- creditors: amounts falling due in more than one year
- creditors: amounts falling due within one year
- debentures
- debtors
- deferred taxation
- depreciation
- development costs
- directors: interests in the company's shares or debentures; remuneration; transactions with company
- dividends
- employees: numbers; remuneration
- exceptional items
- extraordinary items
- finance leases
- fixed assets
- foreign currency translation
- guarantees
- goodwill
- hire of plant and equipment
- investment income
- investments, including details of subsidiaries and other significant shareholdings
- interest payable
- loan redemption: amounts set aside for
- pension commitments
- post-balance sheet events
- provision for liabilities and charges
- rental income
- reserves
- segmental analysis
- share capital
- stocks
- taxation

Figure 10.1 Items in respect of which further information is to be disclosed in notes to the accounts

Provided that the auditors have presented their report without qualifications (see Chapter 3), it is reasonable to assume that companies have fulfilled their obligations with regard to disclosure of information in the notes to the accounts.

Some companies present details of accounting policies in a separate statement outside the notes to the accounts. Other companies, including

S&N, present their accounting policies as note 1 of the notes to the accounts.

As many of the accounting policies and details in the notes have already been referred to in our discussions on the main statements in previous chapters, we shall confine ourselves to the following items from Figure 10.1:

- capital commitments
- contingent liabilities, including guarantees
- foreign currency translation
- pension commitments
- post-balance sheet events
- segmental analysis

Capital commitments

The Companies Act requires disclosure of the aggregate amounts of capital expenditure for which contracts have been entered into but which have not been brought into the accounts, and the amount authorized by the directors but for which no contracts have been entered into. The capital commitments for S&N are shown in Example 10.1.

Example 10.1
Extract from S&N 1997
notes to the accounts

26 CAPITAL COMMITMENTS		
	Group	Company
	1997	1997
	£million	£million
Expenditure committed	22.5	17.5

This means that the parent company has entered into commitments which will involve it in spending £17.5 million in the future; the commitment of the group (i.e. the parent company and subsidiaries) is £22.5 million.

Contingent liabilities

A *contingency* is defined in SSAP 18: Accounting for contingencies as:

> a condition which exists at the balance sheet date, where the outcome will be confirmed only on the occurrence or non-occurrence of one or more uncertain future events. A contingent gain or loss is a gain or less dependent on a contingency.

This concept of contingency is illustrated in Example 10.2.

Example 10.2
Illustration of contingency

Suppose company A agreed to guarantee a debt owed by company B. If company B pays up on time, then company A is not liable. On the other hand, if company B defaults, then company A will have to settle B's debt. If we assume that A has a balance sheet date of 31 December 1998 but B's debt is not due to be paid until 31 January 1999, then at 31 December 1998 A has a contingent liability.

If it seems likely that a loss will arise, it should be provided for by making a charge in the profit and loss account and including an equivalent amount in creditors. In other words, the company has decided that the particular item is no longer 'contingent'. On the other hand, where a company has concluded that it is improbable that the contingent loss will in fact occur, the company is required to show in the notes to the accounts details of the contingent liability.

Example 10.3 shows how S&N has disclosed contingent liabilities.

Example 10.3

Extract from S&N 1997 notes to the accounts

28 CONTINGENT LIABILITIES

At 27 April 1997 there were contingent liabilities in respect of guarantees to third parties amounting to Group £20.1 million (1996 – £20.4 million) and Company £19.3 million (1996 – £18.9 million).

A further illustration, with some very specific details, is shown in Example 10.4.

Example 10.4

Extract from Jarvis Hotels 1997 notes to the financial statements

21 CONTINGENT LIABILITIES AND COMMITMENTS

(a) The group has received a number of tourist board grants which have been used to fund developments within the hotels. The potential clawback of grants is estimated at £279 000 which would crystallize if certain investment return criteria were exceeded or the assets in question were not used or retained for purposes intended when grants were received.

(b) In order to cover obligations under the EU Directive on package holidays, the Company has placed £229 000 in a trust account held with the Bank of Scotland. In the event of the Company's insolvency the monies would be used to refund customers.

(c) The Group has entered into a number of contractual agreements in respect of the hire of plant and equipment installed and used in its hotel premises. There are a large number of agreements in respect of each hotel, of which some provide for accelerated payment of a percentage of outstanding rentals on early termination of the contract.

At 29 March 1997 the group had annual commitments under operating leases as set out below:

	Land and buildings 1997 £million	Other 1997 £million
Operating leases which expire:		
Within one year	29	565
In two to five years	15	846
Over five years	1174	246
	1218	1657

In Example 10.4, Jarvis Hotels has combined the contingent liabilities and commitments into one note.

Foreign currency translation

Companies can be involved in accounting for foreign currencies in two ways:

1 As an individual company, either the parent company or a subsidiary might engage in business transactions which are denominated in foreign currencies.

2 The parent company, or one of the subsidiaries, invests in a foreign subsidiary or branch which keeps its records in the foreign currency, which has implications for the preparation of consolidated accounts.

Both of these situations are considered below.

The individual company

A gain or loss will arise from the settlement of business transactions at exchange rates different from the rates when the transactions were entered into, as illustrated in Example 10.5.

Example 10.5 Foreign exchange transaction gains and loses	A company which has a financial year end of 31 December 1997 entered into the following transactions: (1) On 15 November 1997 it bought machinery from a German company for DM 1 million. The sterling equivalent at 15 November was £350 000 but when the transaction was settled on 15 December 1997 the pound had strengthened against the DM and the company had to pay only £340 000. The gain of £10 000 will be included in the company's profit and loss account for the year ended 31 December 1997. The machinery remains in the balance sheet at a value of £350 000. (2) On 1 December 1997 it sold goods to a French company for FF 2 million. The sterling equivalent at that date was £205 000. Settlement is due on 15 January 1998. At 31 December 1997 the sterling equivalent (i.e. calculated at the foreign exchange rate at that day) was £200 000. The loss on exchange of £5 000 will be charged in the company's profit and loss account for the year ended 31 December 1997. The gain on the German transaction may be termed a *realized gain* because the transaction has been settled, whereas the loss on the French transaction may be termed an *unrealized loss* because final settlement does not take place until after the balance sheet date. Nevertheless, the loss is accounted for in the profit and loss account for the year ended 31 December 1997.

The relevant accounting standard, SSAP 20: Foreign currency translation, classes balance sheet items as either *monetary* (e.g. debtors, loans, creditors, cash) or *non-monetary* (e.g. fixed assets, investments in other companies). The standard uses the term *translation* to describe the process whereby financial data denominated in one currency are expressed in terms of another currency. For accounts purposes:

- When a transaction takes place it is recorded in the books at the rate of exchange at that date (as happened with the two transactions in Example 10.5 with the purchase of the fixed asset (machinery) and the sale of goods).
- Monetary items are retranslated (i.e. recalculated) at the balance sheet date, at the exchange rate ruling at that date; this is referred to as the *closing rate* (in Example 10.5 the amount owed by the French debtor (a monetary asset) was retranslated to £200 000). Gains or losses arising from such translations are included in the current year's profit and loss account, but with a gain on a long-term item (e.g. a loan) prudence must be exercised, for example if there are doubts about the convertibility of the currency in question.

- Non-monetary items are not retranslated at the balance sheet date but are left in the records at the original amount (as happened with the machinery in Example 10.5).

There is one exception to the above, which is where a company has taken out a loan in a foreign currency to finance the purchase of equity investment denominated in a foreign currency. For example, a UK company might take out a loan in French francs in order to buy ordinary shares in a French company.

In that case the company may retranslate the investment (i.e. a non-monetary item) and set the gain or loss against the gain or loss on the foreign loan (a monetary item). These are shown as movements on reserves, thus removing from the profit and loss account any gain or loss on the retranslation of the monetary item (the foreign loan).

The application of the above rules, as applied by Lonrho, is shown in Example 10.6, where we have italicized the relevant descriptions.

<table>
<tr><td>

Example 10.6

Extract from Lonrho 1996 annual report and accounts

</td><td>

Statement on accounting policies

Exchange rates

Foreign currency assets and liabilities and the results for the year are translated into sterling at the rates existing at 30 September. Exchange differences arising from the retranslating of the opening net investment in overseas companies are disclosed as movements on reserves. *Exchange adjustments relating to borrowings which have been used to finance or provide a hedge against foreign equity investments are taken to reserves to the extent that they are matched by exchange movements on those investments.* All other adjustments due to fluctuations arising in the normal course of trade are included in profit before taxation. The principal sterling exchange rates used to translate foreign currency assets and liabilities and the results for the year are:

	1996	1995
Kenya pound	4.3823	4.4038
Malawi kwacha	23.9324	23.9779
South Africa rand	7.0904	5.7788
United States dollar	1.5637	1.5827
Zimbabwe dollar	16.1564	13.9673

</td></tr>
</table>

The first half of the Lonrho note relates to the second foreign currency issue, i.e. the consolidated accounts stage, which is discussed below.

Consolidated accounts

When the accounts of the parent company and its subsidiaries are consolidated to produce the group balance sheet and group profit and loss account, a decision has to be made as to the exchange rates to be used in translating the balance sheet and profit and loss items of a foreign subsidiary from the foreign currency into sterling. SSAP 20 requires that, with special exceptions, the rates to be used are:

- the closing rate for balance sheet items
- the closing rate or the average rate for profit and loss items.

Example 10.7 illustrates the overall effect of the application of these rules.

Example 10.7
Translation of foreign
subsidiary's balance sheet
and profit and loss
account

On 1 January 1997 FI plc bought 100% of the share capital of a Spanish company for £10 million, at the exchange rate of 250 pesetas = £1 prevailing at the time. The investment was equal to the balance sheet value of the Spanish company's assets less liabilities of 2500 million pesetas. (Because of this equality there is no goodwill in this example.) The investment of £10 million can be termed the *opening net investment* in the foreign subsidiary.

At the financial year end, 31 December 1997, the Spanish company's profit and loss account showed a profit of 260 million pesetas and the exchange rate used for translation was 260 pesetas = £1.

Two things have affected the value of FI's investment:

1 The original investment is now worth $\dfrac{2500 \text{ million}}{260}$ = £9.6 million. The peseta has weakened against the pound and the value of the investment has decreased.

2 The Spanish company has made a profit of 260 million pesetas, which is equivalent to $\dfrac{260 \text{ million}}{260}$ = £1 million.

The individual figures making up the subsidiary company's profit (i.e. turnover, expenses) will be included with the parent company's figures to produce a group profit and loss account. The inclusion of the figures for the subsidiary will have the effect of increasing group profits by £1 million.

The difference between the values of the net investment in the Spanish company at the beginning and end of the year, £0.4 million (£10 million – £9.6 million), will be deducted in the consolidated reserves.

The accounting treatments in Example 10.7 illustrate the requirements of the accounting standard for consolidated accounts, which are:

- balance sheet items are translated at the closing rate;
- an exchange difference arising from the retranslation of the opening net investment is dealt with as a movement on reserves;
- the profit and loss items may be translated at either the closing rate or the average rate; where average rates are used, any difference between that rate and the closing rate is to be dealt with as a movement on reserves.

Example 10.6 showed how Lonhro has disclosed this information in its statement on accounting policies. The S&N accounting policy for foreign currencies differs only in that an average rate is used for translation of profit and loss account items. This is shown in Example 10.8.

Example 10.8
Extract from S&N 1997
notes to the accounts

1 ACCOUNTING POLICIES

(g) Foreign currencies

Revenues and costs of overseas companies are included in the consolidated profit and loss account at average rates of exchange during the year with the year end adjustment to closing rates being taken to reserves. Assets and liabilities in foreign currency are translated at year end rates of exchange.

Exchange differences on the retranslation of investments in, and opening net assets of, foreign subsidiary undertakings are dealt with through reserves net of differences on related foreign currency borrowings and swaps. Other gains and losses arising from foreign currency transactions are included in the consolidated profit and loss account.

Pension commitments

Normally the pension scheme run for the benefit of employees is separate from the employing company. The company is responsible for paying contributions, which are charged against its profits. SSAP 24: Pension costs is the accounting standard covering pensions. The pensions costs incurred are charged to a company's profit and loss account. Broadly speaking, the thrust of the accounting standard is to charge the profit and loss account with pension costs over the working lives of the employees, i.e. the costs are matched with the period over which the company benefits from the input of the employees. In the notes to the accounts we can expect to find the company's accounting policy for dealing with pension costs. S&N's accounting policy is shown in Example 10.9.

Example 10.9
Extract from S&N 1997 notes to the accounts

1 ACCOUNTING POLICIES

(h) Retirement benefits
The expected cost of pensions in respect of defined benefit pension schemes is charged to the profit and loss account so as to spread the cost of pensions over the expected remaining service lives of employees in the scheme.

SSAP 24 requires disclosure of the cost and nature of the scheme and details of actuarial valuations. Periodically, valuations of the scheme's assets are made and these are compared with the pension liabilities which have to be met from those assets. In recent years, many schemes have been in surplus, i.e. the scheme's asset base is higher than the pension liabilities which have to be met. SSAP 24 requires that such surpluses should normally be spread over the remaining service lives of the employees. These pension details will usually be found in the notes to the accounts under a heading such as *pension commitments*. The details are presented by S&N under note 5, Employee Costs and Numbers, in the notes to the accounts. Example 10.10 is an extract from this note showing that the main company scheme was in surplus but the Courage scheme was in deficit.

Example 10.10
Extract from S&N 1997 notes to the accounts

5 EMPLOYEE COSTS AND NUMBERS

(iii) Pension commitment
. . . At 1 November 1994 the market value of the assets of the main Company schemes was £515.5 million and the actuarial value of the assets was sufficient to cover 112% of the benefits that had accrued to members. The surplus is being spread over the expected remaining service lives (13 years) of employees in the schemes.

The Courage pension schemes were valued on acquisition in 1995 by qualified actuaries using the projected unit method and the actuarial assumptions used in the Scottish & Newcastle plc schemes valuations at 1 November 1994. The market value of the assets of the schemes was £402.6 million and the actuarial value of the assets was only sufficient to cover 84% of the benefits that had accrued to members. The Company is making special contributions to the Courage schemes in recognition of the funding position.

Post-balance sheet events

SSAP 17: Accounting for post-balance sheet events defines post-balance sheet events as 'those events, both favourable and unfavourable, which occur between the balance sheet date and the date on which the financial statements are approved by the board of directors'. They are classified as:

- *adjusting events*, i.e. events which arise after the balance sheet date, which provide additional evidence relating to conditions at the balance sheet date and, therefore, require adjustment to the figures in the financial statements (an example would be where information is received regarding rates of taxation);
- *non-adjusting events*, i.e. events which arise after the balance sheet date and concern conditions which did not exist at that time but which because of their significance should be disclosed in the notes to the accounts to ensure that the financial statements are not misleading (examples include mergers and acquisitions and changes in rates of foreign exchange).

Example 10.11 shows an example of a favourable, non-adjusting post-balance sheet event being disclosed.

Example 10.11
Extract from British Energy 1996/97, notes to the financial statements

35 POST-BALANCE SHEET EVENT

On 3 June 1997 Nuclear Electric concluded new fuel services contracts with BNFL, with a total value of around £1.5 billion at current prices. The new Nuclear Electric contracts cover the extension of AGR fuel fabrication services from 2000 to 2006 and the provision of reprocessing and storage services in respect of spent fuel arising from its stations not covered by its existing contract. At the same time minor amendments have been made in the terms of existing contracts of Nuclear Electric and Scottish Nuclear with BNFL regarding the fuel services provided for all AGR power stations. Following the signing of these new contracts the Group now has fixed price contracts (subject to RPI indexation) covering the bulk of spent fuel services for the whole of the remaining lives of its existing AGR power stations.

The new contracts combined with the revisions to existing contracts will result in savings in fuel costs of some £10 million in 1997/98.

Segmental analysis

Some authorities take the view that what users of group accounts are interested in is the financial position and results of the group as a whole. Others argue that in order to make a meaningful assessment of a group's position and future performance we need information concerning the different activities and markets in which the group's divisions or subsidiaries are engaged.

Segmental reporting supplies this type of information. Three of the authoritative sources discussed in Chapter 1 have requirements for reporting about the segments of a business. SSAP 25: Segmental reporting identifies the following:

- *class of business*: 'a distinguishable component of an entity that provides a separate product or service';

- *geographical segment*: 'a geographical area comprising an individual country or group of countries in which an entity operates or to which it supplies products or services'.

For geographical segments, the distinction needs to be made between the origin and the destination of turnover.

SSAP 25 requires the following disclosures for each class of business and each geographical segment:

- *turnover*: distinguishing between (i) turnover derived from external customers and (ii) turnover derived from other segments;
- *result*: before accounting for taxation, minority interests and extraordinary items;
- *net assets*.

Such disclosure breaks down the total into helpful segments but because the group itself defines its own segments comparison between groups is not necessarily enhanced.

S&N segmental analysis (note 2 in the notes to the accounts) presents data with regard to both class of business (retail, beer and leisure) and geographical segment (UK and the rest of Europe). The analysis can take up a great deal of room in the report. Thus, for example, in the Stagecoach 1997 annual report segmental analysis covers over two pages. On the other hand, Example 10.12 illustrates how Safeway, which has only one class of business and trades only in the UK, has nevertheless provided a segmental analysis of turnover and profits of its two retail brands.

<table>
<tr><td>**Example 10.12**
Extract from Safeway
1997 notes to the
accounts</td><td colspan="3">Year ended 29 March 1997

1.0 Sales and profit
The group's sole trading activity is grocery retailing which is carried out almost entirely in the United Kingdom. In order to provide shareholders with additional information, the group's sales and operating profit have been analysed between its two retail brands, as set out below:</td></tr>
</table>

	1997 £million	1996 £million
Sales:		
Safeway	6627.8	6031.1
Presto	438.6	468.9
	7066.4	6500.0
Turnover, excluding VAT:		
Safeway	6178.5	5630.1
Presto	411.2	439.3
	6589.7	6069.4
Operating profit:		
Safeway	430.2	368.4
Presto	31.6	31.1
Total	461.8	417.5

Summary

The Companies Act specifies a number of items for which additional information is to be given in notes to the accounts. The objective of providing further details by way of notes is to supplement the information already given for any particular item in the various financial statements which are presented by a company. Companies might also voluntarily provide further details.

Users of accounts will find a great deal of information in the notes. The notes to the accounts section of the annual report is at least as important as the accounts themselves.

Exercises

These exercises are based on the extracts from the S&N 1997 annual report and accounts in Appendix 3.

1 Note 1 of the notes to the accounts sets out the accounting policies but, in common with all companies, S&N does not state that any fundamental accounting principles have been applied. What are the four fundamental principles which are assumed to have been applied in the absence of information to the contrary?

2 What are the company's accounting policies in respect of
  (a) stock valuation?
  (b) retirement benefits?
  Where else in the annual report is information to be found in respect of retirement benefits?

3 For 1997 how much of the group *profit on ordinary activities after taxation* is accounted for by subsidiary companies?

4 How much was owed by the parent company to subsidiaries and by subsidiaries to the parent company at 27 April 1997?

5 What change took place in the average number of employees in each division during the year?

An introduction to the basic interpretation of accounts

Introduction

This book is primarily concerned with the understanding of UK company accounts. We have discussed the sources of authority which companies must follow when preparing their accounts, what items are in the accounts, the ways in which we arrive at valuations for these items, what the various financial statements tell us and how these statements relate to each other. At this stage readers should know what information is in a set of accounts and how to find the information in which they are interested. Usually, the object of retrieving information from a set of accounts is to judge a company's financial position and performance.

However, before looking in more detail at what we can find out about a company's performance and financial position from a set of accounts, it has to be remembered that the figures in the accounts are not the only data we can refer to. We need to make use of whatever information is available, whether from the company itself or from external sources.

Internal sources: the company, in addition to its annual report and accounts, might issue:

- interim reports and summary accounts
- newsletters
- employee reports
- a prospectus (relating to a new issue of shares)
- documents setting out details of a proposed acquisition, merger, demerger or disposal
- marketing catalogues and circulars

External sources: external sources includes:

- Company House, for documents, including annual accounts, which are required to be filed with the Registrar of Companies
- government publications
- company guide books listing information about selected companies
- computer databases, e.g. Datastream
- financial, trade and general press cuttings services
- reports by financial analysts who have visited the company and have built up specialized knowledge of the company and of the industry

To return to the interpretation of the accounts themselves, this involves making comparisons:

- between the actual results of a company for one period and the actual results for a previous period or periods
- between the actual results of one company and the actual results of another company or companies or an industry average
- between the actual results of a company for one period and the forecast results for that period

Which items we choose to compare depends on the perspective we take. For example, lenders are mainly concerned with the company's ability to continue to pay interest on the loans and to repay the loans in due course, whereas shareholders are primarily interested in the return on their investments and the value of the investment. Faced with the large volume of data in a set of accounts, it makes sense to reduce this to a manageable size so as to concentrate on the specific areas in which we are interested in the interpretation of the accounts. The most commonly used technique for this purpose is ratio analysis.

Ratio analysis

The relationship between two items from the financial statements can be expressed either in ratio form or as a percentage. For example, we might need to compare the item *current assets* with the item *creditors: amounts due within one year.* If current assets are £2 million and creditors due within one year are £1 million, the relationship can be expressed as 2:1 or we can say that the creditors are 50% of the current assets.

Ratios are a convenient way of capturing the relationship between two items from the financial statements. We can compare two balance sheet items or two profit and loss account items, or we might compare a balance sheet item with a profit and loss account item. For example, we might compare the item *capital and reserves* with the item *profit after taxation.*

In order to gain the maximum benefit from the process of ratio analysis we need to be selective about which ratios we calculate, otherwise we might produce almost as many ratios as there are figures in the accounts. Different analysts adopt different frameworks for this purpose but a number of key ratios feature in most sets of ratios.

A number of key ratios are discussed below under the following headings:

- solvency ratios
- operating ratios
- investment ratios

The first two types use information from the accounts. The third type, which involves the analysis of investment decisions, i.e. whether to buy or sell shares in the company, extends the analysis by using market price data in addition to data in the accounts themselves.

In general, we need to remember that we are calculating any particular ratio in order to make a comparison, for example with another period and/or another company. This provides a yardstick to enable us to judge whether, in the particular circumstances, results are good or bad or have improved or worsened.

The illustrations of the ratios which follow below are based on the balance sheet and the profit and loss account of the company XYZ plc in Examples 11.1 and 11.2 respectively.

XYZ plc
Balance sheet at 31 December 1997

		£million
Fixed assets		35
Current assets		
Stock	5	
Trade debtors	13	
Bank	12	
	30	
Creditors: amounts falling due within one year		
Trade creditors	5	
Other creditors	9	
	14	
Net current assets		16
Total assets less current liabilities		51
Creditors: amounts falling due after more than one year		12
		39
Capital and reserves		
Issued share capital (£1 shares)		25
Profit and loss account		14
		39

XYZ plc
Profit and loss account for the year ended 31 December 1997

	£million
Turnover	40
Cost of sales	25
Gross profit	15
Administration expenses	(4)
Distribution expenses	(2)
Interest on long-term loan	(1)
Profit on ordinary activities before taxation	8
Tax	(3)
Profit on ordinary activities after taxation	5
Dividends (8p per share)	(2)
Retained profit	3

Solvency ratios

These can be subdivided into two groups:

- short-term solvency ratios
- long-term solvency ratios

We shall consider each group in turn.

Short-term solvency ratios

Current ratio

This is the ratio of current assets to current liabilities (current liabilities being the creditors which fall due for payment in the next 12 months).

Definition: $\dfrac{\text{current assets}}{\text{creditors: amounts falling due within one year}}$

$$= \quad 30{:}14 = 2.1 \text{ or } 46.7\%$$

This indicates whether there are sufficient current assets available to enable the company to pay its short-term creditors.

Quick ratio (or asset test ratio)

Definition: $\dfrac{\text{current assets} - \text{stocks}}{\text{creditors: amounts falling due within one year}}$

$$= \quad \frac{30 \text{ m} - 5 \text{ m}}{14 \text{ m}}$$

$$= \quad 25{:}14 = 1.8 \text{ or } 55.5\%$$

Removing stocks from current assets leaves the liquid assets (bank balance, debtors, short-term investments), i.e. those readily available to meet amounts due to creditors.

The amount of cash available to pay a company's short-term creditors is dependent upon the rate at which stock is sold to customers and the rate at which the debtors pay their bills. The following two ratios are concerned with these rates.

Stock turnover

Definition: $\dfrac{\text{cost of goods sold during the period}}{\text{average stock held}}$

To find the average stock held, we need to know the stock figures at the beginning and end of the year. From the balance sheet above (Example 11.1) we know that the stock at 31 December 1997 is £5 million. For the purposes of illustration let us assume that the stock at 31 December 1996 was £6 million.

$$\text{Therefore in this case average stock} = \frac{6 \text{ m} + 5 \text{ m}}{2} = 5.5 \text{ m}$$

$$\text{Then stock turnover} = \frac{25 \text{ m}}{5.5 \text{ m}} = 4.5 \text{ times}$$

The figure for *cost of goods sold* during the period is not always available and might be defined in different ways by different companies. Hence, for making comparisons between companies some analysts use the turnover figure for the numerator as a crude substitute. Thus in this case it would be:

$$\frac{40 \text{ m}}{5.5 \text{ m}} = 7.3 \text{ times}$$

Debtors' turnover (average collection period for trade debts)

Definition: $\dfrac{\text{trade debtors} \times 365}{\text{credit sales}}$ $\dfrac{13 \times 365}{40.}$

Assuming all sales were credit sales

$$= \frac{13 \text{ m} \times 365}{40 \text{ m}} = 118.6 \text{ days}$$

i.e. on average it takes 118.6 days for debtors to pay.

This seems to be a lengthy period but we have to be careful because we do not know what is usual in the industry concerned.

Creditors' payment period (average payment period for trade creditors)
The amount of cash needed at one time to pay a company's short-term creditors is partly dependent on the length of time the company takes to pay its creditors. An indication of this is given by calculating the average payment period for trade creditors.

Definition: $\dfrac{\text{trade creditors} \times 365}{\text{cost of goods purchased}}$

$$= \frac{5 \text{ m} \times 365}{25 \text{ m}} = 73 \text{ days}$$

i.e. on average, payment is made to trade creditors in 73 days.

As with the debtors' ratio, some analysts use the figure for turnover to substitute for *cost of goods purchased* because the latter figure is not usually available.

Long-term solvency ratios

If a company is to remain solvent in the long term it must be able to meet all liabilities (and not just those due for settlement in the short term). Two ratios provide useful indications of the position: interest coverage ratio and shareholder equity ratio.

Interest coverage ratio

Definition: $\dfrac{\text{profit before interest and tax}}{\text{periodic interest charges}}$

$$= \frac{9 \text{ m} (8 \text{ m} + 1 \text{ m})}{1 \text{ m}} = 9 \text{ times}$$

Currently, the company has profits available to cover the interest on its loans nine times. If the company is unable to meet such interest costs, its solvency is put into question. The higher the level of external financing, generally speaking, the higher will be the level of costs of servicing the loans.

Shareholders' equity ratio

Definition: $\dfrac{\text{shareholders' equity}}{\text{total assets}}$

$$= \frac{39 \text{ m} \times 100}{65 \text{ m}} = 60\%$$

In this case, 60% of the total assets are financed by the shareholders. In general, financial analysts will look for a high proportion as an indication of a company's financial stability. What is 'satisfactorily high' depends on the circumstances of the case.

We are concerned here with the relationship between the different ways in which the company has been financed. This relationship is called the *gearing* of the capital structure of the company and may be expressed in alternative ways; whichever way is used, the terms *low gearing* and *high gearing* describe, respectively, a company relying primarily on finance provided by the shareholders (equity finance) and a company obtaining a high proportion of finance from loans and other external sources.

Operating ratios

The aim of the operating activities of a company is to produce a profit. Two ratios which may be used to assess how a company has performed in its profit-seeking activities are the return on capital employed and the ratio of net profit to sales.

Return on capital employed (ROCE)

There are a number of ways in which this ratio may be calculated and in practice it is necessary to be aware of how the term has been defined, particularly where comparisons between companies are being made. Overall what is looked for is a means of expressing the relationship between the investment made in a company and the profit generated. Two definitions are considered: *return on net assets* and *return on shareholder's equity.*

Return on net assets

Definition: $\dfrac{\text{profit before interest and tax}}{\text{total assets less current liabilities}}$

$$= \frac{9 \text{ m} \times 100}{51 \text{ m}} = 17.6\%$$

In this case, the return on the capital employed is 17.6%. In this example capital employed is the total long-term capital provided, i.e. £39 million + £12 million.

Return on shareholders' equity

Definition: $\dfrac{\text{profit after interest and tax}}{\text{shareholders' equity}}$

$$= \frac{5 \text{ m} \times 100}{39 \text{ m}} = 12.8\%$$

In this case, the return on capital employed is 12.8%. Capital employed is the balance sheet value of the shareholders' capital (i.e. capital and reserves), £39 million.

The balance sheet value of the shareholders' capital employed is £39 million, which has produced a return (profit available for ordinary shareholders) of £5 million, i.e. 12.8%.

A further measure of the company's profit generating ability is to relate the net profit to the turnover, defining net profit as *profit before interest and tax*.

Net profit to turnover

Definition: $\dfrac{\text{profit before interest and tax}}{\text{turnover}}$

$$= \frac{9\ \text{m} \times 100}{40\ \text{m}} = 22.5\%$$

In other words, for every £1 of sales 22.5p is available to pay interest and tax as well as leaving a balance available for the shareholders.

Investment ratios

Investment ratios are used by an investor or potential investor in making a decision whether to buy, sell or hold a particular company's shares. Investment ratios include earnings per share, price/earnings ratio, dividend yield and dividend cover.

Earnings per share (EPS)

Definition: $\dfrac{\text{profit attributable to ordinary shareholders}}{\text{number of ordinary shares}}$

$$= \frac{3\ \text{m}}{25\ \text{m}} = 12\text{p}$$

This figure is to be disclosed in the profit and loss account. The EPS figure is derived from information available in the company's accounts.

The next two ratios go beyond the figures in the financial statements by relating accounting information to the market price of the company's shares. For the purposes of illustration, we will assume that the market price per share is 130p.

  Price/earnings ratio (P/E ratio)

Definition: $\dfrac{\text{market price per ordinary share}}{\text{earnings per share}}$ $\qquad 2.5$

$$= \frac{130\text{p}}{12\text{p}} = 10.8$$

This ratio indicates that the price of the shares is 10.8 times the earnings (i.e. profits). In other words, it gives an idea as to the number of years it would take to cover the price out of the company's earnings.

Dividend yield

Definition: $\dfrac{\text{dividend per ordinary share}}{\text{market price per ordinary share}}$

$$= \frac{8\text{p}}{130\text{p}} = 6.2\%$$

The dividend yield indicates the percentage return (in the form of dividends) the investor is obtaining from his investment valued at today's market price.

Dividend cover ratio

Definition: $\dfrac{\text{profit after taxation and preference dividend}}{\text{ordinary dividend}}$

$$= \frac{5\text{ m}}{2\text{ m}} = 2.5 \text{ times}$$

It is important for the investor to know whether the company will be able to continue to pay dividends at current levels. Some indication of this can be obtained from the dividend cover ratio. In this example, the company's profits which are attributable to ordinary shareholders cover 2.5 years of dividends at the current level.

Ratios in the annual report

Some companies include selected ratios in their annual report. For example, Marks and Spencer include a number of 'key performance measures' as part of a five-year financial summary, as shown in Example 11.3.

Example 11.3
Extract from Marks and Spencer 1996 annual report and accounts

KEY PERFORMANCE MEASURES		1996
Gross margin	Gross profit / Turnover	34.8%
Net margin	Operating profit / Turnover	13.1%
Profitability	Profit before tax / Turnover	13.8%
Earnings per share (Defined by FRS 3)	Standard earnings / Weighted average ordinary shares in issue	23.3p
Earnings per share	Headline earnings / Weighted average ordinary shares in issue	24.3p
Dividend per share		11.4p
Dividend cover	Profit attributable to shareholders / Dividends	2.0
Return on equity	Profit after tax and minority interests / Average shareholders' funds	17.4%
Capital expenditure		£303.3 million

Summary

In carrying out an interpretation exercise it is not necessary to calculate every possible ratio but instead to concentrate on what is relevant to the circumstances. Some matters might be obvious from a reading of the figures in the accounts; it does not need a ratio to conclude that sales figures of £1.5 million for 1996 and £1.0 million for 1997 means that there has been a huge drop in sales!

Remember that the ratios themselves are merely a convenient way to capture the relationship between items. Looking at only one set of accounts or calculating ratios from only one set will rarely be the end of the exercise. Comparison with other years and/or other companies, or with expectations, is an integral feature of interpretation. The basis of interpretation, however, is having a good understanding of the accounts themselves.

There are likely to be differences between companies' accounting policies and valuations which make comparisons between companies difficult. Finally, it must be borne in mind that accounts can be interesting because of what they contain but, on occasions, they can be even more interesting because of what they conceal. Creative accounting is one of the issues discussed in Chapter 12.

Exercises

These exercises are based on the extracts from the S&N 1997 annual report and accounts in Appendix 3.

1 Calculate the interest coverage ratio for S&N for 1997.
2 Can you find any reference to 'interest cover' within the S&N 1997 annual report and accounts? If so, does this confirm your answer to question 1?
3 Calculate the shareholders' equity ratio for the S&N group for 1997.
4 Calculate the net profit to turnover ratio for the S&N group for 1997.
5 Can you find a similar ratio to that in question 4 in the list of Marks and Spencer ratios in Example 11.3? If so, is it worthwhile making a comparison with S&N?

Issues and possible developments in financial reporting

We have seen that the directors of UK companies are required by UK law to prepare accounts which give a true and fair view of the state of affairs of the company and of the results (profit or loss) at the end of the company's financial year; they must also do the same for the group, where there is one. That the accounts be true and fair is a Companies Act requirement, although the term is not defined in the Act. The accounts are summaries of what has happened and should reflect the underlying economic reality of a company's transactions. Accounting standards stipulate that where the legal form of a transaction is different from the substance of the transaction it is the substance of the transaction which should be reflected in the accounts; for example, an asset held on a lease could be brought into the balance sheet even though, legally, it is owned by another party.

This is the objective which UK accountants have when preparing annual financial statements, although the 'substance over form' argument might not be agreed with by UK lawyers or by accountants in countries where different rules are applied.

The issue of accounting standards by the Accounting Standards Board (ASB) is an ongoing process. New standards are published following due discussion. The current ASB discussion papers are listed below:

- accounting for tax
- pension costs in the employer's financial statements
- provisions
- impairment of tangible fixed assets
- earnings per share
- segmental reporting
- derivatives and other financial instruments
- measurements of tangible fixed assets
- discounting in financial reporting: working paper

Three issues emerge from the above comments:

- If the overall objective of accounts is to reflect the underlying economic reality of transactions, to what extent is this affected by companies which do not follow the underlying spirit of the objective and engage in some form of creative accounting?
- Accounts look at what has happened, i.e. they are summaries of past events. Would they be more useful if they were more concerned with the future, for example to include information about future prospects?
- UK company accounts comply with UK regulations. Accountants in other countries apply their national regulations. In an increasingly converging commercial world, to what extent would it be useful to have a convergence of accounting regulations, by way of international harmonization of accounting?

Possible developments

Regulation of creative accounting

There has been a great deal of adverse criticism of the UK system of financial reporting for allowing company managers to present financial statements which have been cosmetically adjusted to present a better picture than the underlying economic reality suggests. The greater the amount of discretion left to management in the adoption of acceptable accounting policies, the greater the possibility for them to be creative in this context.

The creative accounting phenomenon has probably been around for as long as accounting itself but in the last two decades there has been an increase in its use and an increase in the number of books published about it. The best known is probably *Accounting for Growth* by Terry Smith, first published by Century Business in 1992. In the first edition, Smith identified a number of creative accounting techniques engaged in by major companies, including: pre-acquisition write-down, off-balance sheet finance, capitalization of costs, changes in depreciation policy, pension fund surplus and currency mismatching.

Although there have been a number of infamous examples of deliberate presentation of misinformation, in the main creative accounting is simply about presenting a picture in line with company management's perception of what the market wants to see, for example a lower gearing ratio by keeping finance off the balance sheet. Some finance theorists believe that none of this matters because any information that is around is captured in the market price of the company's share and the market can see through any presentational manipulation.

Nevertheless, accounting regulators take the matter seriously and a number of recent accounting scandals have led to measures to narrow the range of 'allowable' creative accounting techniques. One example of the move to curb such practices is FRS 5: Reporting the substance of transactions, which has cut down on the possibilities of using off-balance sheet financing. This process will continue as part of the ASB's continuous updating programme.

It seems likely that the opportunities will be reduced by further regulation. However, users of accounts should remain aware that determined 'creators' might still try to be ahead of the game.

In his book, Terry Smith identified companies which would possibly underperform or even fail. All account users obviously have an interest in what is likely to happen in the future, which leads to the question of whether the financial statements themselves should incorporate a formal statement about the future.

Future prospects as an element in financial reports

Commentators have questioned the usefulness of accounts as they are currently prepared, i.e. based on what has happened in the past. It has been suggested that from an investor's standpoint, faced with decisions as to whether to buy, sell or hold shares, it would be more useful if information was presented which would help investors in making such decisions. Information, both quantitative and qualitative, might include data on current values of assets, the disclosure of more background information, the development of interim financial reports and the presentation of a forecast financial report for the next period.

The ASB, in its *Statement of Principles for Financial Reporting*, published in November 1995, recognizes that, 'to be useful, information must be relevant to the decision-making needs of users'. While also recognizing that information should have predictive value, it states that 'to have predictive value, information need not be in the form of an explicit forecast'. On the other hand, the production of a forecast financial report was a specific suggestion made in *Making Corporate Reports Valuable* (Research Committee of the Institute of Chartered Accountants of Scotland, 1988).

Overall, it is probable that developments in financial reporting will include the extension of the amount of information currently disclosed, possibly including more formal forecasts with regard to the future (in addition to the rosy picture often presented in a chairman's statement; see Chapter 3).

When we discuss any accounting development we need to go beyond our country-specific parameters and consider what is happening elsewhere. For example, with regard to the 'future prospects' issue, it is interesting to note that a report by the Jenkins Committee of the American Institute of Certified Public Accountants, published in 1994, proposes significant disclosures of a forward-looking nature but does not suggest an explicit forecast.

International harmonization of accounting

Accounting is different in countries across the world but for a number of years the increase in cross-border trade and investment has led to programmes of international harmonization of accounting.

Accounting systems in different countries have developed in response to different cultural environments. Within Western Europe two types of business culture may be identified: the 'Anglo-Saxon' model, with large capital markets, institutional investors and corporate growth by means of takeovers; and the 'continental' model, with a much greater influence from banks, the government and family, together with less developed capital markets. To a certain extent this traditional division is becoming less sharp and, as the models' differences break down, so the need for separate country-specific accounting systems can be expected to diminish.

At the same time the growth in international trade and cross-border investment has brought with it a perceived demand for sets of accounts which are comparable regardless of the country from which they are produced. Hence, the development of international programmes of accounting harmonization may be thought of as a process by which the degree of variation in accounting practices is deliberately limited so that any financial statements produced are comparable.

Two of the leading players here are the European Union, which via a series of company law directives has sought to produce comparability of financial statements from companies from different member states, and the International Accounting Standards Committee (IASC). The objective of the IASC is to achieve greater uniformity in the accounting principles which are used by businesses and other organizations for financial reporting around the world. The IASC publishes International Accounting Standards and in 1995 it reached an agreement with the International Organization of Securities Commissions (IOSCO) whereby the IASC is to produce a core set of standards in 1999, and on completion the IOSCO will be in a position to endorse the IASC standards.

Although not an international standard-setting body *per se*, the US Financial Accounting Standards Board (FASB) remains influential in the international context; many European companies present their financial statements in US-type formats, in some cases using US GAAP.

Overall, a narrowing of accounting differences can be looked for so that users of accounts should be in a position to make comparisons on the basis of closer harmonization of accounting practices.

Summary

UK company accounts are prepared by a company's directors. The accounts are required to give a true and fair view, i.e. they are to reflect the underlying economic reality of the company's state of affairs at the end of its financial year and the results for the year. Three issues which might affect the development of UK financial reporting are: the extent to which creative accounting is practised, the move for accounts to be more forward looking and the strengthening of international programmes of accounting harmonization. At the same time, it is likely that there will be an increase in the regulation of accounting, via accounting standards, as a result of these developments.

Appendix 1: Balance sheet formats

Balance Sheet Format 1

A   *Called-up share capital not paid*

B   *Fixed assets*

I   Intangible assets
1 Development costs
2 Concessions, patents, licences, trademarks, and similar rights and assets
3 Goodwill
4 Payments on account

II   Tangible assets
1 Land and buildings
2 Plant and machinery
3 Fixtures, fittings, tools and equipment
4 Payments on account and assets in the course of construction

III   Investments
1 Shares in group undertakings
2 Loans to group undertakings
3 Participating interests (excluding group undertakings)
4 Loans to undertakings in which the company has a participating interest
5 Other investments other than loans
6 Other loans
7 Own shares

C   *Current assets*

I   Stocks
1 Raw materials and consumables
2 Work in progress
3 Finished goods and goods for resale
4 Payments on account

II   Debtors
1 Trade debtors
2 Amounts owed by group undertakings

3 Amounts owed by undertakings in which the company has a participating interest
4 Other debtors
5 Called-up share capital not paid
6 Prepayments and accrued income

III Investments
1 Shares in group undertakings
2 Own shares
3 Other investments

IV Cash at bank and in hand

D **Prepayments and accrued income**

E **Creditors: amounts falling due within one year**

1 Debenture loans
2 Bank loans and overdrafts
3 Payments received on account
4 Trade creditors
5 Bills of exchange payable
6 Amounts owed to group undertakings
7 Amounts owed to undertakings in which the company has a participating interest
8 Other creditors, including taxation and social security
9 Accruals and deferred income

F **Net current assets (liabilities)**

G **Total assets less current liabilities**

H **Creditors: amounts falling due after more than one year**

1 Debenture loans
2 Bank loans and overdrafts
3 Payments received on account
4 Trade creditors
5 Bills of exchange payable
6 Amounts owed to group undertakings
7 Amounts owed to undertakings in which the company has a participating interest
8 Other creditors, including taxation and social security
9 Accruals and deferred income

I **Provisions for liabilities and charges**

1 Pensions and similar obligations
2 Taxation, including deferred taxation
3 Other provisions

J **Accruals and deferred income**
Minority interests

K Capital and reserves

I Called-up share capital

II Share premium account

III Revaluation reserve

IV Other reserves
1 Capital redemption reserve
2 Reserve for own shares
3 Reserves provided for by the articles of association
4 Other reserves

V Profit and loss account
Minority interests

Balance Sheet Format 2

Assets

A Called-up share capital not paid

B Fixed assets

I Intangible assets
1 Development costs
2 Concessions, patents, licences, trademarks, and similar rights and assets
3 Goodwill
4 Payments on account

II Tangible assets
1 Land and buildings
2 Plant and machinery
3 Fixtures, fittings, tools and equipment
4 Payments on account and assets in the course of construction

III Investments
1 Shares in group undertakings
2 Loans to group undertakings
3 Participating interests (excluding group undertakings)
4 Loans to undertakings in which the company has a participating interest
5 Other investments other than loans
6 Other loans
7 Own shares

C Current assets

I Stocks
1 Raw materials and consumables
2 Work in progress
3 Finished goods and goods for resale
4 Payments on account

II   Debtors
      1 Trade debtors
      2 Amounts owed by group undertakings
      3 Amounts owed by undertakings in which the company has a
        participating interest
      4 Other debtors
      5 Called-up share capital not paid
      6 Prepayments and accrued income

III   Investments
      1 Shares in group undertakings
      2 Own shares
      3 Other investments

IV   Cash at bank and in hand

D   Prepayments and accrued income

Liabilities

A   Capital and reserves

I   Called-up share capital

II   Share premium account

III   Revaluation reserve

IV   Other reserves
      1 Capital redemption reserve
      2 Reserve for own shares
      3 Reserves provided for by the articles of association
      4 Other reserves

V   Profit and loss account
      Minority interests

B   Provisions for liabilities and charges

      1 Pensions and similar obligations
      2 Taxation, including deferred taxation
      3 Other provisions

C   Creditors

      1 Debenture loans
      2 Bank loans and overdrafts
      3 Payments received on account
      4 Trade creditors
      5 Bills of exchange payable
      6 Amounts owed to group undertakings
      7 Amounts owed to undertakings in which the company has a
        participating interest
      8 Other creditors, including taxation and social security
      9 Accruals and deferred income

D   Accruals and deferred income

Appendix 2: Profit and loss account formats

Profit and Loss Account Format 1

1 Turnover
2 Cost of sales
3 Gross profit or loss
4 Distribution costs
5 Administrative expenses
6 Other operating income
7 Income from shares in group undertakings
8 Income from participating interests (excluding group undertakings)
9 Income from other fixed asset investments
10 Other interest receivable and similar income
11 Amounts written off investments
12 Interest payable and similar charges
13 Tax on profit or loss on ordinary activities
14 Profit or loss on ordinary activities after taxation
Minority interests
15 Extraordinary income
16 Extraordinary charges
17 Extraordinary profit or loss
18 Tax on extraordinary profit or loss
Minority interests
19 Other taxes not shown under the above items
20 Profit or loss for the financial year

Profit and Loss Account Format 2

1 Turnover
2 Change in stocks of finished goods and in work in progress
3 Own work capitalized
4 Other operating income
5 (a) Raw materials and consumables
   (b) Other external charges
6 Staff costs:
   (a) Wages and salaries

(b) Social security costs

(c) Other pension costs

7 (a) Depreciation and other amounts written off tangible and intangible fixed assets

(b) Exceptional amounts written off current assets

8 Other operating charges

9 Income from shares in group undertakings

10 Income from participating interests (excluding group undertakings)

11 Income from other fixed asset investments

12 Other interest receivable and similar income

13 Amounts written off investments

14 Interest payable and similar charges

15 Tax on profit or loss on ordinary activities

16 Profit or loss on ordinary activities after taxation

Minority interests

17 Extraordinary income

18 Extraordinary charges

19 Extraordinary profit or loss

20 Tax on extraordinary profit or loss

Minority interests

21 Other taxes not shown under the above items

22 Profit or loss for the financial year

Profit and Loss Account Format 3

A Charges

1 Cost of sale

2 Distribution costs

3 Administrative expenses

4 Amounts written off investments

5 Interest payable and similar charges

6 Tax on profit or loss on ordinary activities

7 Profit or loss on ordinary activities after taxation

Minority interests

8 Extraordinary charges

9 Tax on extraordinary profit or loss

Minority interests

10 Other taxes not shown under the above items

11 Profit for the financial year

B Income

1 Turnover

2 Other operating income

3 Income from shares in group undertakings

4 Income from participating interests (excluding group undertakings)

5 Income from other fixed asset investments

6 Other interest receivable and similar income

7 Profit or loss on ordinary activities after taxation
Minority interests
8 Extraordinary income
Minority interests
9 Loss for the financial year

Profit and Loss Account Format 4

A   Charges
1 Reduction in stocks of finished goods and in work in progress
2 (a) Raw materials and consumables
(b) Other external charges
3 Staff costs:
(a) Wages and salaries
(b) Social security costs
(c) Other pension costs
4 (a) Depreciation and other amounts written off tangible and intangible fixed assets
(b) Exceptional amounts written off current assets
5 Other operating charges
6 Amounts written off investments
7 Interest payable and similar charges
8 Tax on profit or loss on ordinary activities
9 Profit or loss on ordinary activities after taxation
Minority interests
10 Extraordinary charges
11 Tax on extraordinary profit or loss
Minority interests
12 Other taxes not shown under the above items
13 Profit for the financial year

B   Income
1 Turnover
2 Increase in stocks of finished goods and in work in progress
3 Own work capitalized
4 Other operating income
5 Income from shares in group undertakings
6 Income from participating interests (excluding group undertakings)
7 Income from other fixed asset investments
8 Other interest receivable and similar income
9 Profit or loss on extraordinary activities after taxation
Minority interests
10 Extraordinary income
Minority interests
11 Loss for the financial year

Appendix 3: Extracts from Scottish & Newcastle 1997 annual report and accounts

Chairman's Statement

Sir Alistair Grant
Chairman

Overall Group results have demonstrated that Scottish & Newcastle's strategic positioning as a major player in beer brands, in pub retailing and in short-break holidays provides a platform for sustained profit growth.

Pre-tax profits have again risen strongly to £372·0m. Earnings per share increased by 17·4% to 45·8p. Your Directors recommend a final dividend of 14·17p per share, an increase of 10·0%.

Our Beer and Retail divisions have continued to exploit the opportunities made possible by the acquisitions of Courage and of Chef & Brewer respectively. Leisure activities were faced with difficulties through a combination of depressed consumer spending in certain of Center Parcs markets and through the translation into sterling of profits derived from Holland, Belgium, France and Germany.

THE ECONOMY

Despite the apparent absence of the 'feel good factor', the British economy, during the year under review, produced conditions beneficial to industrial companies and to their customers. There has been no loosening of the extremely competitive pressures which first emerged after the UK's exit from the ERM but low inflation, relatively low interest rates and some improvement in levels of employment have led to a modest pick up in consumer spending in those sectors upon which our Company relies for its sales and profit growth. By contrast, in continental Europe the combination of structural uncompetitiveness and fiscal policies aimed at meeting the conditions necessary for the introduction of the Euro in 1999 have adversely affected both consumer markets and exchange rates.

Our beer and pub retail businesses have experienced greater sales buoyancy in the southern regions of England than in other areas. Scottish Courage's very much improved portfolio of beer brands combined with the quality of the southern pub estate have enabled our Company to benefit fully from this southern biased level of market demand for our products. Marketing effort and investment in improved pub facilities continue to be directed across the entire UK and there is some evidence that our markets in other regions are beginning to pick up.

The new operational responsibility of the Bank of England for setting interest rates is, we judge, a good omen for the outlook for inflation, possibly less good for levels of consumer expenditure.

DEVOLUTION

The General Election has delivered an incontrovertible mandate to the new Labour Government and its policies for constitutional change within the UK. There is a clear commitment to a referendum in Scotland to obtain the decision of the electorate on two questions: the introduction of an Assembly and the granting to that Assembly of tax varying powers. In common with most other substantial Scottish based companies, Scottish & Newcastle, although directed from Scotland, derives the greater part of its sales and profits from other areas of the United Kingdom and beyond. A successful company owes its success to seemingly small improvements in economic conditions, management capability, industrial efficiency and marketing effectiveness. Businesses can decline because of correspondingly small adverse movements in each of these critical areas. S&N employs 5,600 people within Scotland and has net assets of over £200m invested in the Scottish market. The implications for our Company of any new and progressive deterioration in any aspect of Scotland's domestic and international competitiveness might be to limit levels of investment and employment in this our home market and to impair our ability to meet competition from companies not so burdened. The electorate might view the power to levy taxes by any Assembly as initially, at least, a theoretical question. In our judgement this power, if granted, might lead to the eventual creation within Scotland of conditions which would inhibit the recruitment and retention of talent, bias investment decisions towards other areas of the UK and make Scottish goods and services significantly uncompetitive.

EUROPEAN MONETARY UNION

Scottish & Newcastle is an international business. Our Center Parcs operations employ 6,000 people in Holland, Belgium, Germany and France. Our Beer Division derives substantial sales in the UK from its marketing of such international brands as Beck's, Holsten, Kronenbourg, Fosters, Miller and Coors.

If the EMU introduction runs to timetable, it is in our interest that it should be restricted to those member states who are fully committed to meeting the real substance of the criteria for convergence and who can act as a sustained test-bed during which the consequences for each EMU member of ceding economic sovereignty can be experienced by them and assessed by others. The current relative strength of the UK economy compared with the long run difficulties which we have experienced in securing sustained growth since the Second World War argues against our putting our prosperity, even perhaps our political stability, at risk through too early participation in the EMU and in the centralist structures which may flow from it. If our representatives can find a more appealing tone and persuasive content for the exposition of our views in Europe we must hope that, at some point, we can be good Europeans within a Europe which has taken on board some of the lessons which we have learned in our efforts to become more efficient and more competitive.

THE BREWING INDUSTRY

The British consumer, despite the burden of duty borne by the UK beer producers, continues to enjoy among the widest range of ales and lagers obtainable through a network of on and off sales outlets at prices which reflect the efficiency of our industry and the competitiveness of our market. British beers and British pubs are consistently among the key attractions quoted by visitors to our country.

Our sector has adapted itself over the past 8 years to the changes imposed as a result of the Beer Orders. It continues to

be important for our customers and for those who work in our industry that the European Commission sees the value of the existing, limited maintenance of the brewery tie continuing into the future.

In a dynamic market new products, new types of outlets and new social habits impose upon producers, distributors and consumers increasing responsibilities. In our lifetime we have seen increasing levels of spending power and of self confidence among young people. We have, and we fully accept a responsibility for ensuring that our products are sold only to those who can legitimately be our customers.

POLITICAL DONATION

As is shown in the Report of the Directors the Company made a contribution of £50,000 to the Conservative Party during the year. In April the Board agreed that it was inappropriate for the Company to make any contribution to any political party and consequently we would not expect to do so in the future.

EMPLOYEES

Sir Alick Rankin retired as Chairman of Scottish & Newcastle plc on 31 January 1997 after thirty seven years service with our Company; his contribution to the expansion and development of S&N has been immense. Long-standing shareholders will recall with admiration and gratitude Alick Rankin's strategic vision in taking this Company forward from its somewhat difficult position as a major but regional brewer to the position of market leadership which was achieved when he and his colleagues realised a long-held ambition with the acquisition of Courage in 1995. A company can be measured in terms of its balance sheet, profit and loss account, stockmarket value, brand share, competitive efficiency. By all these measures the present position of S&N is a testimony to Alick Rankin's leadership. However, it is very probable that he has taken greatest pride in the creation of a company which has grown and prospered without forfeiting the standards which he set for straight dealing and utter reliability.

Ian McAllister, Chairman and Managing Director of Ford Motor Company of Great Britain, joined our Board as a Non-Executive Director on 26 September 1996. Neville Bain, formerly Chief Executive of Coats Viyella, was appointed to our Board as a Non-Executive Director on 26 June 1997.

Throughout the year each of our divisions has pursued energetically opportunities presented through acquisition and investment and the continuing pursuit of new products, new markets and new efficiencies. I would like, on behalf of the Board, to thank our management and staff for their dedication and hard work. Your Company is in an excellent position to maintain the sound progress that has been achieved in the year under review and to continue to invest in the people, brands and productive assets which will secure its sustained growth.

Chief Executive's Review

Brian Stewart
Chief Executive

The last year has been one of achievement for the Group, not just in producing a set of strong financial results but also in developing our longer term brand strength and earnings potential. The initiatives that have been taken have led to improving growth trends and this is evident in each of our divisions.

These improving trends are perhaps most evident in the particularly strong performance in the second half of the year where our results were produced on a genuinely comparable basis. The first half of the year gained comparatively from the acquisition of Courage.

In the second half we saw real turnover growth, accelerating key brand performance and a very positive contribution from our capital investment. It is a trend that has continued into the early weeks of the new financial year.

RETAIL

Our Retail Division has continued to capitalise not only on the excellent sites available following our Chef & Brewer acquisition but also from the development and improvement of our food and beverage offering to our customers. Historically, we have had a lower percentage of food sales than we would have liked in this rapidly growing market. Over the past 12 months there has been tremendous progress with our food sales growing faster than the market in a highly profitable manner.

Development of our retail brands, such as Old Orleans, Rat & Parrot and now Chef & Brewer, together with focused investment in the more traditional community pub area, is generating substantial returns. It is particularly satisfying that the financial return from new investment is not only being maintained but gradually enhanced. We are confident that this can be maintained, particularly with the balance of our increasing investment being spread across a variety of market sectors, not just 'the High Street'.

Since the Courage acquisition, we have had to operate within a tied cap of 2,624 outlets. This will not inhibit our growth as we can see considerable advantage in increasingly concentrating on directly managed branded outlets where our undoubted retailing skills can contribute distinctive benefit. Branded outlets are delivering the best financial performance in the estate and consequently we expect this concentration not only to improve total performance from our tied estate but also the individual contribution of managed houses.

Our investment in training has been reflected in the increasing quality of standards of operation and in formal recognition by the industry. Any introduction of a minimum wage must surely recognise the contribution to employment and the raising of the general skill pool that is increasingly being delivered by training.

The initiatives taken within the division, not only in terms of physical investment but also in the development of operating and management skills at all levels, are consistent with our ambition to be the premier pub retailer.

BEER

In the Beer business, our brand success is indisputable with key brands showing substantial volume and value growth. In the half year results it was highlighted that we had decided to forego loss-making volume and focus on developing a brand value platform. In this process, in the first six months of the year, we lost a modest amount of volume market share. In the second six months we have generally held volume share and seen a significant increase in our value share. Our key brands, the brands that generate real value, have grown strongly at a time when we have held our overall market position. This is very much the essential strategy that the Beer business has espoused for the coming years. Indeed, at this juncture, we are ahead of our expectations encouraged by consumer and customer demands for these key products.

While market projections in volume terms may be relatively static, value is growing ahead of inflation and will continue to grow. Our brand strengths equip us to grow faster still.

Our cost reduction programme is very much in line with expectations. This is no mean achievement, given the scale of integration involved. It is not yet finally concluded but it is a credit to all those involved that it has progressed so smoothly. The disruption and personal consequence of reducing our workforce by almost 900 over the past 12 months may appear a simple statistic but is a considerable trauma for each individual involved.

Our marketing investment has continued to grow in real terms not only in value but also in quality of delivery. Our brand success is not confined purely to the UK. Growth has also come in international markets, particularly the United States where the discerning consumer is increasingly prepared to consider international products. The success of Newcastle Brown Ale in America where we have grown volume sales by 45%, emphasises our capacity as an international brand developer.

The outcome of the Bass/Carlsberg Tetley merger reference has given us little cause for concern given the increasing strength of our brand position. Perhaps we have benefited through the preoccupation of others with that transaction at a time when Scottish & Newcastle and Courage were being integrated.

The new Government has indicated a range of areas which it intends to review in some depth – licensing, the liquid volume in a pint of beer, shatterproof glasses and beer duty. It will be important to deal with each of these issues in a most positive manner.

Building brands is already transforming the business in terms of margins and profits. It is our way ahead.

LEISURE

In Leisure, we have seen the same pattern of strengthening performance as the year has progressed. This has been masked by currency fluctuations with the strengthening of sterling off-setting the early results from our enhancement of the position of Center Parcs in the Benelux.

Center Parcs, in common with the rest of the Group, is intent on positioning its product at the top end of the quality spectrum. In Holland and Belgium to achieve this objective requires increased investment in the existing villages. Early indications of success are the rising trend of occupancy and the improved booking performance in the Dutch market where initial efforts have been focused. In our new German village, occupancy improved in the second half of the year and our bookings into the next financial year are strong. Our new

village development has been a brake on our rate of profit growth but there are now clear indicators that we can achieve our objectives, albeit later than intended.

Performance in the UK has been little short of remarkable. Occupancy in the second half of the year is 90% with our new village at Longleat showing a significantly improved performance. After ten years, in spite of competitive conditions, the UK business demonstrates the real earnings potential of Center Parcs.

Our French market has probably been the most depressed in terms of consumer spending. EMU convergence is undoubtedly extracting a price from the French consumer. In spite of those conditions, our French villages have performed well with occupancy of nearly 90%. While this is slightly down on last year, our capacity has been increased with the construction of new villas and as a result our business in France actually grew during the second half year – a remarkable performance.

In Center Parcs, we have therefore seen the benefits of our strategy of focusing on quality. There is a need to enhance the returns from our investment but undoubtedly considerable progress is being made.

In Pontin's, we have seen rising profits from an increased focus on the more traditional Pontin's market and here too the demand for quality is evident. People are prepared to pay for that quality of offer and the results are encouraging.

Our three divisions have considerable organic growth potential but, equally, they could be extended both domestically and internationally. The characteristic of future development will, however, be investment in businesses giving strong cash flow which allows continued brand development through both marketing and capital spend.

In the Community

Henry Fairweather
Group Personnel and Services Director

Scottish & Newcastle's commitment to the communities and environments in which it operates has always been strong. The Company and its employees devote considerable time, effort and money to charity, community and environment projects.

Direct donations to charity in 1996/97 totalled £525,000. In addition to this, hundreds of local charities and projects were supported by Group companies and individual teams of employees. When all of this activity is taken into account, the total value of support is substantially higher with the Retail Division alone raising £5m from local in-pub activity.

Just a few examples of the many hundreds of projects completed during the year can be outlined here. In keeping with the business's desire to support education and youth and help young people to develop their future working skills, the Company continued to sponsor Understanding Industry. Support involves sponsorship of courses for 16 year old pupils in 10 different schools throughout the UK. Staff from local S&N companies in all three divisions have taken part in courses as session leaders.

A great deal of support was also given to social welfare, covering the elderly, homeless, disadvantaged and disabled. For example, the Company contributed £20,000 towards the establishment of a new cancer research laboratory at the Western General Hospital in Edinburgh, one of the UK's leading centres for cancer research and treatment. Pontin's has been supporting the British Red Cross for over 25 years and in the past year, £25,000 has been raised to provide holidays for the disabled and disadvantaged.

SCOTTISH & NEWCASTLE AND THE ENVIRONMENT

Scottish & Newcastle recognises that almost all its activities impact on the environment to some degree, and that the effective management of environmental affairs is essential.

Our environmental policies are determined at the highest level within the Group. An advisory committee is dedicated to reducing the impact of operations on the environment. In addition each division has a director with specific responsibility for environmental matters. Special consideration is given to energy usage, reducing resource usage, increasing the use of recycled or recovered materials, and waste minimisation. Environmental targets are incorporated in operational business plans.

Some project examples are outlined here: in the light of growing concern over water availability, strenuous efforts have been made to reduce its use in beer production. In 1976 it took 8.8 pints of water to make a pint of beer, this has now been reduced to 6. Over the last 20 years the brewing industry has reduced its energy consumption by 40%, Scottish & Newcastle has consistently been better than the industry average; the Company has introduced a number of energy saving initiatives across the Retail estate which have led to environmental benefits as well as improving customer comfort.

Scottish & Newcastle's commitment to protecting the environment is underlined with direct financial support for suitable projects and initiatives.

The Company has made an annual donation of £50,000 for the last five years to Glasgow Caledonian University to fund a Chair in environment research. The aim of the department is to develop a knowledge and expertise in environmental issues and it is expected to become one of the leading authoritative voices on all matters environmental.

In summary our commitment to the environment encompasses every aspect of our operations and the Company continues to develop an active programme in this area.

Financial Review

Derek Wilkinson
Group Finance Director

SUMMARY

Last year the financial review drew attention to the strong cash generating characteristics of the Group which had been further enhanced by the acquisition of Courage. These characteristics have enabled us to finance internally an increasing level of investment over the last few years. In the financial year ended 27 April we have invested a further £270m, an increase of £40m on the previous year. This investment activity has again been financed from internal cash flow. Gearing levels have reduced and interest cover has increased.

Our performance in 1996/97 is further evidence of the Group's ability to generate an increasingly strong flow of cash to exploit the undoubted opportunities for organic growth that exist in our three trading divisions.

REVIEW OF RESULTS

Group turnover was 12·8% ahead of last year and operating profit 16·7% ahead.

The results for the year included a 52 week contribution from Courage which was acquired on 16 August 1995. Last year's results included a 37 week contribution from Courage with turnover of £885·3m and operating profit of £36·7m.

The Courage beer business is now fully integrated with our own Beer business and, as such, it is no longer possible to identify separately the contribution made.

RETAIL

The year saw further disposals from our Retail estate as we sought to comply with the limit of 2,624 outlets imposed by the MMC following the acquisition of Courage. We began the year with an estate of 2,678 and closed below the MMC limit at 2,592 units with 29 fewer managed houses and 57 fewer tenancies. The need to be net disposers of estate which has acted as a brake on our earnings growth in recent years is now behind us.

Turnover grew by 4·7% to £778·9m and operating profit by 9·0% to £171·6m. The net margin on sales increased again to 22·0%. Margins have increased annually since the acquisition of the Chef & Brewer estate in 1993 as a result of increasing sales levels, a more profitable product mix and rigid control of costs.

Managed Houses The key driver of profit growth was again our managed estate with turnover ahead by 4·8% to £747·6m and operating profit of £148·7m up by 12·1%. Sales per outlet grew by 6·9%.

The development of the former Chef & Brewer estate has again been a strategic priority. We have completed 246 development projects during the year and early indications are that returns are being maintained at a level of c. 25%.

During the year we reduced our cost base further with the centralisation at a new office in Leeds of the management and administration of our estate in the northern half of the country. The rollout of electronic point of sale technology to the Chef & Brewer estate, which is scheduled to be completed in November 1997, continued to result in both better management of the cost base and a lower cost of sales.

Tenancies With a 16% reduction in the average number of units trading, our tenancy division did well to achieve profits of £22·9m, 7·3% below last year.

Average profit per house has continued to increase as we improve the quality of our tenanted estate.

BEER

Including the full year contribution from Courage the Beer Division has increased turnover by 20·5% to £2,167·6m and operating profit by £55·6m or 45·8%. The net margin on sales has increased from 6·8% to 8·2%. Profit growth in the second half year, which is more directly comparable, was 28·8% and turnover growth 5·7%.

While we have experienced some loss of volume due to giving up business previously done at unsatisfactory price levels, the resulting loss of contribution has been more than compensated by real increases in net selling prices in both the On and Take-Home trades. The proportion of price increases conceded in discounts has reduced.

Significant progress has been made in the year with the process of integration and the closure of two breweries in Halifax and Nottingham.

Since August 1995, integration savings arising as a consequence of the Courage acquisition have amounted to £46m with a benefit of £37m accruing in 1996/97. Further savings of £24m are anticipated in 1997/98.

LEISURE

The appreciation of sterling which strengthened on average by 10% against the major European currencies and the continuing low levels of consumer confidence in most northern European countries were the main factors contributing to a fall in operating profit by 10·6% to £76·5m. At constant exchange rates, a more meaningful measure, profits were down by £3·8m or 4·7%.

Encouragingly the trend of profits at Center Parcs, at constant exchange rates, and Pontin's both improved in the second half of the financial year. Center Parcs was only marginally below last year and Pontin's were ahead. Center Parcs benefited from increased occupancy particularly in the UK where more consumer buoyancy is now evident and in Holland where product innovation and the refurbishment programme underway are beginning to achieve results.

Pontin's volumes and tariffs in the second half both increased as a consequence of the accommodation refurbishment programme in our Family Favourite centres.

INTEREST PAYABLE

Interest payable fell by 9·3% from £56·2m to £51·0m due to a reduction in the average level of debt, particularly currency debt, and lower effective interest rates on both sterling and currency borrowings. The strength of the pound relative to other European currencies resulted in a currency benefit of £0·7m.

Interest cover increased from 6·3 times to 8·3 times.

PROFIT BEFORE TAXATION

Profit before tax has increased from £156·9m to £372·0m but last year's figure was after charging a loss on disposals of fixed assets of £0·5m and a provision for reorganisation costs of £150·8m. Prior to any exceptional items profit before tax for 1996/97 is up by 21·4% to £374·1m.

TAXATION

The tax charge of £85·8m represents an effective tax rate of 23·1% relative to last year's rate of 30·1% which was distorted by the exceptional provision for reorganisation costs.

We have continued to benefit from a low effective tax rate on the profits of our overseas subsidiaries although these profits now represent a smaller percentage of total profit earned.

Tax relief on our growing levels of capital expenditure in the UK has increased and some benefit has been derived from the release of prior year over provisions. Given the anticipated increase in the percentage of our profits to be sourced from the UK in 1997/98 we expect a small increase in our effective tax rate.

EARNINGS PER SHARE AND DIVIDENDS

Profit attributable to ordinary shareholders before exceptional items increased by 21·6% to £285·4m. The fully diluted weighted average number of shares in issue increased to 629·4m.

Fully diluted earnings per share were 45·8p, an increase of 17·4% on 1995/96.

A final dividend of 14·17p per share is proposed which, together with the interim dividend of 7·21p, brings the total for the year to 21·38p, an increase of 10·0%. Excluding the impact of exceptional items the total dividend is more than twice covered.

ACQUISITIONS AND DISPOSALS

There were no acquisitions or disposals in the year that have had a material impact on financial performance.

Following the acquisition of Courage on 16 August 1995 for £430m there remained a deferred consideration payable to the Foster's Brewing Group in 1999 or 2000. The deferred consideration was to be based on the increase in value of 10m Scottish & Newcastle ordinary shares over a price of 537p per share.

During the year the Company assigned the liability for the settlement of the deferred consideration to a third party for a payment of £20·2m.

The difference between the original estimated cost of the deferred consideration and the premium paid to assign the liability has been treated as an adjustment to goodwill.

PROPERTY REVALUATION

During the year the Group's licensed and related properties, leisure properties and various other properties were revalued. The revaluation resulted in a surplus over net book value of £106m.

CASH FLOW

	1997 £m	1996 £m
Operating Activities	475	451
Capital Expenditure	(270)	(230)
Investments	18	4
Asset Disposals	35	38
Operating Cash Flow	258	263
Interest, Dividends & Tax	(223)	(215)
Free Cash Flow	35	48

In spite of an increase in capital expenditure to a record level of £270m and a significantly higher level of spend on integration costs, operating cash flow at £258m has remained broadly similar to last year's level. Given the opportunities available within our licensed retail estate and the returns being achieved on development projects the percentage of total investment, allocated to our Retail Division, has increased from 38% to 43%.

Total spend within our Retail Division amounted to £116m of which £79m related to expenditure on development projects and acquisitions, £10m on the installation of electronic point of sale equipment in the former Chef & Brewer estate and a further £27m on maintenance and other smaller projects. The development of branded retail outlets has remained a priority given the higher returns available and the lower risk profile associated with rolling out proven concepts. At the end of the financial year 21% of our managed estate was branded. We anticipate by the year 2000 that the percentage of our estate that is branded will increase significantly.

We have continued to achieve average returns in excess of 25% on our development capital. More importantly these high initial returns are being maintained with the development projects undertaken since the acquisition of Chef & Brewer in 1993 still achieving average returns in excess of 27%. As in all retailing, location is the key ingredient for success. We believe that our estate and particularly the Chef & Brewer estate provides a continuing opportunity for profitable development.

Within Beer the capital spend of £91m included additional brewing and storage capacity at the Tadcaster brewery following the closure of the Home brewery in Nottingham and the former Courage brewery in Halifax. A new mainframe computer was installed at our Head Office in Edinburgh to permit centralisation of data-processing operations. We continued to rationalise our keg population and to install the necessary dispense equipment to roll out the Courage brands into our Retail estate.

Leisure capital spend of £63m was below last year's level of £85m reflecting the decision not to open a new village until higher returns are achieved on the recent village openings and we see some evidence of recovery in the northern European economy.

Spend has been primarily focused on the major upgrading and repositioning initiative being implemented in Holland and Belgium. Due to increasing demand we have increased the number of VIP villas on all villages, introduced child-friendly villas and opened new themed pools on four of our villages. Within the UK we have undertaken a major refurbishment scheme at Sherwood Forest on the villas and the central facilities. This refurbishment follows 10 years of very high occupancy levels since the opening of the Sherwood Forest village in 1987.

Pontin's have continued their programme of upgrading accommodation and central facilities. Further work has been undertaken at Brean Sands and Camber Sands with new projects at Blackpool, Prestatyn and Wall Park.

Each of our trading divisions achieved a positive operating cash flow with Retail and Leisure substantially ahead of last year. Beer cash flow was held back by spend of £60m on exceptional costs associated with integration which peaked during the year.

The cash outflow on interest, dividends and tax increased marginally from £215m to £223m. The cost of dividends increased by 18% as a result of the higher rate of dividend paid and the fact that the shares issued in 1995/96 to finance the Courage acquisition did not qualify for the final dividend paid in September 1995.

Free cash flow, the cash flow before acquisitions, was £35m. Year end net debt decreased from £752·3m to £688·1m, partly as a consequence of the strengthening of the pound, while gearing declined from 36·5% to 31·2%.

FOREIGN EXCHANGE

The Group's reported profits, net assets and gearing are all affected by movements in foreign exchange rates, particularly the Dutch Guilder and the Deutsche Mark. It is Group policy to hedge exposure to cash transactions in foreign currencies for a range of forward periods but not to hedge exposure to the translation of reported profits. Assets denominated in currency are matched by borrowings broadly to the level of Group gearing.

In 1996/97 we have experienced the unusual event of sterling strengthening significantly against the principal European currencies. Average exchange rates relative to the pound have appreciated by c. 10% and year end rates by c. 20%.

The appreciation of sterling has had the following impact on financial performance:
– Leisure operating profit has declined by £5·3m.
– Group profit before tax has been reduced by £4·6m.
– Net assets have fallen by £98m.
– Debt levels are down by £40m.

INTEREST RATE MANAGEMENT

Interest rate exposure is managed within parameters agreed by the Board which stipulate that borrowings where the rate of interest is fixed for a period in excess of 12 months should account for no less than 30% and no more than 70% of total borrowings. To achieve this the Group enters into interest rate swaps, options and forward rate agreements. At 27 April 1997, 52% of borrowings were at rates fixed for periods in excess of 12 months and 48% were at variable rates.

TREASURY POLICY AND CAPITAL STRUCTURE

Treasury policies are reviewed internally by the Board and are managed by the central Treasury Department which provides a service to divisions including overseas subsidiaries.

The policies have, as their key objective, the management of financial risk through investment, borrowing and foreign exchange activities in relation only to the underlying business needs of the Group.

The Treasury Department reports formally on a monthly basis to a Treasury Committee under the Chairmanship of the Group Finance Director and operates within a range of specified authorisation levels and policies. It is subject to regular compliance audits by the Group Review & Audit Department and an annual review by the Group's external auditors.

The Group's policy is to maintain a mix of bank and capital market borrowings that provide sufficient resources to meet its financing requirements over the medium term.

During the year most of the Group's borrowing facilities were reviewed and maturities extended, resulting in an average maturity of 4·3 years on all facilities including overdrafts and debentures.

ACCOUNTING POLICIES

There have been no material changes in accounting policies during the year. Two new Accounting Standards, FRS1 Revised (Cash Flow Statements) and FRS8 (Related Party Disclosures) are applicable to the year being reported. The Group cash flow statement on Page 40 has [of the original] been drawn up to comply with FRS1 and comparatives have been adjusted accordingly. In the case of FRS8 the only transactions that fall to be reported on relate to those with associated undertakings.

YEAR 2000

Planning to cope with the impact of the year 2000 on the Group's key financial and other systems is at an advanced stage.

The Retail Division is in the process of implementing a new financial system which will be fully operational by early in calendar year 1998. Scottish Courage, has adopted the financial systems previously used by Courage which are already year 2000 compatible. Center Parcs implemented a new financial package some two years ago. Other support systems are being progressively replaced.

The funding of these extensive systems changes is being resourced from within existing development budgets.

Report of the Directors

GROUP RESULTS

A detailed analysis of the results for the year is provided in note 2 to the accounts.

DIVIDENDS

The Directors are recommending a final dividend of 14·17p per share to be paid on 1 September 1997 to ordinary shareholders on the register at close of business on 8 August 1997. This would make a total ordinary dividend for the year of 21·38p per share.

BUSINESS REVIEW AND FUTURE DEVELOPMENTS

The Report of the Directors should be read in conjunction with the Chairman's Statement, the Chief Executive's Review and the Financial Review on pages 2 to 25 [of the original] which contain details of the Group's trading during the year and an indication of likely future developments.

AGM SPECIAL BUSINESS

Subject to having the relevant authority in their Articles of Association, listed companies are now permitted to send to those shareholders wishing to receive them Summary Financial Statements for each financial year instead of full Annual Report & Accounts. The Directors consider that it would be in the interests of both shareholders and the Company that the relevant regulation in the Company's Articles be amended so that this flexibility can be made available to shareholders. A Special Resolution (Resolution 9) is therefore being proposed to make the necessary amendment to Regulation 134 of the Company's Articles.

Copies of the full Accounts would however continue to be sent to any shareholders wishing to receive them. The Directors envisage that this new arrangement will be available in respect of the Company's 1998 Report & Accounts and further details will be sent with the Company's Interim Report later this year, including a form enabling shareholders to request a copy of the full Annual Report & Accounts if they should still wish to receive it.

As in previous years, it is proposed to renew the Directors' authority to allot share capital and to permit non pre-emptive issues of ordinary shares in limited circumstances. These authorities are contained in Special Resolutions 10 and 11. Although they are in a shortened form from Resolutions put to shareholders in the past, the effect is to continue the authorities in the form which the Directors have sought over many previous years.

The new allotment authority sought is in respect of up to £17,000,000 nominal of share capital (representing approximately 14% of the Company's present issued ordinary share capital). The pre-emption rights dis-application is sought in connection with any rights issue and in respect of any allotment for cash of up to £6,000,000 nominal of ordinary share capital (representing approximately 5% of the Company's present issued ordinary share capital).

The Directors are not currently aware of any circumstances in which any part of the above authority would be used, but as in previous years, consider it desirable that they should have the flexibility to issue shares from time to time to enable the

Company to take advantage of business opportunities as they arise. Resolutions 10 and 11 will grant the authority and dis-application until the date of next year's Annual General Meeting or 30 September 1998 if sooner.

SHARE CAPITAL

Details of shares issued during the year, including shares issued and options granted under the employee share schemes and shares and options held by the Scottish & Newcastle Employee Share Trust, are contained in note 21 to the accounts.

PAYMENT OF SUPPLIERS

The Company agrees terms and conditions with suppliers before business takes place. The Company's policy and practice is to pay agreed invoices in accordance with the terms of payment. At the year end the amount owed to trade creditors by the Company was equivalent to 31 days of purchases from suppliers.

NOTIFIABLE INTERESTS

As at 30 June 1997 the Company has been notified of the following interests representing 3% or more of the issued ordinary share capital of the Company:

PDFM Ltd:	11·5%
Scottish Widows Fund and Life Assurance Society	3·5%.

DIRECTORS

The names of the current Directors of the Company are set out on pages 26 and 27 [of the original]. Sir Alick Rankin retired as Chairman and as a Director on 31 January 1997 and Sir Alistair Grant succeeded him as Chairman of the Company. I G McAllister, who was appointed a Non-Executive Director on 26 September 1996, retires and, being eligible, offers himself for election. N C Bain, who was appointed a Non-Executive Director on 26 June 1997, retires and, being eligible, offers himself for election. G G Dickson, J H W Fairweather and I G Hannah retire by rotation and, being eligible, offer themselves for re-election.

I G McAllister and N C Bain have no service contracts. G G Dickson, J H W Fairweather and I G Hannah have service contracts which are terminable on 2 years' notice.

No Director had, during or at the end of the year, any material interest in any contract of significance in relation to the Group's business.

The interests of the Directors in the Ordinary Shares of the Company are set out in the Remuneration Committee Report on pages 30 to 34 [of the original].

EMPLOYEE RELATIONS AND INVOLVEMENT

The Company is firmly committed to the principles of employee involvement. A full range of briefing, consultation and bargaining arrangements have been developed in all parts of the Group and these are subject to continual review and improvement.

DISABLED PERSONS

Full and fair consideration has been given to applications for employment made by disabled persons and appropriate training, career development and promotion have been provided in all cases.

POLITICAL AND CHARITABLE CONTRIBUTIONS

During the financial year the Group made political contributions of £50,000 (1996 – £50,000) to the Conservative Party and various charitable contributions totalling £525,000 (1996 – £523,000).

AUDITORS

Ernst & Young have expressed their willingness to continue in office and a resolution proposing their re-appointment and authorising the Board to fix their remuneration will be submitted at the Annual General Meeting.

By Order of the Board
M J Pearey, Secretary
30 June 1997

Report of the Remuneration Committee

REMUNERATION COMMITTEE REPORT

The Company complies with the Best Practice provisions relating to Remuneration Committees as set out in Section A of the Annex to the London Stock Exchange Listing Rules.

The Remuneration Committee comprises Sir Alistair Grant (Chairman), Neville Bain, Sir Malcolm Field and Ian McAllister. It meets at least three times a year and is responsible for setting all elements of Executive Directors' remuneration packages. The Committee is also responsible for establishing the annual targets for the Company's Results Related Bonus Scheme and granting options under the Company's Share Option Schemes, as well as approving participation in, and the operation of, the Company's Long-Term Incentive Plan.

In setting the remuneration package for Executive Directors, the Committee aims to ensure that the total package including benefits is competitive with companies of a similar size, activity and complexity and that accordingly it will attract and retain Executive Directors with the skills to maximise returns for shareholders. The Committee believes that it is important that a significant part of the remuneration package should be clearly linked to measurable Company performance, from which shareholders may benefit. Accordingly, the package attempts to balance base salary with both short and long-term performance incentives. The Committee keeps the total remuneration package and the balance of its various elements under regular review. In establishing its remuneration policy, the Committee gives full consideration to the Best Practice provisions set out in Section B of the Annex to the London Stock Exchange Listing Rules.

The remuneration package for Executive Directors comprises:

BASE SALARY

Individual base salaries are reviewed annually by the Committee and take into account any responsibility changes, as well as external independent advice as to salary levels appropriate to each Director's responsibilities within the Group in the context of comparable organisations.

RESULTS RELATED BONUS SCHEME

The maximum bonus payable to Executive Directors under the Scheme for the year to 27 April 1997 is limited to 40% of base salary and the level of bonus is related to the two objectives of achieved growth in earnings per share and profit before tax and exceptional items. For Executive Directors who are Divisional Chairmen, profit before tax relates to relevant divisional profit before tax and for other Executive Directors to Group profit before tax. At Group level, for the maximum bonus to become payable, earnings per share and profit before tax were required to be 45·9 pence and £375m respectively. The figures achieved for the year were 45·8p in respect of earnings per share and £374·1m in respect of profit before tax and exceptional items. Accordingly, at Group level, the bonus element achieved for the year was 38% of base salary (1996 – 18% of base salary). At divisional level, the bonus element achieved ranged between 19% and 39% of base salary.

PENSIONS AND LIFE ASSURANCE

Executive Directors participate in a Company funded pension scheme, which provides at normal retirement age of 60 and subject to length of service, a pension of up to two thirds of salary at retirement subject to Inland Revenue limits and other statutory rules. Life assurance cover is provided of 4 times salary. The contributions made by the Company to the scheme and the pension entitlement of individual Directors are shown later in this report. Pension entitlement is calculated by reference to base salary only and neither annual bonuses nor benefits in kind are pensionable. Service as a Non-Executive Director is not pensionable.

OTHER BENEFITS

Other Benefits shown later in this report in the table of individual Directors' remuneration comprise the taxable values in respect of the provision of a Company car and fuel, medical insurance, a beer and wines and spirits allowance and subscriptions to professional and trade bodies. The appropriation of shares to each Executive Director under the Profit Sharing Scheme up to the annual maximum initial market value of £8,000 is not shown under Other Benefits but the relevant shares are included in the table of beneficial shareholdings of Directors.

LONG-TERM INCENTIVE PLAN

This Plan, which was introduced in May 1995, provides, at the discretion of the Committee, ordinary shares in the Company up to a value of 30% of current salary to Executive Directors, as well as to selected managers. These shares, or an appropriate proportion, are allocated after 3 years dependent upon the Group's performance against all other companies in the FT-SE 100. The measure of performance is Total Shareholder Return, comprising the difference between the share price at the start of the Plan and that at the end of the Plan plus the dividends paid during the 3 years of the Plan. This return will be compared with that of all other companies in the FT-SE 100 over the same period and the Company's placing will determine the extent of the allocation. If the performance is in the top 30 of the FT-SE 100, then an allocation of shares will be made in full. If the performance is in the bottom 30 of the FT-SE 100, then no allocation will be made. An intermediate performance will produce a proportion of shares, with 2·5% being released for each position in the rank above 70th in the FT-SE 100 that the Group achieves.

SHARE SCHEMES

Executive Directors may participate in the Company's Profit Sharing, Executive Share Option and Savings-Related Share Option Schemes.

Executive Directors participate in both the 1984 and the 1994 Executive Share Option Schemes. The 1984 Scheme expired in 1994 and no further options can be granted thereunder, but options may still be exercised under the 1984 Scheme for a period of 10 years from the original date of grant. A proportion of options under the 1984 Scheme granted between 17 January 1992 and 28 July 1994 were granted at a discount of 15% to the then market price, but may only be exercised at this discounted price if growth in the Company's earnings per share is equal to or greater than the increase in the Retail Prices Index, plus 10% over any 5 consecutive financial years of the Company prior to exercise. Options under the 1994 Scheme may only be exercised if the Company's growth in earnings per share is equal to or greater than the increase in the Retail Prices Index plus 6% over any 3 consecutive financial years of the Company prior to exercise. Options are granted at the market price at the date of grant and not at a discount. As indicated above, options will not normally be exercisable at the earliest before a period of 3 years from the date of grant.

Options may be granted to Executive Directors up to a total value of 4 times earnings. The initial grant of options would normally be made over a 3 year period. Thereafter further options may be granted to maintain the value of options at the date of grant at a figure equivalent to 4 times earnings.

Options granted under the Savings-Related Option Scheme are not subject to a performance condition, but require a savings contract to be entered into for 3 or 5 years and for options to be exercised within 6 months of the termination of that savings contract. Options under the Savings-Related Option Scheme are available generally to all eligible employees and can be granted at a discount of up to 20% of the market price at the time of grant. There is a current maximum limit on savings of £250 per month.

Under the Profit Sharing Scheme, in which all eligible employees participate, shares may be appropriated to Executive Directors up to a current maximum initial market value in a tax year of £8,000. These shares are held by the Trustees of the Scheme and can be transferred tax free to participants after a period of 3 years.

SERVICE CONTRACTS

The Chairman has been appointed as Non-Executive Chairman from 1 February 1997, subject to termination of that appointment by either party on one year's notice. Non-Executive Directors are appointed for an initial term of 3 years, renewable for a further term of 3 years.

The Committee considers that the standard period of notice for Executive Directors should be 1 year. In certain instances, a newly appointed Executive Director may be offered a 3 year fixed term contract, but would thereafter revert to a 1 year notice basis. After 3 years service with the Group (whether or not as an Executive Director), the period of notice for Executive Directors is progressively increased for each complete year of service up to the completion of 15 years' service, whereupon a maximum 2 year notice period is achieved. Also, an Executive Director aged 50 years or more is entitled to 2 years' notice, provided that 5 years' full-time prior service with the Group has been completed. The Committee believes that these arrangements are necessary in order to recruit Executive Directors of a suitable calibre and also to take into account the position of Executive Directors who have served the Company over a substantial period of time. All present Executive Directors have more than 15 years' service with the Group and accordingly have service contracts which are terminable on 2 years' notice. In the event of the termination of any service contract or appointment by the Company, the Committee would ensure that legally appropriate mitigation factors would be fully applied to any compensation that may be payable.

G G Dickson, J H W Fairweather, I G Hannah, I G McAllister and N C Bain are proposed for re-election or election at the forthcoming Annual General Meeting. Messrs. Dickson, Fairweather and Hannah have service contracts which are terminable on 2 years' notice. I G McAllister and N C Bain have no service contracts.

DIRECTORS' REMUNERATION AND INTERESTS

Total Emoluments

	1997 £000	1996 £000
Fees to Non-Executive Directors	50	45
Salaries and Other Benefits	1,634	1,661
Results Related Bonuses	500	256
Contributions to Pension Scheme and Life Assurance	137	148
Compensation for Loss of Office (Mr A M Mowat)	–	150
	2,321	**2,260**

Individual Emoluments

	Salaries and Fees		Bonuses		Other Benefits		Pension & Life Assurance Contributions		Total Emoluments	
	1997 £000	1996 £000	1997 £000	1996 £000	1997 £000	1996 £000	1997 £000	1996 £000	1997 £000	1996 £000
CHAIRMAN										
Sir Alick Rankin (to 31/01/97)	88	115	–	–	10	13	1†	2†	99	130
Sir Alistair Grant (from 01/02/97 as Chairman)	44	18	–	–	1	–	1†	–	46	18
CHIEF EXECUTIVE AND DEPUTY CHAIRMAN										
B J Stewart	385	348	146	63	14	14	38	37	583	462
EXECUTIVE DIRECTORS										
J A Dalgety	189	89	35	24	9	4	17	9	250	126
G G Dickson	242	207	95	37	19	8	22	21	378	273
J H W Fairweather	168	144	62	26	13	7	15	15	258	192
I G Hannah	243	219	87	39	10	10	24	22	364	290
T J Hemmings (to 28/04/96)	–	192	–	35	–	7	–	16	–	250
A M Mowat (to 30/09/95)	–	211*	–	–	–	5	–	6	–	222
R Summers (to 24/06/95)	–	27	–	–	–	3	–	2	–	32
D M Wilkinson	200	179	75	32	14	9	19	18	308	238
NON-EXECUTIVE DIRECTORS										
Sir Malcolm Field	22	20	–	–	–	–	–	–	22	20
I G McAllister (from 26/09/96)	13#	–	–	–	–	–	–	–	13	–
Lord Nickson (to 31/08/95)	–	7	–	–	–	–	–	–	–	7
TOTALS	**1,594**	1,776	**500**	256	**90**	80	**137**	148	**2,321**	2,260

*Includes compensation for loss of office. †Life assurance only. #Paid to Ford Motor Company.

PENSION ENTITLEMENTS

The pension entitlements earned by the current Directors during the year were as follows:

	Complete Years of Service at 27 April 1997	Increase in Accrued Pension During the Year to 27 April 1997 £000	Accumulated Total Accrued Pension at 27 April 1997 £000
B J Stewart	20	26	186
J A Dalgety	24	25	82
G G Dickson	18	21	110
J H W Fairweather	27	13	82
I G Hannah	16	18	118
D M Wilkinson	22	14	103

SHARES

The beneficial interests of the Directors in the 20p ordinary shares in the Company at 28 April 1996 and 27 April 1997 are shown below.

Name	Fully Paid Ordinary Shares 1997	1996
N C Bain (at date of appointment)	6,000	6,000
J A Dalgety	7,855	7,292
G G Dickson	60,018	12,278
J H W Fairweather	69,284	66,407
Sir Malcolm Field	1,142	1,142
Sir Alistair Grant	5,000	5,000
I G Hannah	18,897	17,995
I G McAllister	–	–
B J Stewart	154,476	55,853
D M Wilkinson	92,095	88,075

Certain of the interests in the fully paid shares include shares held as participants in the Profit Sharing Scheme.

Executive Directors also have an interest as potential beneficiaries along with other employees in 2,781,164 ordinary shares held by the Trustee of the Scottish & Newcastle Employee Share Trust at 27 April 1997.

EXECUTIVE AND SAVINGS-RELATED SHARE OPTIONS

Option Holdings	Options Held at 27 April 1997		Dates Exercisable		Options Exercisable at 27 April 1997	
	Number	Weighted Average Exercise Price – p	Earliest	Latest	Number	Weighted Average Exercise Price – p
J A Dalgety	109,849	538	22/07/91	02/07/06	38,118	403
G G Dickson	82,991	594	16/12/96	02/07/06	6,675	535
J H W Fairweather	130,225	406	22/07/91	02/07/06	102,646	353
I G Hannah	103,509	524	17/01/95	02/07/06	36,639	362
B J Stewart	107,429	573	16/12/96	02/07/06	10,361	535
D M Wilkinson	157,964	466	21/08/92	02/07/06	96,176	384

Movement in Option Holdings	Options Held at 28 April 1996	Options Granted During Year	Options Exercised During Year	Weighted Average Exercise Price – p	Weighted Average Market Price at Date of Exercise – p	Gain on Exercise – £	Options Held at 27 April 1997
J A Dalgety	76,792	33,057	–	–	–	–	109,849
G G Dickson	160,961	24,851	102,821	360·25	666	314,375	82,991
J H W Fairweather	117,727	14,684	2,186	343	675·5	7,268	130,225
I G Hannah	77,593	25,916	–	–	–	–	103,509
B J Stewart	296,311	27,158	216,040	375	677	652,441	107,429
D M Wilkinson	138,985	22,258	3,279	343	675·5	10,903	157,964

Options granted to Directors during the year under the Executive Option Scheme were granted at an option price of 664p which was the market price at the date of grant. Options were granted during the year to Messrs. Fairweather and Wilkinson under the Savings-Related Option Scheme at an option price of 545p. The market price at the date of grant was 678p.

The aggregate of the amount of gains made by Directors on the exercise of options during the year totalled £984,987. All shares acquired by Directors on the exercise of such options were retained by Directors, save for the sale, where necessary, of sufficient shares to provide the exercise cost.

The market price of the Company's ordinary shares at 25 April 1997 was 672p. The highest and lowest market prices during the year to 27 April 1997 were 700p and 629·5p respectively. The Register of Directors' Interests, which is open to inspection, contains full details of Directors' shareholdings and options.

LONG-TERM INCENTIVE PLAN

Name	Maximum Number of Shares Held in Plan at 28 April 1996	Shares Added[†] During Year to 27 April 1997	Maximum Number of Shares Held in Plan at 27 April 1997
J A Dalgety	5,502	8,819	14,321
G G Dickson	11,616	11,549	23,165
J H W Fairweather	8,253	7,883	16,136
I G Hannah	12,227	12,076	24,303
B J Stewart	19,871	19,689	39,560
D M Wilkinson	10,089	9,976	20,065

[†]Includes re-invested dividends.

No shares have yet been allotted under the Long-Term Incentive Plan and the number of shares which may be allotted to Executive Directors at the first possible allotment in 1998 and in subsequent years will be dependent upon the level of achievement of the performance criteria explained earlier in the Committee's Report.

Save as disclosed above, no Director had an interest in any other shares or debentures of the Company or its subsidiaries and no change occurred in the interests of Directors between 27 April 1997 and 30 June 1997.

EXTERNAL APPOINTMENTS

The Company encourages its Executive Directors to become Non-Executive Directors of other leading companies as it believes that the exposure to other companies and the wider knowledge and experience gained benefit the Company. Subject to there being no conflict of interest and to the time spent being reasonable, Executive Directors are permitted with Board agreement to take up two such appointments. The fees for appointments may, at the discretion of the Board, be retained by the Director.

NON-EXECUTIVE CHAIRMAN

The Chairman does not participate in the Company's share schemes, Bonus Scheme, Long-Term Incentive Plan or Pension Scheme, but receives life and medical insurance and the provision of a car.

NON-EXECUTIVE DIRECTORS

Non-Executive Directors receive a fee only plus their expenses for attending Board and other Company meetings. A small additional fee is paid where a Non-Executive Director chairs a

Board Committee. They do not receive any other benefits from the Company and their fees are set by the Board (excluding Non-Executive Directors) within the aggregate limit agreed by shareholders.

Sir Alistair Grant
Chairman, Remuneration Committee
30 June 1997

CORPORATE GOVERNANCE

The Company's Audit Committee operated with 2 Non-Executive Directors until the additional appointment of I G McAllister to the Committee on 26 September 1996. Sir Alistair Grant ceased to be a member of the Audit Committee on his appointment as Chairman on 1 February 1997 and for the remainder of the financial year the Committee operated with 2 Non-Executive Directors. N C Bain was appointed a Non-Executive Director of the Company on 26 June 1997 and became a member of the Audit Committee. The Audit Committee therefore now operates with 3 Non-Executive Directors. Other than in respect of the periods referred to above when the Audit Committee operated with 2 Non-Executive Directors the Company has complied throughout the financial year with the Cadbury Committee's Code of Best Practice.

The Report of the Remuneration Committee, arising out of the Greenbury Report on Directors' remuneration and in accordance with Stock Exchange Listing requirements, is set out on pages 30 to 34 [of the original] following the Report of the Directors.

INTERNAL FINANCIAL CONTROL
The Board is responsible for the Group's system of internal financial control and has established a control structure to provide reasonable, but not absolute, assurance against material misstatement or loss. The key procedures within the control structure are:

- The Group operates a decentralised divisional structure. Each division and its constituent operating units have formal management structures with clear definition of responsibility and which operate within well defined policies.
- There is comprehensive financial reporting. Budgets covering profits, cashflows and capital expenditure are prepared annually and are approved by the Board. Actual results are reported monthly and are compared against budget and last year. Revised forecasts are prepared and reviewed quarterly.
- There is a structured process for appraising and authorising capital projects. This process includes clearly defined authorisation levels. Projects are subject to post invest-

ment appraisals.
- The Group has a Group Review and Audit Department which reports to the Audit Committee. The annual audit plan is approved by the Audit Committee and covers business performance and internal controls in all divisions and functions. Reports are produced for each audit undertaken.
- Treasury transactions are controlled by a Central Treasury Department. The Department reports monthly to a Treasury Committee under the chairmanship of the Group Finance Director and operates within a range of specified authorisation levels and policies approved by the Board. The department is subject to regular compliance audits by the Group Review and Audit Department and an annual review by the Group's external auditors.

The Board has reviewed the appropriateness and the effectiveness of the system of internal financial control in operation during the financial year. No material weaknesses have been identified.

GOING CONCERN
After making enquiries the Directors have a reasonable expectation that the Company has adequate resources to continue operating for the foreseeable future. For this reason, the going concern basis was adopted in preparing the accounts.

REPORT BY THE AUDITORS TO SCOTTISH & NEWCASTLE PLC ON CORPORATE GOVERNANCE MATTERS
In addition to our audit of the accounts we have reviewed the Directors' statements above concerning the Company's compliance with the paragraphs of the Cadbury Code of Best Practice specified for our review by the London Stock Exchange and their adoption of the going concern basis in preparing the accounts. The objective of our review is to draw attention to any non-compliance with Listing Rules 12.43(j) and 12.43(v).

We carried out our review in accordance with guidance issued by the Auditing Practices Board, and assessed whether the Directors' statements on going concern and internal financial control are consistent with the information of which we are aware from our audit. That guidance does not require us to perform the additional work necessary to, and we do not, express any opinion on the effectiveness of either the Company's system of internal financial control or its corporate governance procedures nor on the ability of the Company to continue in operational existence.

Opinion

With respect to the Directors' statements on internal financial control above other than the opinion on effectiveness, which is outside the scope of our report, and going concern above, in our opinion the Directors have provided the disclosures required by the Listing Rules referred to above and such statements are consistent with the information of which we are aware from our audit work on the accounts.

Based on enquiry of certain Directors and officers of the Company, and examination of relevant documents, in our opinion the Directors' statement above appropriately reflects the Company's compliance with the other paragraphs of the Code specified for our review by Listing Rule 12.43(j).

Ernst & Young, Chartered Accountants
Edinburgh 30 June 1997

Directors' Responsibilities and Auditors' Report

STATEMENT OF DIRECTORS' RESPONSIBILITIES

The Directors are required by law to prepare accounts which give a true and fair view of the state of affairs of the Company and of the Group as at the end of the financial year and of the profits for that year. They are also responsible for ensuring that proper and adequate accounting records have been kept and that appropriate procedures have been followed for safeguarding Group assets and preventing and detecting fraud and other irregularities. Appropriate accounting policies which follow generally accepted accounting practice have been applied consistently in the preparation of the accounts and reasonable and prudent judgements and estimates have been made. The accounts have been prepared on a going concern basis.

REPORT OF THE AUDITORS

To the members of Scottish & Newcastle plc

We have audited the financial statements on pages 38 to 57 [of the original] which have been prepared under the historical cost convention as modified by the revaluation of certain fixed assets and on the basis of the accounting policies set out on pages 42 to 43. We have also examined the amounts disclosed relating to the emoluments, share options and long-term incentive plan interests of the Directors, which form part of the report to shareholders by the Remuneration Committee on pages 30 to 34.

Respective responsibilities of directors and auditors

As described above the Company's Directors are responsible for the preparation of the accounts. It is our responsibility to form an independent opinion, based on our audit, on those accounts and to report our opinion to you.

Basis of opinion

We conducted our audit in accordance with Auditing Standards issued by the Auditing Practices Board. An audit includes examination, on a test basis, of evidence relevant to the amounts and disclosures in the accounts. It also includes an assessment of the significant estimates and judgements made by the Directors in the preparation of the accounts, and of whether the accounting policies are appropriate to the Group's circumstances, consistently applied and adequately disclosed.

We planned and performed our audit so as to obtain all the information and explanations which we considered necessary in order to provide us with sufficient evidence to give reasonable assurance that the accounts are free from material misstatement, whether caused by fraud or other irregularity or error. In forming our opinion we also evaluated the overall adequacy of the presentation of information in the accounts.

Opinion

In our opinion the accounts give a true and fair view of the state of affairs of the Company and of the Group as at 27 April 1997 and of the profit of the Group for the 52 weeks then ended and have been properly prepared in accordance with the Companies Act 1985.

Ernst & Young, Chartered Accountants
Registered Auditor
Edinburgh 30 June 1997

GROUP PROFIT AND LOSS ACCOUNT
52 Weeks Ended 27 April 1997

	Notes	1997 £m	1996 £m
Turnover	2	**3,349·2**	2,968·9
Net operating costs	4	**(2,924·1)**	(2,604·5)
Operating profit	2	**425·1**	364·4
Loss on disposal of fixed assets	3	**(2·1)**	(0·5)
Reorganisation costs	3	**–**	(150·8)
Profit on ordinary activities before interest		**423·0**	213·1
Interest payable	7	**(51·0)**	(56·2)
Profit on ordinary activities before taxation		**372·0**	156·9
Taxation on profit on ordinary activities	8	**(85·8)**	(47·3)
Profit on ordinary activities after taxation	9	**286·2**	109·6
Preference dividends on non-equity shares		**(0·8)**	(1·0)
Profit attributable to ordinary shareholders		**285·4**	108·6
Ordinary dividends on equity shares	10	**(131·3)**	(119·2)
Profit/(loss) retained		**154·1**	(10·6)

	Notes	Pence	Pence
Basic earnings per ordinary share	11	**46·5**	18·5
Dilution effect of options and convertible cumulative preference shares		**(0·7)**	(0·2)
Effect of loss on disposal of fixed assets		**–**	0·1
Effect of reorganisation costs		**–**	20·6
Fully diluted earnings per ordinary share excluding exceptional items		**45·8**	39·0

GROUP AND COMPANY BALANCE SHEETS

At 27 April 1997

	Notes	GROUP 1997 £m	1996 £m	COMPANY 1997 £m	1996 £m
Fixed assets					
Tangible assets	12	**2,966·9**	2,901·9	**1,519·5**	1,412·4
Investments	13	**226·0**	239·2	**1,196·3**	1,216·5
		3,192·9	3,141·1	**2,715·8**	2,628·9
Current assets					
Stocks	14	**149·6**	158·9	**132·6**	141·2
Debtors	15	**450·8**	469·2	**906·1**	1,028·6
Cash and short-term deposits	16	**73·0**	104·0	**25·6**	56·7
		673·4	732·1	**1,064·3**	1,226·5
Creditors Amounts falling due within one year	17	**1,166·5**	1,332·8	**1,513·8**	1,623·8
Net current liabilities		**(493·1)**	(600·7)	**(449·5)**	(397·3)
Total assets less current liabilities		**2,699·8**	2,540·4	**2,266·3**	2,231·6
Less:					
Creditors Amounts falling due after more than one year	18	**409·2**	338·1	**298·5**	213·7
Provisions for liabilities and charges	20	**82·9**	142·8	**82·9**	142·8
		2,207·7	2,059·5	**1,884·9**	1,875·1
Capital and reserves					
Equity share capital	21	**183·6**	180·5	**183·6**	180·5
Non-equity share capital	21	**12·4**	15·0	**12·4**	15·0
Called up share capital		**196·0**	195·5	**196·0**	195·5
Contingent equity share capital	21	**–**	21·1	**–**	21·1
Equity reserves					
Share premium account	22	**831·3**	818·3	**831·3**	818·3
Revaluation reserve	23	**312·8**	218·9	**189·3**	146·8
Other reserves	24	**(433·3)**	(352·1)	**(48·3)**	(45·5)
Profit and loss account	25	**1,300·9**	1,157·8	**716·6**	738·9
		2,207·7	2,059·5	**1,884·9**	1,875·1

The financial statements on pages 38 to 57 [of the original] were approved by the Board on 30 June 1997 and signed on its behalf by:

Sir Alistair Grant Chairman
D M Wilkinson Finance Director

GROUP CASH FLOW STATEMENT

52 Weeks Ended 27 April 1997

	Notes	1997 £m	1997 £m	1996 £m	1996 £m
Net cash inflow from operating activities	30		475·0		451·1
Returns on investments and servicing of finance					
Interest received		5·8		5·0	
Interest paid		(52·0)		(63·9)	
Preference dividends paid		(0·8)		(0·7)	
Net cash outflow for returns on investments and servicing of finance			(47·0)		(59·6)
Taxation			(52·2)		(50·7)
Capital expenditure and financial investment					
Purchase of tangible fixed assets		(270·1)		(230·0)	
Purchase of investments		(42·0)		(63·8)	
Sale of tangible fixed assets		35·2		38·2	
Realisation of investments		59·5		67·8	
Net cash outflow for capital expenditure and financial investment			(217·4)		(187·8)
Acquisitions and disposals					
Purchase of business		(20·2)		(429·8)	
Net cash acquired with business		–		4·1	
Purchase of investment in associated undertaking		–		(0·4)	
Net cash outflow for acquisitions and disposals			(20·2)		(426·1)
Equity dividends paid			(123·3)		(104·4)
Net cash inflow/(outflow) before use of liquid resources and financing			14·9		(377·5)
Management of liquid resources					
Movement in short term deposits with banks			1·0		49·9
Financing					
Issues of ordinary share capital		9·8		362·4	
Proceeds of loan capital		194·0		221·1	
Repayment of loan capital		(185·0)		(186·3)	
Net cash inflow from financing			18·8		397·2
Increase in cash in the period	31		34·7		69·6

Liquid resources comprise term deposits of less than one year.

STATEMENT OF TOTAL RECOGNISED GAINS AND LOSSES
52 Weeks Ended 27 April 1997

	1997 £m	1996 £m
Profit attributable to ordinary shareholders	285·4	108·6
Revaluations	109·1	(19·0)
Exchange adjustments	(107·0)	(18·9)
Total recognised gains and losses for financial year	287·5	70·7

NOTE ON HISTORICAL COST PROFITS AND LOSSES
52 Weeks Ended 27 April 1997

	1997 £m	1996 £m
Reported profit on ordinary activities before taxation	372·0	156·9
Realisation of property revaluation deficits of previous years	(2·2)	(9·2)
Historical cost profit on ordinary activities before taxation	369·8	147·7
Historical cost profit/(loss) for the year retained after taxation and dividends	151·9	(19·8)

RECONCILIATION OF MOVEMENTS IN SHAREHOLDERS' FUNDS
52 Weeks Ended 27 April 1997

	1997 £m	1996 £m
Profit attributable to ordinary shareholders	285·4	108·6
Ordinary dividends	(131·3)	(119·2)
Other recognised gains and losses relating to the year (net)	2·1	(37·9)
New share capital issued	13·5	362·4
Contingent share capital	(21·1)	21·1
Contribution to employee share trust	(3·7)	–
Goodwill on acquisitions	0·9	(114·8)
Goodwill on disposals	2·4	–
Net additions to shareholders' funds	148·2	220·2
Shareholders' funds at 28 April 1996	2,059·5	1,839·3
Shareholders' funds at 27 April 1997	2,207·7	2,059·5

NOTES TO THE ACCOUNTS

1 ACCOUNTING POLICIES

(a) Basis of Preparation

The accounts are prepared under the historical cost convention except that certain properties are included at valuation.

Net surpluses arising from professional valuations which are undertaken on a regular basis are taken direct to revaluation reserve. The accounts are prepared in accordance with applicable accounting standards.

(b) Basis of Consolidation

(i) The Group accounts consolidate those of the Company and its subsidiary undertakings for the period of 52 weeks (53 weeks when necessary) ending on the Sunday nearest 30 April.

(ii) On the acquisition of subsidiary undertakings or businesses, fair values are attributed to the underlying net tangible assets acquired. Goodwill, being any excess of the consideration over the fair values, is taken to reserves and, where appropriate, relief under S.131 of the Companies Act 1985 is taken in respect of shares issued in consideration for the acquisition of subsidiary undertakings. The profit or loss on the disposal of a business is stated after taking account of any purchased goodwill previously written off through reserves. Results of subsidiary undertakings acquired during the year are included from the dates of acquisition.

(iii) Undertakings, other than subsidiary undertakings, in which the Group has an investment representing not less than 20 per cent of the voting rights and over which it exerts significant influence are treated as associated undertakings. The Group accounts include the appropriate share of the results and reserves of these undertakings.

(iv) No profit and loss account is presented for Scottish & Newcastle plc as provided by S.230 of the Companies Act 1985.

(c) Depreciation

(i) Freehold land is not depreciated.

(ii) Industrial freehold properties are depreciated over their estimated useful lives of 40 to 50 years. Freehold licensed, non-industrial and leisure properties are not depreciated, it being Group policy to maintain them to such standard that the estimated residual values, based on prices prevailing at the time of acquisition or subsequent valuation, are at least equal to their book values.

Any permanent diminution in the value of such properties is charged to the profit and loss account as appropriate.

(iii) Buildings held on lease are depreciated over the unexpired term only when such term is 30 years or less in the case of leisure properties and 50 years or less in the case of other properties.

(iv) Other tangible assets are written off over their estimated useful lives as follows:

Fittings:
Licensed and related properties – 5 to 15 years
Leisure – 7 to 15 years

Vehicles, plant and equipment:
Malting and brewing plant – 20 to 30 years
Kegging, bottling and canning plant – 5 to 20 years
Commercial vehicles and private cars – 3 to 6 years
Containers and other equipment – 3 to 15 years
Leisure plant – 10 to 15 years

(d) Interest Capitalisation

The cost of the development of holiday villages includes interest on construction costs up to the time of opening.

(e) Stock Valuation

Stocks are stated at the lower of cost or net realisable value. The cost of raw materials and consumables is actual cost. The cost of finished goods and work in progress comprises materials, excise duty where appropriate, labour and attributable production over-heads.

(f) Deferred Taxation

Deferred taxation is provided on the liability method on all timing differences which are expected to reverse in the future, calculated at the rate at which it is estimated that tax will be payable. Advance corporation tax, which is expected to be recoverable in the future, is deducted from deferred tax or, if appropriate, included in debtors.

(g) Foreign Currencies

Revenues and costs of overseas companies are included in the consolidated profit and loss account at average rates of exchange during the year with the year end adjustment to closing rates being taken to reserves. Assets and liabilities in foreign currency are translated at year end rates of exchange.

Exchange differences on the retranslation of invest-ments in, and opening net assets of, foreign subsidiary undertakings are dealt with through reserves net of differences on related foreign currency borrowings and swaps. Other gains and losses arising from foreign currency transactions are included in the consolidated profit and loss account.

(h) Retirement Benefits

The expected cost of pensions in respect of defined benefit pension schemes is charged to the profit and loss account so as to spread the cost of pensions over the expected remaining service lives of employees in the scheme.

(i) Leases

Operating lease rentals are charged to the profit and loss account on a straight line basis over the term of the lease.

(j) Turnover

Turnover is sales, including recovery of duty where appropriate, rents receivable and other trading income of the Group, after eliminating intra-Group transactions and excluding VAT and property disposals.

2 SEGMENTAL ANALYSIS

	1997			1996		
	Turnover £m	Operating Profit £m	Net Operating Assets £m	Turnover £m	Operating Profit £m	Net Operating Assets £m
Class of business						
Retail	778·9	171·6	1,289·4	744·2	157·4	1,114·6
Beer	2,167·6	177·0	751·1	1,798·1	121·4	658·0
Leisure	402·7	76·5	1,008·6	426·6	85·6	1,154·9
	3,349·2	425·1	3,049·1	2,968·9	364·4	2,927·5

	1997			1996		
	Turnover £m	Operating Profit £m	Net Operating Assets £m	Turnover £m	Operating Profit £m	Net Operating Assets £m
Geographical area of operation						
UK	3,054·2	376·2	2,400·2	2,652·2	306·3	2,096·4
Rest of Europe	295·0	48·9	648·9	316·7	58·1	831·1
	3,349·2	425·1	3,049·1	2,968·9	364·4	2,927·5

The analysis of turnover by destination is not materially different from that presented above. Beer turnover is after eliminating UK inter segment sales of £163·2m (1996 – £148·0m).

	1997 £m	1996 £m
Net operating assets comprise:		
Net assets	2,207·7	2,059·5
Adjusted for: net debt	688·1	752·3
dividends	87·5	79·5
taxation	65·8	36·2
Net operating assets	3,049·1	2,927·5

3 EXCEPTIONAL ITEMS

During the year there was a loss on disposal of fixed assets of £2·1m (1996 – £0·5m). Taxation on the loss was a credit of £2·1m (1996 – £nil).

The reorganisation costs in 1996 of £150·8m related to the Beer Division. Tax relief on the reorganisation costs was £25·2m.

4 NET OPERATING COSTS

	1997 £m	1996 £m
Change in stocks of finished goods and work in progress	7·8	(7·0)
Own work capitalised	(6·0)	(5·9)
Raw materials and consumables	911·8	803·4
Custom and excise duties	758·0	604·0
Employee costs (note 5)	535·7	511·4
Depreciation	123·7	112·6
Operating lease rentals – plant and machinery	8·7	9·9
– land and buildings	35·1	36·0
Income from investments	(8·8)	(8·9)
Share of profit of associated undertakings	(7·4)	(2·7)
Other operating charges	565·5	551·7
	2,924·1	2,604·5

The auditors' remuneration was £0·6m (1996 – £0·9m) for audit services and £0·2m (1996 – £0·2m) for non-audit services.

5 EMPLOYEE COSTS AND NUMBERS

(i) **Employee costs**	1997 £m	1996 £m
Wages and salaries	450·9	428·7
Social security costs	46·4	46·6
Other pension costs	30·9	30·0
Employee profit sharing scheme	7·5	6·1
	535·7	511·4

(ii) **Number of employees**	1997	1996
The average numbers of employees during the year were:		
Retail	26,610	27,747
Beer	7,865	9,198
Leisure	10,534	10,926
Group central functions	267	250
	45,276	48,121

(iii) Pension commitment

The Group funds a number of pension schemes which are administered through independent trusts. The total pension costs for the Group were £30·9m (1996 – £30·0m) and for the Company £28·4m (1996 – £27·2m).

The main Company schemes are defined benefit schemes and pension costs relating to these schemes are assessed in accordance with the advice of qualified actuaries using the projected unit method. Apart from the Courage schemes, the latest actuarial valuations were made at 1 November 1994. The valuations assumed a long-term interest rate yield of 9%, a growth in dividend income of 4·5% per annum, earnings growth of 6·5% per annum and increases in pensions of 4% per annum. *At 1 November 1994 the market value of the assets of the main Company schemes was £515·5m and the actuarial value of the assets was sufficient to cover 112% of the benefits that had accrued to Members. The surplus is being spread over the expected remaining service lives (13 years) of employees in the schemes.*

The Courage pension schemes were valued on acquisition in 1995 by qualified actuaries using the projected unit method and the actuarial assumptions used in the Scottish & Newcastle plc schemes valuations at 1 November 1994. The market value of the assets of the schemes was £402·6m and the actuarial value of the assets was only sufficient to cover 84% of the benefits that had accrued to Members. The Company is making special contributions to the Courage schemes in recognition of the funding position.

6 DIRECTORS' REMUNERATION

Information concerning directors' emoluments, shareholdings and options is shown in the Report of the Remuneration Committee on pages 30 to 34 [of the original].

7 INTEREST PAYABLE

	1997 £m	1996 £m
Bank loans and overdrafts	50·7	53·7
Other	5·0	8·3
	55·7	62·0
Deposits and other interest receivable	(4·7)	(4·5)
Capitalised	–	(1·3)
	51·0	56·2

8 TAXATION ON PROFIT ON ORDINARY ACTIVITIES

	1997 £m	1996 £m
Based on profit for the year		
Corporation tax at 33%	77·3	40·0
Deferred taxation	2·8	(2·6)
Overseas taxation	4·2	9·5
Taxation on the share of profit in associated undertakings	1·5	0·4
	85·8	47·3

The effective rate of taxation has been reduced by £20·2m (1996 – £15·8m) as a result of capital allowances exceeding depreciation, and by £13·2m (1996 – £9·4m) in respect of adjustments relating to prior years. The 1996 effective rate of taxation was affected by the reorganisation provision (note 3).

9 PROFIT ON ORDINARY ACTIVITIES AFTER TAXATION

	1997 £m	1996 £m
Parent Company	112·3	(19·5)
Subsidiary Undertakings	169·5	126·8
Associated Undertakings	4·4	2·3
	286·2	109·6

10 ORDINARY DIVIDENDS ON EQUITY SHARES

	1997 £m	1996 £m
Interim 7·21p per share (1996 – 6·55p)	44·2	40·1
Proposed final 14·17p per share (1996 – 12·88p)	87·1	79·1
	131·3	119·2

11 EARNINGS PER SHARE

Basic earnings per share have been calculated on the average number of ordinary shares in issue during the year, namely 614·1 million (1996 – 585·6 million) and earnings of £285·4m (1996 – £108·6m).

Fully diluted earnings per share excluding exceptional items have also been calculated since, in the opinion of the Directors, this is a more representative indicator of the trading performance of the Group. Fully diluted earnings per share excluding exceptional items allows for the full exercise of all outstanding options and the conversion of convertible cumulative preference shares and is based on 629·4 million shares (1996 – 608·8 million) and adjusted earnings of £288·5m (1996 – £237·5m).

12 TANGIBLE ASSETS

	Licensed and Related Properties £m	Breweries, Warehouses and Other Properties £m	Leisure Properties £m	Vehicles, Plant and Equipment £m	Total £m
GROUP					
Cost or valuation					
At 28 April 1996	1,404·1	302·0	1,282·1	910·6	3,898·8
Transfers	(7·5)	6·1	–	1·4	–
Additions	109·9	6·7	43·7	106·4	266·7
Disposals	(33·1)	(27·2)	(20·3)	(115·2)	(195·8)
Revaluation	125·8	(1·0)	(19·2)	–	105·6
Exchange adjustments	–	(0·3)	(159·9)	(19·9)	(180·1)
At 27 April 1997	1,599·2	286·3	1,126·4	883·3	3,895·2
Depreciation					
At 28 April 1996	265·9	73·1	123·2	534·7	996·9
Transfers	–	–	–	–	–
Provided during the year	32·0	4·6	18·8	68·3	123·7
Disposals	(17·7)	(25·9)	(6·3)	(111·2)	(161·1)
Exchange adjustments	–	–	(16·9)	(14·3)	(31·2)
At 27 April 1997	280·2	51·8	118·8	477·5	928·3
Net book value at 28 April 1996	1,138·2	228·9	1,158·9	375·9	2,901·9
Net book value at 27 April 1997	1,319·0	234·5	1,007·6	405·8	2,966·9
COMPANY					
Cost or valuation					
At 28 April 1996	631·1	298·5	355·5	778·5	2,063·6
Transfers	(7·5)	6·1	–	1·4	–
Additions	39·8	6·6	21·1	94·3	161·8
Transfers from/(to) subsidiary undertakings	8·1	–	(2·0)	(0·3)	5·8
Disposals	(19·4)	(27·2)	(1·0)	(108·5)	(156·1)
Revaluation	19·2	(1·0)	19·8	–	38·0
At 27 April 1997	671·3	283·0	393·4	765·4	2,113·1
Depreciation					
At 28 April 1996	99·1	72·6	33·9	445·6	651·2
Transfers	–	–	–	–	–
Provided during the year	14·3	4·5	6·4	57·6	82·8
Transfers from/(to) subsidiary undertakings	1·4	–	(0·8)	(0·1)	0·5
Disposals	(8·6)	(25·9)	(0·3)	(106·1)	(140·9)
At 27 April 1997	106·2	51·2	39·2	397·0	593·6
Net book value at 28 April 1996	532·0	225·9	321·6	332·9	1,412·4
Net book value at 27 April 1997	565·1	231·8	354·2	368·4	1,519·5

	GROUP			COMPANY		
	Licensed and Related Properties £m	Breweries, Warehouses and Other Properties £m	Leisure Properties £m	Licensed and Related Properties £m	Breweries, Warehouses and Other Properties £m	Leisure Properties £m
The net book value of properties comprises:						
Freehold	1,138·1	225·0	801·7	512·1	222·5	265·8
Leasehold over 50 years	100·9	4·7	75·3	37·8	4·7	75·3
Leasehold under 50 years	80·0	4·8	130·6	15·2	4·6	13·1
	1,319·0	234·5	1,007·6	565·1	231·8	354·2
For those properties included at cost or valuation, the equivalent historical cost figures at 27 April 1997 are:						
Historical cost	1,346·8	285·4	1,070·4	533·6	282·1	342·7
Depreciation based on cost	280·2	51·8	118·8	106·2	51·2	39·2
Net historical cost value	1,066·6	233·6	951·6	427·4	230·9	303·5

	GROUP £m	COMPANY £m
Cost or valuation of properties comprises:		
Valuation at May 1993	15·6	9·2
Valuation at April 1997	2,176·6	886·8
At cost	368·9	255·1
	2,561·1	1,151·1

The Group's principal leisure, licensed and non-industrial properties have been valued at 27 April 1997 by a panel of external chartered surveyors. The basis of valuation was open market value for existing use and was last carried out in 1993. The valuation disclosed a total net surplus of £105·6m. A total of £107·6m has been added to revaluation reserve, while £2·0m, representing permanent diminutions in value below historic cost, has been charged against profits. Industrial properties, including breweries and warehouses, are included at depreciated historic cost due to their specialised nature.

13 INVESTMENTS

	Shares in Subsidiary Undertakings £m	Associated Undertakings £m	Other Investments £m	Trade Loans £m	Total £m
GROUP					
At 28 April 1996		23·2	18·8	197·2	239·2
Additions		–	1·1	40·9	42·0
Disposals, repayments and provisions		–	(1·0)	(60·1)	(61·1)
Share of revaluation surplus in the period		1·5	–	–	1·5
Share of retained profit in the period		4·4	–	–	4·4
At 27 April 1997		29·1	18·9	178·0	226·0
COMPANY					
At 28 April 1996	981·6	18·9	18·8	197·2	1,216·5
Additions	–	–	1·1	40·9	42·0
Disposals, repayments and provisions	(1·1)	–	(1·0)	(60·1)	(62·2)
At 27 April 1997	980·5	18·9	18·9	178·0	1,196·3

Other investments in both the Group and the Company include £11·4m (1996 – £12·2m) in respect of 2·8 million ordinary shares of 20p each in Scottish & Newcastle plc. These shares are held by the Scottish & Newcastle Employee Share Trust (note 21).

Trade loans in both the Group and the Company are net of provisions of £23·1m (1996 – £35·0m). During the year £1·6m (1996 – £6·2m) was provided for through the profit and loss account and £13·5m (1996 – £4·6m) was written off against provisions.

Scottish & Newcastle plc, the principal company, is incorporated in Great Britain and registered in Scotland. The subsidiary undertakings contributing significantly to the results and assets of the Group are as follows:

	Business	Country of Incorporation	Country of Operation
Center Parcs N.V.	Holiday Centres	Netherlands	Netherlands, Belgium, France, Germany and Great Britain
Cleveland Place Holdings PLC	Public Houses	Registered in England	Great Britain
The Chef & Brewer Group Limited	Public Houses	Registered in England	Great Britain
Huggins & Company Limited	Public Houses	Registered in England	Great Britain

The above companies are wholly owned and Cleveland Place Holdings PLC is held directly by Scottish & Newcastle plc.

The principal associated undertaking is a 50% holding of the equity shares in the Public House Company Limited, the parent company of a property investment group which operates in the UK.

14 STOCKS

	GROUP		COMPANY	
	1997 £m	1996 £m	1997 £m	1996 £m
Raw materials and consumables	53·4	54·5	51·6	52·1
Work in progress	6·5	6·6	6·2	6·2
Finished goods and goods for resale	89·7	97·8	74·8	82·9
	149·6	158·9	132·6	141·2

15 DEBTORS

	GROUP		COMPANY	
	1997 £m	1996 £m	1997 £m	1996 £m
Trade debtors	227·7	237·1	212·7	224·6
Other debtors	37·1	44·4	26·3	33·6
Prepayments	136·3	130·4	110·3	109·2
Amounts owing by associated undertakings	9·3	18·0	9·3	18·0
Amounts owing by subsidiary undertakings	–	–	509·7	564·2
Advance corporation tax	21·8	19·8	21·8	19·8
Deferred tax	18·6	19·5	16·0	59·2
	450·8	469·2	906·1	1,028·6

Other debtors include £6·7m (1996 – £7·8m) and prepayments £3·7m (1996 – £2·0m) due after more than one year. The advance corporation tax and deferred tax are all recoverable after more than one year.

16 CASH AND SHORT TERM DEPOSITS

	GROUP		COMPANY	
	1997 £m	1996 £m	1997 £m	1996 £m
Cash	55·7	82·1	25·6	56·2
Short term deposits	17·3	21·9	–	0·5
	73·0	104·0	25·6	56·7

17 CREDITORS: AMOUNTS FALLING DUE WITHIN ONE YEAR

	GROUP		COMPANY	
	1997	1996	1997	1996
	£m	£m	£m	£m
Loan Capital (note 19)	29·3	104·4	16·2	96·9
Bank overdrafts	331·0	424·5	428·0	521·9
Trade creditors	169·4	184·4	138·5	155·1
Current taxation	105·8	75·0	59·4	27·5
Other taxes and social security costs	137·3	139·7	106·9	112·1
Dividends	87·5	79·5	87·5	79·5
Other creditors	128·0	137·4	89·1	93·5
Accruals and deferred income	178·2	184·9	114·7	133·9
Amounts owing to associated undertakings	–	3·0	–	3·0
Amounts owing to subsidiary undertakings	–	–	473·5	400·4
	1,166·5	1,332·8	1,513·8	1,623·8

Bank overdrafts are unsecured.

18 CREDITORS: AMOUNTS FALLING DUE AFTER MORE THAN ONE YEAR

	GROUP		COMPANY	
	1997	1996	1997	1996
	£m	£m	£m	£m
Loan Capital (note 19)	400·8	327·4	295·0	209·0
Corporation tax	0·4	0·5	–	–
Other creditors	4·5	5·6	–	0·1
Accruals and deferred income	3·5	4·6	3·5	4·6
	409·2	338·1	298·5	213·7

19 LOAN CAPITAL

	GROUP		COMPANY	
	1997	1996	1997	1996
	£m	£m	£m	£m
Not wholly repayable within five years				
Repayable by instalments	15·3	33·4	8·9	12·6
Repayable otherwise than by instalments	82·3	119·3	50·7	49·5
Wholly repayable within five years	332·5	279·1	251·6	243·8
	430·1	431·8	311·2	305·9
Instalments not due within five years	5·2	10·0	2·1	4·2
Amounts due are repayable as follows:				
Bank loans				
More than five years	24·9	25·0	21·8	19·2
Between two and five years	298·6	114·3	239·3	75·7
Between one and two years	13·3	76·4	1·4	71·7
Less than one year (note 17)	28·8	103·4	16·1	96·7
	365·6	319·1	278·6	263·3

	GROUP		COMPANY	
	1997	1996	1997	1996
	£m	£m	£m	£m
Other loans				
More than five years	60·3	99·5	31·0	34·5
Between two and five years	3·3	4·9	1·5	1·5
Between one and two years	0·4	7·3	–	6·4
Less than one year (note 17)	0·5	1·0	0·1	0·2
	64·5	112·7	32·6	42·6
Loan capital – more than one year (note 18)	400·8	327·4	295·0	209·0
Other loans comprise				
9·75% unsecured bonds 2006	15·1	15·1	15·1	15·1
6·9% private placements 2004	15·9	19·4	15·9	19·4
7·9% redeemable debenture stock 2008	28·2	66·5	–	–
Others	5·3	11·7	1·6	8·1
	64·5	112·7	32·6	42·6

Bank loans

Currency bank borrowings are £31·5m and £28·7m are repayable by instalments, with final instalments due between 1997 and 2003. The remaining £2·8m are repayable by lump sum in 2000. Interest rates ranged between 2·9% and 11·5%.

Sterling bank borrowings are £334·1m and £42·2m are repayable by instalments, with final instalments due between 1997 and 2001. The remaining £291·9m are repayable by lump sum between 1997 and 2004. Interest rates, after taking account of interest rate swaps, ranged between 5·9% and 8·5%.

Other loans

The 7·9% redeemable debenture stock 2008 was fair valued at acquisition on 1 November 1993. The nominal value is £21·5m and the nominal rate of interest is 12·125%.

Loan capital

Borrowings of £51·6m are secured on fixed and other assets.

20 PROVISIONS FOR LIABILITIES AND CHARGES

	Acquisition £m	Reorganisation £m	Pensions £m	Deferred Tax £m	Total £m
GROUP					
At 28 April 1996	10·6	71·3	60·9	–	142·8
Transfer from debtors	–	–	–	(19·5)	(19·5)
Profit and loss account	–	–	–	2·8	2·8
Utilised during year	(8·1)	(41·3)	(10·5)	–	(59·9)
Exchange adjustment	–	–	–	(1·9)	(1·9)
Transfer to debtors	–	–	–	18·6	18·6
At 27 April 1997	2·5	30·0	50·4	–	82·9
COMPANY					
At 28 April 1996	10·6	71·3	60·9	–	142·8
Transfer from debtors	–	–	–	(59·2)	(59·2)
Profit and loss account	–	–	–	43·2	43·2
Utilised during year	(8·1)	(41·3)	(10·5)	–	(59·9)
Transfer to debtors	–	–	–	16·0	16·0
At 27 April 1997	2·5	30·0	50·4	–	82·9

Deferred Taxation

	GROUP			COMPANY		
	Capital Allowances £m	Other Timing Differences £m	Total £m	Capital Allowances £m	Other Timing Differences £m	Total £m
At 28 April 1996	0·1	(19·6)	(19·5)	–	(59·2)	(59·2)
At 27 April 1997	0·1	(18·7)	(18·6)	–	(16·0)	(16·0)
Full provision would have been At 28 April 1996	87·5	(33·4)	54·1	82·5	(75·3)	7·2
At 27 April 1997	136·6	(37·4)	99·2	94·4	(34·5)	59·9

The full provision for other timing differences, in both the Group and the Company, includes an advance corporation tax debtor of £21·8m (1996 – £19·8m). The potential tax liabilities which might arise in the event of the disposal of revalued properties, or for capital gains deferred, are not quantified as the Directors do not consider them to constitute timing differences after taking account of expected reinvestment reliefs.

21 SHARE CAPITAL

	Authorised		Issued and fully paid	
	1997 £m	1996 £m	1997 £m	1996 £m
Equity share capital				
Ordinary shares of 20p each	141·5	141·2	123·5	122·7
Special deferred shares of 20p each	60·1	57·8	60·1	57·8
	201·6	199·0	183·6	180·5
Non Equity share capital				
Cumulative preference shares of £1 each				
4·6% + tax credit	3·9	3·9	3·9	3·9
6·425% + tax credit	7·0	7·0	7·0	7·0
7% convertible	1·5	4·1	1·5	4·1
	12·4	15·0	12·4	15·0

Cumulative Preference Shares

These shares confer on the holders priority in the payment of dividends and repayment of capital. The dividends are at the fixed rates indicated in the table. On a winding up the holders are entitled to a repayment of the amount paid up on their shares. The holders of preference shares are not normally entitled to attend or vote at general meetings of the Company unless the preference dividends are six months in arrears or if a resolution is to be proposed which affects the rights of the preference shares. The convertible preference shares are convertible in the years 1997 to 1999 on the basis of 10 ordinary shares for every £22 in nominal amount of preference shares.

During the year

2·6 million 7% £1 convertible preference shares were converted into 1·1 million ordinary shares and 11·6 million special deferred shares. The special deferred shares are balancing shares of nil rights necessitated by the conversion of shares of a higher nominal value into a lower nominal value.

2·7 million ordinary shares of £0·5m nominal value were issued at a consideration of £13·5m pursuant to options exercised under the Employee Share Option Schemes. £3·7m of this consideration was provided by the Company through a contribution to the Employee Share Trust.

Employee Share Schemes

At 27 April 1997, options granted and outstanding under the Savings-Related Share Option Schemes amounted to 8·9 million ordinary shares. These options are exercisable at varying dates up to 28 August 2002, at prices ranging from 332p to 692p per share.

At 27 April 1997, options granted and outstanding under the Executive Share Option Schemes amounted to 3·7 million ordinary shares. These options are exercisable at varying dates up to 4 December 2006, at prices ranging from 301p to 666p per share.

he Scottish & Newcastle Employee Share Trust is used to acquire shares which will, at a later date, be allocated to employees through one of the employee benefit schemes. At 27 April 1997 the Trust held 2·8 million shares (1996 – 2·8 million), with a market value of £18·7m (1996 – £19·9m). The Trust has waived its rights to receive dividends.

At 27 April 1997 2·1 million ordinary shares were held for employees by the Trustees of the Employee Profit Sharing Scheme.

Contingent Share Capital

As part of the acquisition of the Courage business in 1995, Scottish & Newcastle plc agreed to pay to the Foster's Brewing Group in either 1999 or 2000 a sum equal to the increase in value of ten million of the Company's shares over 537p per share. Scottish & Newcastle plc had the option of settling this consideration either by the issue of ordinary shares or in cash. At 28 April 1996 an estimate of the consideration (£21·1m) was included in the balance sheet as contingent share capital. During the current financial year the Company's liability for the contingent consideration was assigned to a third party for a consideration of £20·2m. Consequently, contingent share capital has been reduced to nil and a goodwill adjustment of £0·9m has been made to reserves.

22 SHARE PREMIUM ACCOUNT

	GROUP £m	COMPANY £m
At 28 April 1996	818·3	818·3
Premium on shares issued – employee options	13·0	13·0
At 27 April 1997	831·3	831·3

23 REVALUATION RESERVE

	GROUP £m	COMPANY £m
At 28 April 1996	218·9	146·8
Revaluation	107·6	40·0
Revaluation arising in associated undertaking	1·5	–
Transferred to profit and loss account (note 25)	2·2	2·5
Exchange adjustments	(17·4)	–
At 27 April 1997	312·8	189·3

24 OTHER RESERVES

	GROUP £m	COMPANY £m
At 28 April 1996	(352·1)	(45·5)
Contribution to employee share trust	(3·7)	(3·7)
Goodwill on acquisition	0·9	0·9
Goodwill on disposals	2·4	–
Exchange adjustments – on assets	(121·0)	–
– on borrowings	40·2	–
At 27 April 1997	(433·3)	(48·3)

The cumulative amount of goodwill written off, net of goodwill on disposals, is £583·8m (1996 – £587·1m).

25 PROFIT AND LOSS ACCOUNT

	GROUP £m	COMPANY £m
At 28 April 1996	1,157·8	738·9
Profit/(loss) for year retained	154·1	(19·8)
Transferred from revaluation reserve (note 23)	(2·2)	(2·5)
Exchange adjustment	(8·8)	–
At 27 April 1997	1,300·9	716·6

26 CAPITAL COMMITMENTS

	GROUP		COMPANY	
	1997 £m	1996 £m	1997 £m	1996 £m
Expenditure committed	22·5	44·1	17·5	33·1

27 OPERATING LEASE RENTALS

	LAND & BUILDINGS		OTHER	
	1997 £m	1996 £m	1997 £m	1996 £m
Group annual commitments under non-cancellable operating leases are:				
Leases expiring				
within one year	0·6	0·3	2·3	2·2
within two to five years	2·2	2·7	3·2	2·9
in over five years	33·8	35·0	2·0	1·5
	36·6	38·0	7·5	6·6

28 CONTINGENT LIABILITIES

At 27 April 1997 there were contingent liabilities in respect of guarantees to third parties amounting to Group £20·1m (1996 – £20·4m) and Company £19·3m (1996 – £18·9m).

29 ASSOCIATED UNDERTAKINGS

Transactions with associated undertakings were:

	1997 £m	1996 £m
Sales to associated undertakings	118·4	89·3
Purchases from associated undertakings	21·0	22·0

30 NET CASH INFLOW FROM OPERATING ACTIVITIES

	1997 £m	1996 £m
Operating profit	425·1	364·4
Share of profit of associated undertakings	(7·4)	(2·7)
Dividends from associated undertakings	1·5	–
Depreciation	123·7	112·6
Provisions against investments	1·6	6·2
(Increase)/decrease in stocks	7·9	(11·5)
Decrease in debtors	12·5	37·3
Decrease in creditors	(30·0)	(15·1)
Net cash inflow from ordinary operating activities	534·9	491·2
Reorganisation costs	(41·3)	(19·9)
Utilisation of acquisition and pensions provisions	(18·6)	(20·2)
Net cash inflow from operating activities	475·0	451·1

The reorganisation costs of £41·3m relate to the £150·8m of Beer Division reorganisation costs charged as an exceptional item in 1996. The prior year reorganisation costs of £19·9m comprise £3·4m relating to the Retail Division and £16·5m relating to the Beer Division.

31 RECONCILIATION OF NET CASHFLOW TO MOVEMENT IN NET DEBT

	1997 £m	1996 £m
Increase in cash	34·7	69·6
Cash inflow from change in loan capital	(9·0)	(34·8)
Cash inflow from change in liquid resources	(1·0)	(49·9)
Change in net debt resulting from cashflows	24·7	(15·1)
Loans acquired with business	–	(14·6)
Exchange	39·5	3·9
(Increase)/decrease in net debt	64·2	(25·8)
Net debt at 28 April 1996	(752·3)	(726·5)
Net debt at 27 April 1997	(688·1)	(752·3)

32 ANALYSIS OF NET DEBT

	At 28 April 1996 £m	Cash flow £m	Exchange £m	At 27 April 1997 £m
Cash	82·1	(25·4)	(1·0)	55·7
Bank overdrafts	(424·5)	60·1	33·4	(331·0)
Net cash	(342·4)	34·7	32·4	(275·3)
Short term deposits	21·9	(1·0)	(3·6)	17·3
Loan capital	(431·8)	(9·0)	10·7	(430·1)
Net debt	(752·3)	24·7	39·5	(688·1)

	1997 £m	1996 £m	1995 £m	1994 £m	1993 £m
Assets employed					
Fixed assets	**3,192·9**	3,141·1	2,773·0	2,573·9	1,951·6
Net current liabilities	**(493·1)**	(600·7)	(535·3)	(486·4)	(198·5)
Loan capital (over one year)	**(400·8)**	(327·4)	(345·8)	(333·3)	(266·9)
Creditors (over one year) and provisions	**(91·3)**	(153·5)	(52·6)	(79·4)	(63·0)
	2,207·7	2,059·5	1,839·3	1,674·8	1,423·2
Financed by					
Share capital	**196·0**	216·6	179·7	179·3	157·7
Share premium and reserves	**2,011·7**	1,842·9	1,659·6	1,495·5	1,265·5
	2,207·7	2,059·5	1,839·3	1,674·8	1,423·2
Turnover	**3,349·2**	2,968·9	2,021·5	1,759·8	1,514·4
Operating profit	**425·1**	364·4	312·6	257·8	226·5
Profit/(loss) on disposal of fixed assets	**(2·1)**	(0·5)	(1·0)	1·6	(4·0)
Reorganisation costs	**–**	(150·8)	–	–	(13·9)
Profit on ordinary activities before interest	**423·0**	213·1	311·6	259·4	208·6
Interest payable	**(51·0)**	(56·2)	(47·6)	(37·6)	(26·1)
Profit before taxation	**372·0**	156·9	264·0	221·8	182·5
Taxation	**(85·8)**	(47·3)	(66·0)	(57·8)	(49·3)
Profit after taxation	**286·2**	109·6	198·0	164·0	133·2
Preference dividends on non-equity shares	**(0·8)**	(1·0)	(1·1)	(1·2)	(1·6)
Profit attributable to ordinary shareholders	**285·4**	108·6	196·9	162·8	131·6
Ordinary dividends on equity shares	**(131·3)**	(119·2)	(97·3)	(85·2)	(70·8)
Profit/(loss) retained	**154·1**	(10·6)	99·6	77·6	60·8
Basic earnings per 20p ordinary share – pence	**46·5**	18·5	36·4	33·7	29·8
Fully diluted earnings per 20p ordinary share, excluding exceptional items – pence	**45·8**	39·0	36·2	32·6	32·2
Dividends per 20p ordinary share – pence	**21·38**	19·43	17·96	16·79	15·98
Dividend cover excluding exceptional items – times	**2·1**	2·0	2·0	1·9	2·0

Prior year figures have been restated to reflect the bonus element incorporated in the 1993/94 and 1995/96 rights issues.

Scottish & Newcastle Personal Equity Plans and Low Cost Share Dealing Service

The Scottish & Newcastle Single Company and General PEPs are open to existing and prospective UK shareholders in Scottish & Newcastle.

A low cost share dealing service for ordinary shares in Scottish & Newcastle is available to ordinary shareholders through stockbrokers Hoare Govett.

If you would like further information on either the PEPs or Share Dealing service please write to, or telephone, the Company Secretary's Department at Abbey Brewery, 111 Holyrood Road, Edinburgh, EH8 8YS. Telephone 0131-556 2591, extension 2250.

Ordinary Shareholdings at 27 April 1997

	Shareholdings		Total shares held	
Shares of 20p each	Number	%	Number	%
Up to 2,500	36,111	84·66	26,274,789	4·26
2,501 to 10,000	4,539	10·64	20,314,700	3·29
10,001 to 50,000	1,064	2·49	24,172,586	3·91
50,001 to 200,000	511	1·20	53,503,770	8·67
200,001 to 500,000	230	0·54	72,658,097	11·77
500,001 to 1,000,000	89	0·21	63,935,116	10·35
Over 1,000,000	110	0·26	356,589,602	57·75
	42,654	100·00	617,448,660	100·00

Ordinary Shares

The closing prices of our shares during the course of the year were:

29 April 1996	691·0p
25 October 1996 (low)	629·5p
14 March 1997 (high)	700·0p
25 April 1997	672·0p

Capital Gains Tax Information

The sale of shares by a UK shareholder may give rise to a Capital Gains Tax liability. As the Finance Act 1988 charges only gains made since 31 March 1982, shareholders may find the following capital gains values helpful:

	At 31 March 1982	
Ordinary Shares	52·5p	164·4p*
4·6% Cumulative Preference Shares	37·5p	
6·425% Cumulative Preference Shares	54·5p	

*164·4p is the adjusted price for shareholders who subscribed for their full entitlement under the rights issues in October 1993 and May 1995.

Registered Office

Abbey Brewery, 111 Holyrood Road, Edinburgh EH8 8YS. Telephone 0131-556 2591.

Registrars

Bank of Scotland, Registrar Department, Apex House, 9 Haddington Place, Edinburgh EH7 4AL. Telephone 0131-243 5187.

Notice of Meeting

Notice to Ordinary Shareholders

Notice is hereby given that the Annual General Meeting of Scottish & Newcastle plc will be held at the Sheraton Grand Hotel, 1 Festival Square, Edinburgh, on Thursday 28 August 1997 at 11.30 am for the following purposes:

Resolution 1 To consider and adopt the Report of the Directors and the accounts for the 52 weeks to 27 April 1997

Resolution 2 To declare a dividend

Resolution 3 To re-elect G G Dickson as a Director

Resolution 4 To re-elect J H W Fairweather as a Director

Resolution 5 To re-elect I G Hannah as a Director

Resolution 6 To elect I G McAllister as a Director

Resolution 7 To elect N C Bain as a Director

Resolution 8 To re-appoint Ernst & Young as auditors and to authorise the Board to fix their remuneration.

As special business to consider and, if thought fit, pass the following Resolutions 9 to 11 as Special Resolutions.

Resolution 9 That Article 134 of the Company's Articles of Association be amended by adding the words "any member to whom a Summary Financial Statement is sent in accordance with the Statutes nor to" after the words "Provided that this Article shall not require a copy of these documents to be sent to" in Article 134.

Resolution 10 That the authority and power conferred on the Directors by paragraph 11 (C)(1) of Article 11 of the Company's Articles of Association in relation to the allotment of relevant securities up to a nominal amount, specified as the Section 80 Amount, be renewed for the period ending on the date of the next Annual General Meeting or on 30 September 1998, whichever is the earlier,and for such period, the Section 80 Amount shall be £17,000,000.

Resolution 11 That the authority and power conferred on the Directors by paragraph 11(C)(2) of Article 11 of the Company's Articles of Association in relation to the allotment of equity securities wholly for cash in connection with a rights issue and also up to a nominal amount specified as the Section 89 amount be renewed for the period ending on the date of the next Annual General Meeting or on 30 September 1998, whichever is the earlier, and for such period, the Section 89 amount shall be £6,000,000.

Abbey Brewery   By Order of the Board
Holyrood Road   M J Pearey
Edinburgh   Secretary
EH8 8YS
29 July 1997

The Annual Report & Accounts are sent to all shareholders, but only ordinary shareholders are entitled to attend and vote or be represented at the Annual General Meeting.

A member entitled to attend and vote may appoint one or more proxies to attend and, on a poll, vote on his behalf. A proxy need not be a member of the Company. To be effective, the enclosed form of proxy should be lodged at the office of the Company's Registrars not later than 48 hours before the time of the meeting.

To be entitled to attend and vote at the meeting and any adjournment thereof of not more than 48 hours (and for the purpose of the determination by the Company of the number of votes a member may cast) members must be entered on the Company's register of members no later than 11.30 am on Tuesday 26 August 1997 being 48 hours before the time fixed for the meeting. If the meeting shall be adjourned for more than 48 hours after the date of the original meeting, then to be so entitled to attend and vote members must be entered on the Company's register of members at the time which is 48 hours before the time of that adjourned meeting.

The following documents are available for inspection at the Registered Office of the Company during normal business hours and on the day of the meeting at the place of the meeting from 15 minutes prior to the meeting until its conclusion:

(i) The register of Directors' share interests kept pursuant to Section 325 of the Companies Act 1985.

(ii) Copies of all contracts of service under which Directors are employed by the Company or any of its subsidiaries.

Appendix 4: Solutions to the exercises

Chapter 2

1 The sources of authority are as follows:

- Code of best practice for the report of the remuneration committee;
- Companies Act for the balance sheet;
- Accounting standards (FRS 1) for the cash flow statement.

2 The S&N Five-year Record contains details, *inter alia*, of assets employed, turnover, operating profit, profit before and after taxation, together with information on dividends, for each of the past five years.

3 Shareholder information (see Appendix 3) gives details regarding S&N shares. The total of shareholdings at 27 April 1997 was 42,654. The closing price on 25 April 1997 was 672.0p. The closing price on 29 April 1996 was 691.0p.

4 The section *In the Community* (see Appendix 3) refers to S&N and the environment. The policy is 'determined at the highest level . . . an advisory committee is dedicated to reducing the impact of operations on the environment . . . each division has a director with specific responsibility for environmental matters'.

5 Certain headings are not common to both companies. This may be because the information is found elsewhere (e.g. the Bass chairman's statement is in the *Annual Review and Summary Financial Statement*). S&N does not contain information for US shareholders because, unlike Bass, its shares are not quoted on the New York Stock Exchange.

Chapter 3

1 You might expect to find a business review and future developments in the report of the directors. S&N, however, have chosen to cross-refer users from this report to pages 2 to 25 (original pages) of the annual report and the chairman's statement, the chief executive's review, and the financial review which are contained therein, together with the operational reports of the three divisions of the group.

2 The financial review and the report of the directors give the total ordinary dividend for the year as 21.38p, which according to the financial review is an increase of 10%.

3 The long-term incentive plan is described in the report of the remuneration committee. The performance of S&N is to be compared with all other companies in the FT-SE 100 share index.

4 The auditors' report carries the name of Ernst & Young. Resolution 8 for the 1997 AGM (see notice of meeting) is to reappoint Ernst & Young as auditors and to authorize the Board to fix their remuneration. The auditors present an unqualified report (i.e. they state that in their opinion the accounts show a true and fair view).

5 The directors of S&N state in the corporate governance section of the annual report that they have every expectation that the company will continue operating for the foreseeable future (i.e. in other words, S&N is a going concern).

Chapter 4

		£million
1 £3780.1 million	Fixed assets	2715.8
	Current assets	1064.3
		3780.1

		£million
2 £1658.6 million	Creditors: amounts falling due within one year	1166.5
	Creditors: amounts falling due after more than one year	409.2
	Provisions for liabilities and charges	82.9
	Total	1658.6

	£million
3 Fixed assets	2628.9
Net current liabilities	(397.3)
Total assets less current liabilities	2231.6

4 Fixed assets are assets intended for use on a continuing basis in a company's activities; they are not intended for resale. Current assets are assets which a company holds on a short-term basis. The main items found under the current assets heading are stocks, debtors and cash.

5 Assets £3780.1 million (see solution 1) – liabilities £1895.2 million (1513.8 + 298.5 + 82.9) = capital £1884.9 million.

Chapter 5

1 The most likely answer might simply be that none have been bought. However, when the company acquires other businesses it is possible that an intangible asset called *goodwill* will arise. This happens when the price paid (the 'consideration') for the shares of the company acquired exceeds the face value of the assets less liabilities in that company. Goodwill, being an asset, could then appear on the group balance sheet. However, we are informed in note 1(b) that where goodwill arises 'it is taken to reserves', meaning it is deducted, hence reducing the *reserves* figure.

2 Vehicles are part of the S&N fixed assets and are found under fixed assets in the balance sheet heading *tangible assets*. Note 12 gives the figures in respect of vehicles under the heading *vehicles, plant and equipment*. In a different context vehicles might be classed as a

current asset, for example in the case of a motor dealer, who would have acquired them with the intention of selling them and would hold them as part of stock.

3 Company: tangible assets

	cost or valuation £million	depreciation £million	net book value £million
At 28 April 1996	2063.6	651.2	1412.4
Additions/disposals during the year	49.5	(57.6)	107.1
At 27 April 1997	2113.1	593.6	1519.5

4 The difference between the investment figures is £970.3 million (£1196.3 million – £226.0 million)

From note 13, it can be seen that the items making up the difference are:

	£million
shares in subsidiary undertakings (company £980.5 million; group nil)	980.5
associated undertakings (company £18.9 million; group £29.1 million)	(10.2)
	970.3

The £980.5 million is the book value of the shares in the subsidiary undertakings, which appears in the balance sheet of the parent company but which is replaced in the group accounts by the actual assets and liabilities found in the subsidiaries' balance sheets.

The £10.2 million is the difference between the value of the investment in associated undertakings which appear in the balance sheet of the parent company and the group's share of the gains made since the acquisition of the associated undertakings. During the current year the gains consist of a share in the revaluation surplus, £1.5 million, and a share of profit of £4.4 million.

5 Short-term deposits are current assets and would be found under the heading *current assets* in the group balance sheet. They are shown in the balance sheet under the item *cash and short-term deposits*. The amount of short-term deposits, £17.3 million, is shown in note 16.

Chapter 6

1 An example is a government grant which has been received in respect of a fixed asset bought by the company. The grant might be received in year 1 but the benefit has to be spread over the life of the asset, which might extend over 1–5 years.

2 The amounts for the item *accruals and deferred income* are found under creditors. The amounts, which are given in notes 17 and 18, are:

	Group £million	Company £million
Creditors: amounts falling due within one year	178.2	114.7
Creditors: amounts falling due after more than one year	3.5	3.5

(Note: because the question did not specify group or company, in this case the information has been given for both.)

3

	£million	
Nominal value	0.5	In equity share capital within the total of £183.6 million*
Premium	13.0	In share premium account within the total of £831.3 million
	13.5	

*In the analysis in note 21, share capital, the nominal value (£0.5 million) of the new shares issued will be part of the total of ordinary shares of 20p each, £123.5 million.

4 It is shown under *capital and reserves* under the heading *profit and loss account* £1300.9 million. In note 25, it can be seen that the £154.1 million is added to the balance at 28 April 1996, £1157.8 million, to become part of the year end balance of £1300.9 million.

5 The underlying relationship in the balance sheet is: assets – liabilities = capital. Assets – liabilities must have increased by £154.1 million to match the increase in capital which results from the profit of £154.1 million.

Chapter 7

1 £3349.2 million.

2 Turnover is defined under accounting policies, note 1(j), as follows:
Turnover is sales, including recovery of duty where appropriate, rents receivable and other trading income of the Group, after eliminating intra-group transactions and excluding VAT and property disposals.

3 The accruals principle implies that all items of *revenues* and *expenses* are recognized in the profit and loss account when they are earned or incurred and not when money is received or paid.

An example is if goods are sold in a company's financial year ended 31 December 1997 but are not paid for until 1998; their sale is included in the turnover figure in the 1997 profit and loss account because the sale was made in that year. It is then necessary to match this sale with the cost of the goods (as part of the expenses figure).

In the case of S&N, as with all companies, the turnover and the operating costs are calculated on the accruals basis and the operating costs are matched with the turnover to which they relate.

4

	£million
The 1997 turnover is	3349.2
The 1996 turnover is	2968.9
The increase is	380.3

This represents an increase of $\frac{380.3}{2968.9} \times 100 = 12.81\%$

5

	£million
Dividends on non-equity (i.e. preference) shares	0.8
Dividends on ordinary shares	131.3
	132.1

6 Two analyses are given in note 2, *segmental analysis*.

		£million
(i) By class of business, i.e.	retail	744.2
	beer	1798.1
	leisure	426.6
		2968.9

		£million
(ii) By geographical area of operation, i.e.	UK	2652.2
	Rest of Europe	316.7
		2968.9

7 £177.0 million (shown in note 2, *segmental analysis*, in the column headed *Operating profit*).

8 £123.7 million (shown in note 4, *net operating costs*).

The depreciation charged in the 1997 profit and loss account, £123.7 million, is added to the accumulated figure for depreciation in the balance sheet. The details are set out in note 12, *tangible assets*, under *Group: Depreciation*.

9

	£million	
Interest payable (net)	51.0	(in group profit and loss account)
Less		
Income from investments	8.8	(in note 4, *net operating costs*)
	42.2	

10 Employee costs £535.7 million (in note 4, *net operating costs*).

Directors' remuneration £2.3 million (in report of the remuneration committee, under *total emoluments*).

Chapter 8

1 S&N, in common with all large UK companies, produces a cash flow statement in compliance with the requirements of the accounting standard FRS 1. The underlying reason is that a company produces a statement which focuses upon the impact of its activities on its cash position. It is of vital importance to any company that it is able to generate cash and to control its cash flow in such a way that it does not have short- or long-term liquidity problems.

2 Purchase of tangible fixed assets
Purchase of investments
Sale of tangible fixed assets
Realization of investments.

3 Interest paid £52.0 million. (This appears under the heading *Returns on investments and servicing of finance*.)

4

	£million
Tax paid 1997	52.2
Tax paid 1996	50.7
Increase	1.5

5 The figure in the 1997 group balance sheet for the item *cash and short-term deposits* is £73.0 million. As can be seen from note 16, this includes a figure for cash of £55.7 million. The £55.7 million is the cash held at the end of the financial year, i.e. 27 April 1997, whereas the amount of £34.7 million shown in the cash flow statement is the increase during the year.

6 The charge for depreciation is a means of spreading the cost (or valuation) of a fixed asset over its useful life and does not represent a cash flow from the business. Hence, to arrive at a cash flow which has been generated by the operating activities, the depreciation (which had originally been deducted in arriving at the operating profit) must be added back.

7 The figure in the profit and loss account represents the dividend that is taken (or is to be taken) from the current year's profits. However, during the year the dividends that have actually been paid, and therefore are a cash flow, are:

	£million
Final dividend for 1996 paid during 1997	79.1
Interim dividend for 1997 paid during 1997	44.2
	123.3

The details are set out in note 10, *ordinary dividends on equity shares*, where reference needs to be made to the columns for both 1996 and 1997.

8 The main factor contributing to the difference is the *cash outflow for the purchase of a business*, £429.8 million.

9 From the financial review (see Appendix 3), under the heading cash flow, we can see that capital expenditure per division for 1997 has been as follows:

	£million
Retail division	116
Beer division	91
Leisure division	63
	270

10

		£million
From shareholders		9.8
From borrowings	(194.0 − 185.0)	9.0
Net cash inflow from financing		18.8

Chapter 9

1 The aim is to inform users of the annual report and accounts of all the gains and losses which have been recorded during the year. Each of the figures on the statement will have been shown elsewhere but the statement brings them all together.

2

	£million	
Profit attributable to ordinary shareholders	285.4	(A)
Revaluations	109.1	(B)
Exchange adjustment	(107.0)	(C)
	287.5	

(A) In the group profit and loss account.

(B) In *revaluation reserve* in the group balance sheet.
Details of the movement during the year are shown in note 23, *revaluation reserve*, including:

Revaluation	107.6
Revaluation arising in associated undertakings	1.5
	109.1

APPENDIX 4: SOLUTIONS TO THE EXERCISES

(C) In *revaluation reserve* in group balance sheet.
Details are set out in note 23, *revaluation reserve*, and include:
exchange adjustment   (17.4)

In *other reserves* in group balance sheet.
Details are set out in note 24, *other reserves*, and include:
exchange adjustments – on assets   (121.0)
                    – on borrowings   40.2

In *profit and loss account* in group balance sheet.
Details are set out in note 25, *profit and loss account*
and include:
exchange adjustment   (8.8)
                                                  (107.0)

Note that the profit and loss account as an item in the balance sheet is simply part of the capital and reserves.

3 The main cause of the difference arises when assets are revalued. If a revaluation surplus is produced, depreciation will have to be provided on the higher value, i.e. more depreciation and, hence, less profit in the profit and loss account. To calculate what the profit would be under pure historical cost rules we would have to add back the extra depreciation charge. In the case of S&N the reverse is the case (for the year we are looking at) and the lower charge for depreciation is deducted.

4 The reason for the deduction is set out in note 21, *share capital*, under the heading *contingent share capital*. At 28 April 1996, S&N included £21.1 million under share capital. It subsequently transpired that an issue of share capital would no longer be required and, hence, the £21.1 million was deducted at 27 April 1997. The item *contingent share capital* is unusual but the note explains how it has been dealt with by S&N.

5 The other recognized gains and losses relating to the year are set out in the statement of total recognized gains and losses. The items are:

	£million
Revaluations	(19.0)
Exchange adjustments	(18.9)
	(37.9)

Chapter 10

1 Going concern principle, accruals principle, consistency principle, prudence principle.

2 From note 1(e), *stock valuation*:
Stocks are stated at the lower of cost or net realisable value. The cost of raw materials and consumables is actual cost. The cost of finished goods and work in progress comprises materials, excise duty where appropriate, labour and attributable production overheads.

From note 1(h), *retirement benefits*:
The expected cost of pensions in respect of defined benefit pension schemes is charged to the profit and loss account so as to spread the cost of pensions over the expected remaining service lives of employees in the scheme.

Other information in respect of retirement benefits:

- In the Report of the Remuneration Committee, under *Pension and Life Assurance*, scheme details for executive directors are given.
- Under *Directors' Remuneration and Interest*, details for individual directors are set out under the title *Individual emoluments*.
- In the notes to the accounts see note 5, *employee costs and numbers* (iii) Pension commitment.
- See note 20, *provision for liabilities and charges*. Details are given of opening balances, movements during the year and closing balance of the provision for pensions.

3 From note 9, *profit on ordinary activities after taxation*:
Subsidiary undertakings £169.5 million.

4 From note 17, *creditors: amounts falling due within one year*:
Amounts owing to subsidiary undertakings £473.5 million.
From note 15, *debtors*:
Amounts owing by subsidiary undertakings £509.7 million.

5 From note 5, *employee costs and numbers*:

(iii) Retail	Decrease	1137	(27 747 – 26 610)
Beer	Decrease	1333	(9198 – 7865)
Leisure	Decrease	392	(10 926 – 10 534)

Chapter 11

1 $\dfrac{\text{Profit before interest and tax}}{\text{Periodic interest charges}} = \dfrac{423.0}{51.0} = 8.3 \text{ times}$

2 In the Financial Review (see Appendix 3), under *interest payable*, it is stated:
'interest cover increased from 6.3 times to 8.3 times.'

3 $\dfrac{\text{Shareholders' equity}}{\text{Total assets}} = \dfrac{(2207.7 - 12.4)}{3192.9 + 673.4} \times 100 = \dfrac{2195.3}{3866.3} \times 100$
$$= 56.8\%$$

4 $\dfrac{\text{Profit before interest and tax}}{\text{turnover}} = \dfrac{423.0 \times 100}{3349.2} = 12.6\%$

5 Marks and Spencer lists a 'profitability' ratio of 13.8%. We would need to examine Marks and Spencer accounts to verify that the definitions of the individual terms correspond. Marks and Spencer and S&N have entirely different activities: it would be more useful to compare S&N with other similar companies.

References

Accounting Standards Board (1995) *Statement of principles for financial reporting*, London: Accounting Standards Board. Reproduced in Coopers & Lybrand (1997)

Accounting Standards Board (1996) *Measurement of tangible fixed assets*, London, Accounting Standards Board. Reproduced in Coopers & Lybrand (1997)

American Institute of Certified Public Accounts (1994) 'Improving Business Reporting – A Customer Focus', *The Jenkins Report*, New York: American Institute of Certified Public Accountants

Auditing Practice Boards (1995) 'Disclosures Relating to Corporate Governance', *Bulletin 95/1*, London Auditing Practice Board

Cadbury Report (1992) *Report of the Committee on the Financial Aspects of Corporate Governance*, London: Gee

Cooper & Lybrand (1997) *Accounting Standards 1998*, London, Coopers & Lybrand

Institute of Chartered Accountants of Scotland (1998) *Making Corporate reports more valuable*, Edinburgh: Institute of Chartered Accountants of Scotland

Smith, T. (1992) *Accounting for Growth*, London: Century Business

Glossary of terms

The following explanations of terms occurring in this book are intended to be user friendly.
Readers requiring precise legal definitions should refer to appropriate sources.

accounting policies	particular policies decided upon by individual companies in regard to their treatment of items included in their accounts
accounting principles	basic assumptions on which accounts are prepared (e.g. prudence)
accounting standards	rules and regulations for the measurement and/or disclosure of particular types of transactions
accruals principle	recognition of revenues and expenses when they are earned and incurred rather than when payment is made
accrued expenses	expenses which have been incurred in one period but which have not been paid by the balance sheet date (e.g. wages)
accumulated depreciation	cumulative amount by which an asset has been depreciated
acquisition	purchase of something (e.g. takeover of a company)
actuarial value	value calculated by an independent expert (i.e. a qualified actuary)
allowable expenses	expenses accepted for taxation purposes
alternative accounting rules	rules in UK company law permitting the application of current cost principles
amortization	spreading the value of an asset over its expected life by periodic charges against profit (usually refers to intangible assets; see also *depreciation*)
appropriate, to	to set funds aside for a specific purpose
appropriation of profits	how profits have been used for specific purposes (e.g. dividends)
articles of association	a company's internal rules (e.g. concerning issue of shares, meetings, etc.)
assign, to	to transfer
associated undertaking	a company in which an investing company has a significant influence but which is not a subsidiary company
auditors	appropriately qualified and registered persons or firm appointed to carry out an audit
authorized share capital	amount of share capital which a company is authorized to issue in accordance with its statutes
bad debts	debts which will not be paid
base salary	contractual salary before additions of bonuses, share options, etc.
bearer bond	the bearer or holder of the bond has the right to interest and eventual repayment
bonus issue	issue of extra free shares to shareholders by transferring balances from reserves to share capital
bonus shares	issue of extra free shares to shareholders by transferring balances from reserves to share capital

book value	value recorded in company's accounts
breakdown of figures	showing figures in detail, item by item
bring into account, to	to include in the accounts
called-up share capital	the amounts that the shareholders have been asked to pay in respect of share capital that has been issued
capital expenditure	money spent on fixed assets (e.g. equipment)
capital instruments	financial instruments (e.g. bonds) used to raise finance
capitalization issue	issue of extra free shares to shareholders by transferring balances from reserves to share capital (i.e. bonus issue)
capitalization of goodwill	act of bringing goodwill into a balance sheet
capitalization of interest	adding the cost of borrowing (i.e. the interest paid) required to finance the acquisition or making of a fixed asset to the value of the asset reflected in the balance sheet
carrying value	monetary amount at which an asset or liability is included in a balance sheet
clawback	money taken back
closing rate	rate of exchange at the balance sheet date
compliance	acting in accordance with rules and regulations
concessions	rights to exploit minerals or sell goods or services
consideration	something given in payment, not necessarily money (e.g. could be in the form of shares)
consignment stock	goods held in order to be sold on behalf of another company or returned if unsold
consolidated accounts	accounts which reflect the combined results and financial position of a group
contingency	something which may possibly take place but which depends on the occurrence or non-occurrence of a particular event
continuing operations	operations in which a company continues to be engaged
convention	an accepted procedure or rule (e.g. the historical cost convention)
convertible debt	form of loan to a company which can be converted into shares at a later date on terms fixed when the stock is issued
convertible loan stock	form of loan to a company which can be converted into shares at a later date on terms fixed when the stock is issued
convertible preference shares	preference shares which carry the right to be converted into ordinary shares on terms fixed when the preference shares are issued
corporate governance	the system of conduct of the affairs of a company by its directors
corporation tax	UK tax on companies
cost of sales	cost of goods sold
creditworthiness	extent to which person or undertaking is considered able to pay for goods or services
creditor	person or undertaking to whom money is owed for goods or services or for an outstanding loan
cumulative preference shares	preference shares which carry a right to the payment of dividends in arrears if a company has been unable to pay in a particular period
current assets	assets which a company holds on a short-term basis; the main items found under this heading are stocks, debtors and cash (compare *fixed assets*)
current liabilities	amounts owing for payment within one year (also known as creditors: amounts falling due within one year)

debenture	loan stock, usually at a fixed rate of interest
debtor	person or undertaking who owes money for goods or services or for an outstanding loan
default, to	not to pay when due (i.e. not to repay a loan at the due date)
deferred income	receipts of income into a company in one accounting period which, however, relate to a subsequent period
deferred shares	shares with rights to receive dividends only after ordinary shareholders have received a predetermined level of dividend, or to receive a dividend after an agreed future date
demerger	separation of an undertaking into different companies
depreciable asset	asset able to be used over more than one accounting period and so able to be depreciated
depreciation	spreading the value of an asset over its expected life by periodic charges against profits (usually used with reference to tangible assets (see also *amortization*)
derivatives	financial instruments such as futures and options
development costs	costs involved in producing new or improved goods and/or services
diminution	decrease
disclose, to	to provide or report information
disclosure	declaring or reporting of information
discontinued operations	operations which have been terminated (e.g. on sale of a business or part of a business)
dividend cover	profit available to ordinary shareholders divided by the total of ordinary dividends (i.e. a measure of by how much current dividends are covered by current profits)
doubtful debts	debts which may not be paid
earnings per share	profit available to ordinary shareholders divided by the number of ordinary shares in issue
emoluments	salaries and fees and other benefits (usually refers to directors or other office holders)
equity capital	amount of capital raised through the issue of shares which carry the main risk, usually the ordinary shares
equity dividends	dividends paid to holders of ordinary shares
equity investments	investments in ordinary shares
equity reserves	reserves attributable to the equity shareholders (usually the ordinary shareholders)
exceptional items	items which arise as a result of the normal business activity of a company but which are unusual because of their size or nature and which are therefore shown separately in the accounts
exchange adjustments	adjustments made for differences in monetary value which result from changes in exchange rates
exchange differences	differences in monetary value arising from changes in exchange rates
exposure draft	outline of proposed accounting standard for comment by interested parties
extraordinary items	large or unusual items which arise not as a result of the ordinary business activity of a company
face value	value written/stated on share certificate
factoring	system whereby a company's debts are collected by another person or company at a discount in exchange for a lump sum

finance leases	leasing arrangements whereby substantially all the risks and rewards incidental to ownership of an asset are transferred to a company, the lessee; assets acquired under such arrangements are brought into the lessee's balance sheet even though in strict legal terms the ownership lies elsewhere
finance, to	to provide or obtain funds
finished goods	goods ready for sale
fixed assets	assets intended for use on a continuing basis in a company's activities: they are not intended for resale (compare *current assets*)
format	the way in which information is set out
freehold	property held without time limit on ownership
gearing	ratio of a company's finance from loans and other external sources to finance from shareholders (USA: *leverage*)
going concern	company which is likely to continue operating for the foreseeable future
golden handshake	usually large amount of money given to certain employees on end of employment
goodwill	an intangible asset arising where the value of a business exceeds the value of the identifiable net assets
gross figure	amount before deductions (e.g. tax) have been made
group	a parent company and its subsidiaries
group undertakings	enterprises or companies which belong to a group (i.e. subsidiaries)
hedge, to	to guard against risk
historical cost	original cost of purchase or production of an asset (also *historic cost*)
immaterial item	item of little or no importance
institutional shareholders	financial undertakings such as insurance companies which invest in shares of other companies
intangible assets	assets which do not have a physical form (e.g. goodwill, patents)
interest capitalization	adding the cost of borrowing (i.e. the interest paid) required to finance the acquisition or making of a fixed asset to the value of the asset as reflected in the balance sheet
interim dividend	dividend paid during the financial period, usually at the end of a half-year
interim report	report given before the end of the financial year, usually at a half-year period
investee company	company (subsidiary or associated company) in which another company has invested
investment income	dividends and interest on an investment
investment property	property held by a company for investment purposes
irredeemable	without a fixed date for repayment
issue price	price at which shares or bonds are issued
issued and fully paid-up share capital	amount of share capital which a company has actually issued (compare the amount it is authorized to issue)
lease	payment made to use assets acquired under lease arrangements
leased assets	assets used under contractual arrangements for a period of time in exchange for payment
leasehold	right to land and/or buildings granted for a specific period by legal contract or lease
lessee	person or undertaking to whom a lease is granted

lessor	person or undertaking granting a lease
limited liability	the liability of a shareholder to contribute capital up to an agreed amount; the limit is the part of a share's nominal value which has been called; once a share has been issued and fully paid there is no further liability
liquid assets	current assets, stocks and work in progress
liquid resources	cash and assets which can be readily changed into cash (e.g. short-term investments)
listed company	a company which is listed on the Stock Exchange and in which shares can be bought and sold
listing rules	regulations which have to be followed in order for shares to be traded on the Stock Exchange
loan capital	long-term sources of company funds raised by borrowing rather than from shareholders
long term	more than twelve months
market value	value (e.g. of shares) if sold at the current price on market
material item	item of importance or significance
materiality	degree of significance, the extent to which something is important
merger	combination of two or more undertakings into a new undertaking
minority interest	the proportion of a subsidiary's worth which does not belong to the group
movement	change
negotiable instrument	a financial document (security) which can be transferred to someone else on payment
net current assets	excess of current assets over current liabilities
net current liabilities	excess of current liabilities over current assets
net figure	amount after deductions have been made (compare *gross figure*)
net realizable value	monetary value of goods after allowing for deductions for costs incurred in selling
non-cumulative preference shares	preference shares without the right to receive dividend payments in arrears should a company be unable to pay in a particular period
non-equity share capital	amount raised through the issue of shares other than ordinary shares (e.g. preference shares)
non-executive director	director who is not a full-time employee of the company but who attends board meetings and gives advice
obsolescence	the fact of being no longer useful
off-balance sheet finance	finance which is not shown on the balance sheet
on the face of	included in (e.g. the balance sheet)
operating leases	leasing arrangements which enable one company, the lessee, to use an asset in return for a lease rental payment (which is charged in the company's profit and loss account)
operating profit	profit resulting from the ordinary business activities of a company
operating property	property occupied by a company as part of its normal business activity (compare *investment property*)
ordinary shares	shares with rights to profits and repayment after the payment of preferential rights and usually with voting rights (also known as *equities*)
overdraft	money withdrawn from the bank in excess of money held in an account

parent company	a company which controls another company, possibly by holding a majority of voting rights
participating interest	shareholding in another company in order to exercise some control or influence
payments on account	a part payment or deposit before final payment for goods and/or services
pension liabilities	amount required for future payment of pensions
post-balance sheet events	events which occur between the balance sheet date and the date on which the financial statements are approved by the directors
preference shares	shares with rights which give them preference over other shares (e.g. a right to a fixed dividend)
preliminary expenses	expenses involved in forming a company (e.g. legal costs)
prepayments	expenses which have been paid in one period but the benefits of which extend to a future period (e.g. insurance premiums)
private placement	offering an issue of shares directly to a potential buyer
promulgation	official announcement (e.g. of a law or rule)
prospectus	notification offering shares in a company
provisions	amounts retained for certain or likely future liabilities
qualified report	audit report which expresses reservations
quoted company	a company which is listed on the Stock Exchange and in which shares can be bought and sold
realize, to	to convert into cash
realized gain	where a transaction resulting in gain takes place and is settled within the accounting period
recognize, to	to acknowledge formally or officially
reconcile, to	to make two or more figures or accounts agree
reconciliation	act of getting figures or accounts to agree
redeemable	which will be repaid (e.g. a debenture loan)
redeemable preference shares 可赎回优先股.	preference shares which carry the right to be repaid at a predetermined time on terms fixed when the redeemable preference shares are issued
redemption	repayment of a loan or debt
redundancy payment	compensation payment to employee on losing job
remuneration	payment for work or services provided
residual value	value of an asset at the end of its useful life
resolution	proposal put to a meeting (e.g. to reappoint the auditors)
retirement benefits	payments to retired employees (i.e. pensions)
retranslation	recalculation of values expressed in another currency
return	income from an activity or from money invested
revaluation	further valuation of an asset (i.e. updating of value)
revaluation reserve	a reserve in the balance sheet which reflects surpluses arising from the revaluation of assets
revenue	amount earned from sales and/or services and/or investments
scrap value	value of an asset if sold for scrap (i.e. at end of its useful life)
secured loan	loan for which repayment is guaranteed by something valuable being deposited by the borrower with the lender
segment	part, section or area of business activity
service contract	contract between a company and a director detailing terms and conditions of employment
set against, to	to put one amount against another

share capital	amount contributed by the owners of a company by way of investment in shares either when a company is set up or at any time later
share option scheme	right to buy or sell shares in the company at a future date at a certain price
share premium	difference between the nominal value and the issue price of a share
shareholders' funds	the capital and reserves of a company
short term	usually less than twelve months
solvency	ability to pay debts as they become due for payment
subsidiary company	a company which is controlled by another company, possibly by the latter holding a majority of its shares
substance over form	the accounting practice whereby transactions or events are recorded in accordance with their underlying economic reality rather than their strict legal form (e.g. an asset acquired under a finance lease)
summary accounts	shortened version of the annual report and accounts
tangible assets	assets which have a physical existence (compare *intangible assets*)
trade creditors	undertakings which are owed money by the company in question arising from trading activities
trade debtors	debtors who owe money to a company arising from trading activities
trademark	name registered by a manufacturer for exclusive use
translation	restatement of values expressed in one currency in another currency
true and fair view	information which accurately reflects what has taken place (i.e. is correct and not misleading)
turnover	amounts derived from the sale of goods or services net of trade discounts and VAT
undertaking	a company or enterprise
underwriting	guaranteeing (e.g. to purchase shares in a new issue in the event of the issue not being fully subscribed)
unqualified report	auditors' report which confirms that accounts show a true and fair view
unsecured loan	loan which has not been guaranteed by something valuable being deposited by the borrower with the lender
useful life	estimated time during which equipment, for example, will be used
work in progress	value of goods which are in the process of being manufactured (i.e. they are not yet complete)
working capital	capital for everyday working of a company (the excess of current assets over current liabilities, i.e. cash, stocks, debtors less creditors)
write down, to	to enter a lower value than the existing recorded value
write off, to	to cancel a debt or remove an asset from the accounts

Index